**Special Interests
and
Policymaking**

Special Interests and Policymaking

Agricultural Policies and Politics in Britain and the United States of America, 1956–70

Graham K. Wilson
Department of Government,
University of Essex

JOHN WILEY & SONS

London · New York · Sydney · Toronto

Library of Congress Cataloging in Publication Data:

Wilson, Graham K.
 Special interests and policymaking.

 Based on the author's thesis, Oxford.
 Bibliography: p.
 Includes index.
 1. Agriculture and state—Great Britain—
History. 2. Agriculture and state—United States
—History. 3. Pressure groups—Great Britain—
History. 4. Pressure groups—United States—
History. I. Title.
HD1927.1956.W55   338.1'841   77-684
ISBN 0 471 99495 2

Text set in 11/12 pt Photon Times,
printed by photolithography,
and bound in Great Britain
at The Pitman Press, Bath

Preface

I have always been fascinated by theories—pluralist, Marxist, elitist, or even democratic—which attempt to show in whose interests governments act, and explain why. It is an empirical contribution to debates around such theories that I offer this study.

I chose to study agricultural subsidies for two reasons. The first is that I have been interested in the countryside since childhood. The second is that I believe that the different social sciences can, in fact, be of use to each other. Agriculture has been studied extensively by sociologists and economists. Indeed, had economists not written cogent, critical studies of farm subsidies, it would have been less interesting to study the politics of such subsidies.

I am indebted to many people and organizations for their help. The British Social Science Research Council kept me solvent while the American Council of Learned Societies paid for a lengthy stay in the United States which was essential. The Fellows and Warden of Nuffield College provided a congenial and productive environment in which to work. Many politicians, civil servants, and pressure group officials, listed in the bibliography, gave generously of their time and were astonishingly open. Mrs. Bayes typed the book speedily and well. Mr. Nevil Johnson and Mr. L. J. Sharpe acted as university and college supervisers for the thesis on which this book is based (as did Professor Herbert Nicholas for a time). I feel that I owe a particular debt of gratitude to Professor Anthony King (University of Essex) and Mr. Philip Williams (Nuffield College) who read earlier drafts with great care and provided many useful suggestions.

Finally, my parents provided much encouragement and this book is dedicated to them.

GRAHAM K. WILSON
University of Essex, 1976

Contents

Introduction   Farm Policies and Interest Group Theory   .   .   .   1

PART I

1   British Subsidies; Feather-beds for Whom?   13
2   British Farmers; Minority Power?   19
3   Agricultural Interest Groups in Britain   30
4   The Policy Process in Britain   42

PART II

5   Policy in America; Change without Reform   57
6   The American Interest Groups   75
7   The Executive and Agriculture   104
8   Congress and Agriculture   128
9   Conclusions; State Power and Minority Benefits   .   .   .   163

Appendix   179

Bibliography   183

Index   201

Introduction

Farm Policies and Interest Group Theory

No social or economic system has succeeded in managing agriculture perfectly. A free market for farm products can produce, both in practice and in theory, most undesirable results. Introductory economics textbooks are fond of the 'cobweb diagram', which shows how farmers responding rationally to the price level can produce alternately huge surpluses and drastic shortages.[1] Yet the opposite to the market system, the Soviet system of state farms, collectivization, and a centrally planned economy, has equally well-known failings which result in lower yields per acre and greater inefficiency than are common under similar geographic conditions in the West.[2] From the Second World War to the 1970s, both the United States and Western Europe were also troubled by a multifaceted 'farm problem' whose symptoms included real poverty, low farm incomes and profits, a rapid movement from the land to the city, and, above all, large unsold surpluses of agricultural produce.

There are certain obvious characteristics of agriculture which make it more difficult to govern that many industries. Farming is usually carried on by a large number of relatively small units, with no control or even significant influence over the general level of prices or output. Yet so important is the skill and effort of the individual farmer, as well as the variations in soil from farm to farm, that agriculture has proved unsuited to the large-scale organization. Not only are there difficulties in administering state farms in socialist economies but there are very few joint stock companies operating farms in the West. The structure of the industry, therefore, makes its process of responding to changes in conditions more complex than in industries dominated by a few large companies.

Ironically, farmers have had to respond to greater changes than people in most industries. Throughout the Western world, farmers have had to contend with the effects not only of the traditional uncertainties of weather and crop yields but of a technological revolution. Increased use of machinery and fertilizers has raised yields per acre and per worker dramatically. The technological revolution in agriculture and greater use of machinery created a situation in which many farmers faced low or even decreasing marginal costs of production. That is to say, many farmers with larger holdings in the West have found it profitable both to expand the size of their holdings and to sell at prices which farmers with less capital and smaller holdings find disastrously low.

These trends have had radical implications for the structure of agriculture. Under free market conditions with farmers behaving like rational economic men, an automatic reduction in the numbers of farms would result from the comparatively low wages and profits in agriculture. Farmers with smaller, unprofitable holdings would move to other occupations, selling their holdings to the owners of larger, more profitable farms. The trend would continue until farm incomes were once more comparable to those enjoyed in other sectors.

To a certain extent, these trends have been observable in both Britain and the United States. Average farm incomes have lagged behind those of the rest of the population, showing the plight of numerous small farmers. Many farmers, tormented by a constant struggle to remain solvent, have left the industry. There are several reasons, however, why the market has not worked in a textbook manner. The ties between a farmer and his land and his reluctance to lose his independence have persuaded many farmers that it is worth staying on, even when they could earn more in a factory. Moreover, many farmers have been able to supplement their meager incomes from agriculture with earnings from other sources such as tourism or, in the United States, work in the city. Agriculture also provides a few benefits such as housing or farm produce which do not appear in financial returns. Finally, farmers have obtained a great variety of grants and subsidies from their governments, a few of which have benefited the smaller farmer.

Many policy-makers would concede that it is one of the prime functions of government to ease such painful changes as the flight from the land. Few would concede that governments have the duty, or even the ability, to halt such profound changes in the structures of their economies. Yet the irony of agricultural policy in Britain, the United States, and the European Economic Community is that negligible effort has gone into helping farmers retrain or shift to new occupations. The drift of farm policy throughout the Western world has been to try to maintain farm prices and incomes at some level justified either by history or by comparisons with the rest of the economy, and not into helping farmers shift into different, more profitable occupations.

Part of the reason for this was the difficulty of disentangling two pressures on farm prices and incomes. The first of these, outlined above, was the long-term change in the structure and techology of farming, a change which governments could arrest only at enormous cost. The second, however, was short-term, chance factors, such as coincidental run of good harvests round the world, the selling off of strategic reserve stocks by one country, or unusually benign weather.

Had farm subsidies merely ironed out short-term price fluctuations, they would have been unassailable. As we have seen, the case against a pure, free market system in agriculture has long been accepted by economists. Opposition to any attempt by government to reduce short-term price fluctuations would be the purest form of dogmatism. Price stability helps not only the farmer, who can plan his investment and production with greater certainty, but also the consumer who is protected from rocketing prices during shortages. Critics of farm subsidies contend that farm subsidies have gone far beyond either smoothing short-term fluctuations or easing social change, and have attempted to preserve artifically outmoded production patterns and prices. The critics' case[3] rests on a number of points.

In the first place, it is argued, agricultural subsidies, like other forms of protection, defy the 'laws' of comparative advantage. When Britain subsidizes the production of wheat which could be grown at lower cost abroad, it misuses resources such as land, labour, and capital which it could better employ in other industries, such as machine tools, the car industry, or chemicals. The point has equal force within one country as well as between them. When the American cotton programmes delayed the movement of cotton westward out of the traditional producing areas by a mixture of subsidies and government controls, a similar waste of resources was involved.

In the second place, farm subsidies distort production patterns within agriculture. If farmers are encouraged to produce wheat which cannot be sold, they are simultaneously discouraged from producing commodities such as soya beans which may be in short supply. Certain forms of agricultural subsidies make the problem worse. The American cotton programmes, for example, subsidized farmers by raising the price of cotton far above its 'natural' market level. One major consequence of raising the price, however, was to discourage consumption of American cotton. Consumers turned either to manmade fibres or alternative sources of supply. Thus farm subsidy policies which relied on raising the market price both encouraged unnecessary production and discouraged consumption. This was a prescription for massive surpluses of unsold stocks, which, of course, afflicted the United States for most of the postwar period.

Finally, the evidence always has been clear that agriculture is an industry in which low profits are made. British agriculture has depended on government grants and subsidies for half its net income in the postwar period, and the situation has been much the same in the United States. Most economists and businessmen would see this lack of profitability as a *prima facie* argument against making heavy investment in the industry. Unless there are compelling reasons to the contrary, unprofitable industries do not make good investments. Yet, in both Britain and the United States, governments have directed massive amounts of money into the industry. Most would conclude that this is economic nonsense.

The defenders of farm subsidies have, of course, argued that agriculture is a special case to which traditional economic analyses do not apply. Arguments about comparative advantage are specious they contend in a world in which every country protects its farmers, and the real or fair price of farm produce is undiscoverable because world trade is dominated by dumping. Some 'liberal' American economists,[4] little enamoured of the market system, have argued that as farmers will not readily leave their farms a reduction in their prosperity endangers the stability of the entire economy. Every depression, it is said, 'has been farm bred and farm led'. British agricultural pressure groups have argued that the higher domestic levels of production which subsidies make possible make a vital contribution to the balance of payments through import saving.[5]

All these defences seem suspect. It is true that world trade in agricultural produce has been more and more distorted by higher subsidies, while trade in industrial commodities has been liberalized. The answer to this problem would seem to be for all countries to reduce agricultural protection, not increase or maintain it. Government policies aimed at avoiding depressions may find more useful targets for expenditure than farm subsidies. Even the 'import saving' argument in Britain is suspect. Modern British agriculture itself imports many of its inputs (such as fertilizer and feed grain), and whether or not agricultural expansion achieves a *net* reduction in imports is highly uncertain. Moreover, agriculture is one of Britain's least profitable industries. More than half of the industry's net income usually comes from government grants and subsidies. There exists, therefore, a *prima facie* case that agriculture was not a good investment for government, and that more valuable production for saving imports or expanding imports could have been achieved by investing the same amount of money elsewhere. Finally, it is far from clear that a trading country like Britain should follow such autarchic economic policies as import saving.

Yet, to some, agricultural subsidies have been an instrument not of economic but of social policy. The farmer has often been seen by progressives, particularly in the United States, as one of the victims of capitalism. Supporting New Deal farm legislation, Fiorello LaGuardia, for example, told Congress that 'It is the exploited masses that now require the attention of this Congress, and in this great army of exploited masses is to be included the farmer'.[6] The comparatively low levels of farm incomes and the existence of rural poverty, particularly in the United States, are undeniable. The tragedy is that while rural poverty has often been used to justify the enormously expensive farm subsidy policies of Britain and the United States, very little of this has benefited the rural poor or farmers with low incomes. Though British and American farm subsidies differ considerably in the form they take, in both countries subsidies have gone primarily to farmers who enjoy incomes well above the national average. Schultze argues convincingly that the main effect of farm subsidies has been to raise the price of farm land, again benefiting mainly the rich.[7] The poorest farmers have benefited little.

Many have concluded, therefore, that there is little economic or social justification for farm subsidies. Even the environmental effects of farm subsidies can be criticized. Modern commercial agriculture is often unsightly, and can involve the destruction of hedgerows and wildlife or the ploughing up of areas such as the Downs to the detriment of the character of the countryside.

It is only fair to say that all these criticisms of agricultural subsidies are contentious. Many government officials, politicians, and even a few economists believe that agricultural subsidies are good, not only for farmers but for consumers and the public at large. In spite of the best attempts of economists, even the most basic questions about farm policy have no commonly accepted answer. D. Gale Johnson, the American economist, has pointed out that no government could give a defensible answer to such basic questions as 'How much has net farm income been increased as a result of national farm programmes?' and 'What is the cost to consumers and taxpayers of the existing farm products?'.[8]

It is hard to deny the cogency of the arguments of critics of agricultural policies. However, it ill behoves a political scientist to give a definitive answer to questions about agricultural policy which have divided economists. It is true that most economists who have studied farm policies disapprove of them, but the number of critics is no proof that policies are inadvisable. Fortunately, the political scientist need not provide the definitive answer. All that we need note is that in spite of the enormous amounts of money involved in the late 1960s, some £438 million per annum in Britain[9] and $6 billion per annum in the United States,[10] no generally convincing justification for them has been established. In short, though we cannot prove that farm subsidies are *against* the public interest, the inability of their friends to establish that subsidies are *in* the public interest suggests the need for political explanation.

If, however, we accept that agricultural subsidies have been clearly neither in the national economic interest nor justified by widely held conceptions of social justice, a remarkable political problem emerges for us to solve. It would seem unlikely that governments would maintain widely criticized policies without some sort of political pressure. Yet farmers are a rare, and decreasing, breed in contemporary societies. Less than 5 per cent of the workforce in both the United Kingdom and the United States are employed in agriculture. Farmers are, therefore, both a small minority and immensely successful in attracting government help. How can this apparent paradox be resolved?

The enormous geographical, cultural, and institutional differences between the United Kingdom and the United States suggest that it would be unwise to start by looking for one explanation common to both countries. Different factors may well explain the success of British and American farmers.

In a sense, these differences are the point of this book. Political scientists have long believed that both the power of organized interests and the ways in which they pursue their goals differ from country to country. Differences in political systems produce differences in the power and behaviour of organized interests. As is so often the case in political science, the fact that a controversy has long existed has not meant that systematic attempts have been made to settle it. Very few, if any, systematic attempts have been made to compare the power of special interests in different countries. One barrier to systematic comparison was the specialized, institutional (rather than the policy) focus of most political scientists. This institutional focus meant that, though a variety of influences might help the cause of an interest, they were rarely all considered within the same study. A little terminological precision is necessary to establish this point.

Discussions of interest group politics are bedevilled by a confusion in the use of the term 'interest group' or 'pressure group'. 'Interest group' is used sometimes to refer to people who have an interest in common, even if they may be unaware of it, and sometimes to the organization with rules, officers, membership lists, etc., which seek to represent them. In this study, the people with an interest in common, such as farmers, are called a 'special interest'; the term 'interest group' is reserved for the organizations which seek to represent them. This raises the obvious possibility that a special interest may succeed not through the workings of an agricultural interest group, but through other political advantages it enjoys, such as having representation in the legislature or the belief that its members are a strategic floating vote in elections.

It has long been debated whether the British or American system of government are the more susceptible to the influence of special interests. Until the 1950s, however, the debate was somewhat one-directional. Britons frequently claimed that their American cousins lived under the shadow of special interests. Not only did Americans often accept these charges (with their common disarming trait of accepting the unique wickedness of the United States) but both they and the British agreed that the reasons why this should happen were entirely obvious. The British had centralized, hierarchically controlled government presided over by one of two political parties differentiated by broad, ideological issues of principle and the social class of their supporters. The Americans, however, lacked almost all these antidotes to the power of special interests. Ill-disciplined parties composed of parochially minded legislators, the (alleged) absence of any ideology to bind the parties, the weakness of class divisions among the electors and the corresponding importance of ethnicity and localism, and the separation of powers and the consequent non-hierarchical, ill-coordinated nature of American government, all supposedly aided by the development in the United States of a type of politics which consisted almost entirely of the politics of special interests.

The interpretation of American politics in terms of interest group politics reached its peak with 'group theorists' such as Truman, Key, and Dahl.[11] Key was the most forceful of the three: 'The study of politics,' he wrote, 'must rest on an analysis of the objectives and composition of interest groups within a society.'[12] There are obvious links between the success of the group theorists in winning acceptance for their empirical perspective on politics and those who, after Tocqueville, praised interest groups as organizations which would help the citizen withstand the pressures of contemporary society and relate meaningfully to his government. Thus the line between group theorists describing reality and celebrating an ideal became blurred. Sometimes the same writer, for example Robert Dahl, was both a writer of empirical studies of the workings of American democracy and celebrant of the pluralist political system as an ideal. Lesser writers carried this blurring of factual analysis and prescription to more ludicrous limits. Two concluded an empirical study of pressure groups with the remarkable finding that 'American democracy has achieved a political system [interest group pluralism] which political philosophers have long dreamed about but never effectively worked out in theory'.[13]

More important for our purposes was the tendency for group theorists at the height of their self-confidence in the 1950s and early 1960s to export their model to other countries. Interest groups, it was discovered, flourished in the most suprising places, such as the Soviet Union. One country, however, whose politics it was widely agreed could be understood better with greater attention to the role of interest groups was Britain. In an influential article published in 1956,[14] Samuel Beer argued that interest groups were more important in Britain than the United States. British interest groups recruited a higher proportion of potential members than those in the United States; they enjoyed greater legitimacy and had a closer relationship with government (particularly Whitehall) than did their American counterparts.

The most relevant extension of pluralist analysis to Britain for this book by an American was an article by J. Roland Pennock.[15] Using the example of agricultural subsidies, Pennock argued that organized interests could be more, not less, successful in Britain than in the United States. Pennock tried to demonstrate that farm subsidies were higher in Britain than in the United States and provided a novel explanation, too. British parties were more highly disciplined than American ones and yet had the same need to 'bid for the support of interest groups'. Farmers were thought by British politicians to be of massive strategic importance in deciding the outcomes of elections. They could, therefore, obtain large subsidies from the Labour and Conservative parties, who feared that the cost of refusing the farmers' requests could be as high as the loss of a General Election.

Many criticisms can be made of Pennock's argument. His estimates of the costs of agricultural subsidies are incomplete, and Barry has made telling criticisms of Pennock's concept of bargaining.[16] Yet though this study disagrees with Pennock's conclusions, he deserves credit for being one of the first political scientists to make a rigorous study of the effects of similar policies in two countries and thereby make a systematic comparison of the powers of a special interest under different political systems.

This book not only discusses more fully Pennock's explanation but adds to it. Pennock, perhaps because of shortages of space, dealt with only one plausible explanation for the political success of British farmers—electoral competition. Though nothing approaching a theory to explain the success of British interest groups has ever been formulated, there is some agreement on the relevant factors.[17]

The first set of factors of relevance may be termed 'political resources'. Pennock points to an important resouce which British special interests may enjoy: the belief that its members are a group of great strategic importance in deciding the outcome of a General Election. Other political resources which special interests may enjoy are having representation within a governing class or group (as land-owners were in Britain in the nineteenth century) or cultural prestige or sympathy. All these benefits are enjoyed without forming any organization to foster the cause of a special interest.

Most studies of special interest politics in Britain, however, have focused on the activities of interest groups as organizations. The very fact that some interests have an organization staffed by highly trained, expert, articulate staff is thought to give them an advantage. Such organizations keep a close watch out for government policies detrimental to their members and are in a position to dissuade government from implementing them. British interest groups enjoy privileged access to Whitehall departments, where their expertise is respected and they enjoy the status of authoritative spokesmen for the section of society they represent. At least, British interest groups have the opportunity to persuade governments; at best, they may negotiate with them.

A third factor which may benefit the political power of some specialist interest groups is the nature of the British policymaking process itself. Recent studies of Whitehall politics[18] have emphasized not only that ministries have a close working relationship with interests they govern, but that they accept a duty to further their interests' causes. The Department of Education and Science not only governs education but is a spokesman for it; the Department of Trade not only administers trade policy but advocates more liberal trade agreements in the interests of British exporters; and the Ministry of Agriculture, Fisheries and Food (MAFF) acts as the Whitehall spokesman for the farmers' cause. Behind the Whitehall façade of opinionless civil servants serving either the public interest or the instructions of political masters, a pluralist conflict goes on between ministries advocating contending interests. The success of a special interest may well be explained by it having the good fortune to be represented by a ministry that identifies with its cause and is headed by a powerful, persuasive minister. Thus, special interests in Britain may have many reasons other than interest groups for their success.

As is so often the case, more complete theories exist to explain the success of American than of British special interests. These are summarized in terms of an 'iron triangle' whose sides are the relevant interest groups, Congressional committees which consider legislation governing their members, and government departments which implement it.[19] All make their contribution to the power of a special interest.

American interest groups are usually thought to have an even greater variety of weapons at their disposal than their British counterparts. As well as the opportunity to persuade Congress or Executive of the justice of their cause, interest groups in the United States have political 'shots in their locker'. At the very least, these include the opportunity to punish enemies and reward friends through campaign contributions or the use of the group's organization in election campaigns. It has long been considered a possibility that, unlike British interest group leaders, those in the United States have the ability to switch their members' votes between political candidates.

The possibility that offending a special interest may cause a real loss of campaign contributions, votes, and help in election campaigns gives politicians in the United States good cause to avoid offending them. A recent study of Congress argues that the basic rule of Congressional behaviour is to keep in step with constituents' wishes and interests.[20] This would enable us to make a number of predictions about how Congress handles agricultural legislation. It would seem reasonable to expect Congressmen representing rural areas to vote in favour of farm subsidies, and possibly even barter support for other issues in exchange for help in adopting legislation favourable to the farmer. Furthermore, a little knowledge of Congressional procedure would suggest that legislators from rural areas have a major opportunity to help farmers. The very Congressional committees which control farm legislation and the appropriations to implement them are almost completely composed of Senators and Congressmen whose constituents include a sizeable number of farmers. As Congress is expected in the overwhelming majority of cases to endorse the decisions of its committees, the potential for control of farm legislation by legislators elected by farmers is obvious.

The final side of the 'iron triangle' consists of the government agencies responsible for administering a policy of concern to a special interest. In the case of agriculture, the relevant department is the United States Department of Agriculture (USDA). Students of American government have argued that there are compelling reasons why agencies and departments must be responsive to the special interests with which they deal. Because the Congressional committees which handle a department's legislation and its appropriation requests are composed of legislators elected by the special interest it governs, failure to please its 'clientele' can result in rejection of its legislation, reductions in the funds available, and loss of status, power, and suzerainty for the agency.

The different explanations for the success of special interests in the United Kingdom and the United States are not necessarily conflicting. Indeed, as the triangular explanation for the success of special interests in the United States makes clear, the analytically distinct reasons for their success may be complimentary in practice. Yet even if the explanations are complimentary, the political scientist will still wish to know what weight to attach to each. For example, though the agricultural interest groups of the United States may make some contribution to explaining the political success of American farmers, their strength in Congress may be more important. Alternatively, the continuance of farm subsidies may be better attributed to the devotion of the USDA to the farmers' cause.

Any estimate of the importance of any one factor is likely to be imprecise. At best, any valuation would be on ordinal, not an interval, scale. Estimating that one factor is more important than others is, however, better than merely cataloguing all influences without some guide to their significance. The way we shall proceed, therefore, is to describe the broad lines of policy and then to examine the applicability to agriculture of the major explanations for the success of special interests in Britain and the United States.

Notes

1. R. G. Lipsey, *An Introduction to Positive Economics,* Weidenfeld and Nicholson, London, 1974, pp. 138–140.
2. R. D. and B. A. Laird, *Soviet Communism and Agrarian Revolution,* Pelican Books, London, 1970, Chaps. 6 and 8; Alec Nove, *The Soviet Economy,* George Allen and Unwin (Minerva), London, 1968, p. 335.
3. Vide D. Gale Johnson, *World Agriculture in Disarray,* Fontana World Economic Issues, London, 1973; Richard W. Howarth, *Agricultural Support in Western Europe,* Institute for Economic Affairs, Research Monograph 25, London, 1971.
4. John Kenneth Galbraith, 'Economic preconceptions and farm policy', *American Economic Review,* March, 1954.

5. Economic Development Committee for Agriculture, *Agriculture's Import Saving Role*, National Economic Development Office, London, 1969.
6. Reprinted in Howard Zinn (Ed.), *New Deal Thought*, Bobbs Merrill, New York, 1966, p. 227.
7. Charles Schultze, *The Distribution of Farm Subsidies; Who Gets the Benefits?*, Brookings Institution Staff Paper, Washington DC, 1971, p. 23.
8. Quoted in Timothy Edward Josling *et al., Burdens and Benefits of Farm Support Policies*, Trade Policy Research Centre, London, 1972, p. 4.
9. Howarth, op. cit.
10. United States Congress, Senate Committee on Agriculture and Forestry, 89th Congress, First Session, *Farm Programs and Dynamic Forces in Agriculture*, Tables 4 and 5; Luther G. Tweeten, Earl O. Heady, and Leo U. Mayer, *Farm Program Alternatives, Farm Incomes and Public Costs under Alternative Commodity Programs for Feed Grains and Wheat*, Ames Center for Agricultural and Economic Development, CAED Report 18, 1963.
11. David Truman, *The Governmental Process, Political Interests and Public Opinion*, Alfred Knopf, 1951; V. O. Key, *Politics, Parties and Pressure Groups*, Crowell Company, New York 1964; Robert Allen Dahl, *A Preface to Democratic Theory*, Phoenix Books New York, 1963, and *Democracy in the United States, Promise and Performance*, 2nd ed., Rand McNally, Chicago, 1972.
12. Key, op. cit., p. 24.
13. R. Joseph Monsen and Mark W. Cannon, *The Makers of Public Policy, American Power Groups and Their Ideologies*, McGraw-Hill, New York, 1965, p. 23.
14. Samuel Beer, 'Pressure groups and parties in Britain', *APSR*, **50** (1956).
15. J. Roland Pennock, '"Responsible Government", separated powers and special interests, agricultural subsidies in Britain and America', *APSR*, **56** (1962).
16. Brian Barry, 'Comments on the "Pork Barrel" and Majority Rule', *Journal of Politics*, **33**, 1971.
17. For major earlier works on British interest groups see S. E. Finer, *Anonymous Empire*, Pall Mall Press, London 1962; Samuel Beer, *Modern British Politics*, Faber and Faber London, 1965; Harry Eckstein, *Pressure Group Politics: The Case of the British Medical Association*, George Allen and Unwin London, 1960; J. B. Stewart, *British Pressure Groups, Their Role in Relation to the House of Commons*, Oxford University Press, Oxford and London, 1958; H. H. Wilson, *Pressure Group, The Campaign for Commercial Television*, Secker and Warburg, Harlow, 1961; J. W. Grove, *Government and Industry in Britain*, Longmans, London, 1962; Robert J. Lieber, *British Politics and European Unity, Parties, Elites and Pressure Groups*, University of California Press, Berkeley, 1970.
18. Hugh Heclo and Aaron Wildavsky, *The Private Government of Public Money*, MacMillan, London, 1974; Edward Boyle and Anthony Crosland, *The Politics of Education*, Harmondsworth, Penguin Books, 1971.
19. Such accounts may be found in any textbook; a specific application of the 'iron triangle' to agriculture is Theodore Lowi's 'How the farmers get what they want', *The Reporter*, 21 May, 1964.
20. David, Mayhew, *Congress, The Electoral Connection*, Yale University Press, New Haven and London, 1974.

PART I

Chapter 1

British Subsidies; Feather-beds for Whom?

From the mid 1950s until the United Kingdom's entry into the European Economic Community (EEC), the British system of agricultural subsidies was one of the simplest in the world. It was also commonly thought to be the least economically damaging subsidy system which could be employed.

At its prime in the mid 1950s, the system was essentially one of *deficiency payments*. The Ministry of Agriculture, Fisheries, and Food (MAFF) promised farmers that if prices for their products fell below a certain level, the 'guaranteed price', the Government would make up the difference with a payment from the Treasury. The advantages of such a system were threefold. First, because the price to the consumer was not raised artificially, consumption was not discouraged as it would have been had the Government raised the price in the market-place. Second, as the cost was paid out of general tax revenue, deficiency payments did not have the regressive effect on incomes which artificially high market prices do. It was the taxpayer, assessed on the basis of his ability to pay, and not the consumer, who is not, who met the cost. Finally, deficiency payments were a comparatively inconspicuous form of subsidy. An increase in farm subsidies was not accompanied by an increase in prices in the shops, which consumers would notice; it was unlikely even to be accompanied by an increase in taxes.

Deficiency payments had disadvantages, too. Critics pointed out that they benefited farmers who produced the most, as deficiency payments were made on each unit produced. Yet the farmers who produce the most are usually the richest farmers, with the highest incomes and large holdings. Deficiency payments did little to help the small farmer with a low output, low income, and little prospect of obtaining capital to improve his farm. A pressing problem for the Government was that so long as deficiency payments were operated in conjunction with the traditional British policy of an 'open door' for imports, there was no real check on

13

their cost. If foreign suppliers sold wheat in Britain at low prices because they could not sell it elsewhere, the price of wheat in Britain would slump, the gap between the price the government had 'guaranteed' farmers and the price farmers obtained in the market would widen, and the cost to the Treasury would mushroom.

By and large, the critics of deficiency payments won the day, and throughout the 1950s and 1960s the British subsidy system became progressively less one based purely on deficiency payments. The 1957 Agriculture Act marked a significance shift in policy with its provisions for many more grants to farmers for investment and modernization. Investment grants, it was thought, would help British agriculture become more competitive and so reduce the future costs of deficiency payments.[1] Moreover, whereas deficiency payments went to farmers for no specific purpose so that they could be spent on consumer goods for the farmhouse as easily as on the farm itself, investment grants were tied to approved farm improvements. In more optimistic moments, the Government hoped for a steady reduction in the cost of deficiency payments as farms became more efficient and competitive with foreign suppliers.

The trend away from reliance on deficiency payments continued in the 1960s. By 1969, the cost of deficiency payments was but one-third of the total cost of agricultural subsidies, compared with 70 per cent in 1955–56. Grants for farm improvements more than trebled between 1966–67 and 1971–72.[2]

If the Government had hoped for a speedy reduction in the costs of farm subsidies as investment grants made British farming more efficient, it was to be disappointed. Indeed, the cost of subsidies shot up from £151·2 million in 1960–61 to £225·5 million in the next crop year, remaining around the £200 million mark thereafter. This unplanned increase in costs reflected the depressing effect on British prices of massive world surpluses. (Much of the world's population remained hungry but too poor to buy these surpluses.) Action was delayed by negotiations to enter the EEC, but when it came it was dramatic. In 1963, the British Government, almost unnoticed, breached one of the basic principles of British trading policy since the repeal of the Corn Laws—that there should be an open door for imports of cheap foodstuffs, particularly from the Dominions. The sharp rise in costs convinced policy-makers that deficiency payments and an 'open door' for imports could not co-exist in an era of large surpluses on world commodity markets. Typically, the 'open door' was partially closed, while deficiency payments were only slightly modified.

The main method the Government used to limit the cost of deficiency payments was the *minimum import price* (m.i.p.). Britain's problem in limiting the cost of deficiency payments by restricting imports was that foreign suppliers might retaliate against British exports. It was felt, therefore, that any restrictions must be acceptable to foreign suppliers; the minimum import price was. Its aim was to force foreign suppliers to charge more for their exports to Britain than they would have done. In case they refused to comply the British Government took powers to impose tariffs. Faced with the choice of keeping the profits from higher prices or seeing them imposed by tariffs and the profits kept by the British Exchequer, foreign suppliers strove manfully to keep up prices. The powers to impose tariffs remained unused, but the principle of British trade, that food should be bought at the cheapest possible price, was breached.

The domestic counterpart to the minimum import price was the *standard quantity*. Under this arrangement, the Government no longer accepted an unlimited obligation to subsidize domestic production. Instead, if the output of cereals was beyond the 'standard quantity', reductions were made in deficiency payments.

The final step away from reliance on deficiency payments came when the Government ended the practice of making payments to the Milk Marketing Board in 1963. Henceforth, milk production was to be subsidized exclusively by the manipulation of the market (and so the price) by the Monopolist Board.

By and large, these changes were regretted by agricultural economists, not only because of their effects but because they made the task of calculating the cost of agricultural subsidies infinitely more difficult. Were the question to be merely what the cost of agricultural subsidies was to the Government, the answer would be simple (see Table 1).

Table 1   Total estimated cost to the Exchequer of agricultural subsidies[3]

Year	Total estimated cost (£ millions)
1958–59	241·4
1959–60	256·1
1960–61	262·9
1961–62	342·6
1962–63	309·6
1963–64	293·9
1964–65	264·3
1965–66	236·6
1966–67	229·1
1967–68	261·5
1968–69	265·4
1969–70	277·1
1970–71	269·0

Though Table 1 shows that agricultural subsidies have been a steadily important item in public expenditure, it clearly does not show the total value of agricultural subsidies. As we have seen, even before Britain joined the EEC, the tendency had been to transfer the cost of farm subsidies away from the taxpayer and onto the consumer. Minimum import prices and the activities of marketing boards cost the Exchequer nothing, but may well have had a significant effect on farm incomes. The most systematic attempt to estimate the value of all forms of farm subsidy in Britain has been made by Richard Howarth.[4]

Howarth used the technique, long established in agricultural economics, of comparing the value of British agricultural output valued at domestic prices (paid in the market or guaranteed by the Government) with those prevailing in world markets. Subsidies were taken to be the difference between the two. Howarth's estimates include, therefore, not merely exchequer payments to farmers as deficiency payments but estimates of the effects of such 'hidden' subsidies as those generated by marketing boards or minimum import prices.

His conclusions are striking. Howarth calculated that in the late 1960s, whereas exchequer cost of price supports was £121·5 million, the total cost to the community was £320·4 million. As Howarth commented, 'Put in another way, the budgetary cost of agricultural price supports in Britain is equivalent to well under half (39 per cent) the estimated total cost borne by the community.' Howarth put the total cost of agricultural support, including not only price supports in the late 1960s but investment and improvement grants, etc., at an average level of £438 million.

There are, unfortunately, many problems with the method Howarth uses. To say that the subsidies are equivalent to the difference between domestic and world market prices is to make a number of questionable assumptions. It is far from clear that world prices are fair prices. Too often in the 1960s, world prices were set by competitive dumping, in which governments vied with each other in paying export subsidies to their farmers. It is also to assume that the level of British production, determined by the value of subsidies paid, has no effect on world market prices. While this may be true of cereals, it is almost certainly not true of eggs, for example, in which Britain is self-sufficient. Finally, the method assumes that there *is* a world market price with which the domestic price can be compared. This is not true of liquid milk which, because of the nature of the product, is scarcely traded at all between nations. Economists like Howarth are forced to use prices of milk products such as dried milk as a substitute, a comparison of very dubious validity as such products are usually made from surplus milk production.

All this is very frustrating for the policy analyst. On the one hand, the techniques used to measure 'hidden' farm subsidies are open to serious criticism. On the other hand, policy-makers have placed increasing reliance on such subsidies, and they cannot be neglected. As Howarth neglects other 'subsidies' to agriculture such as its relief from local government property taxes and inheritance taxes, perhaps it is as well to let his conclusions stand. Tentative conclusions are better than unanswered questions.

It has long been argued in British farming circles that agricultural subsidies are merely compensation for the fact that agriculture, unlike other industries, did not benefit from tariff protection. A 10 per cent tariff on imports of foreign cars, it is argued, has the same effect as a 10 per cent subsidy paid by the Exchequer. There is much to commend such arguments, but they do not alter the fact that agriculture has been treated as a special case. Even using the most sophisticated measure of the value of subsidies to an industry, 'effective protection',[5] which allows for the impact on an industry of tariffs on its inputs, it still seems that farming was almost 50 per cent more protected than manufacturing industry.[6]

Whether or not such special treatment is justified is, of course, a matter of opinion. There are many farmers who believe sincerely that their industry's well-being is vital to the national interest, not because of some vague belief in rural values or society but because of the contribution the industry makes to the balance of payments through saving imports. This argument has even won some official endorsement. Indeed, Ashton argues that: 'In the last analysis, it can be said that balance of payments considerations have been the main determinant of the size of the agricultural industry in the last decade.'[7]

It is worth reiterating some of the objections to import saving stated in the Introduction. Opponents of farm subsidies have argued that money invested in agriculture could have been invested more profitably in other industries. They note that British manufacturing industry has suffered from underinvestment and that, partly because of this, it has lost ground in both domestic and foreign markets. The machine tool is a prime example. Other economists have argued that agricultural expansion has itself required a significant rise in imports such as feed grains. It is possible, too, that by reducing imports from foreign suppliers the agricultural expansion that subsidies made possible reduced opportunities for British exporters. The willingness of countries to buy from Britain is determined to a significant degree by their ability to sell to Britain.

Deciding the rights and wrongs of such arguments is not a task for political scientists, who may take sardonic amusement from the fact that economics is not such a certain subject as they had been led to suppose. At the very least, however, it cannot be argued that agricultural subsidies are obviously in the public interest and that they are so obviously to the benefit of the nation's economy that political explanations for their existence are superfluous.

One further general justification for farm subsidies remains. It is that farm subsidies are an instrument of social justice, not economic policy, channelling money to rural areas in which incomes are lower than in manufacturing industry and amenities such as schools, housing, and transport are below the national average.

One does not have to be insensitive to the problems of the small farmer or farmworker to see the flaws in such an argument. Government aid to the industry has done little to help those most in need. In fact, figures collated by the Ministry of Agriculture show that 49·2 per cent of government payments to farmers go to the already affluent producer—the 23 per cent of farmers who employ over four men the year round. Farms which employ no more than two full-time men receive in contrast only 18·0 per cent of subsidies, though they account for 64 per cent of the agricultural holdings in Britain.[8] Those who defend farm subsidies on the grounds that they benefit the small farmer should remember that he has not been their primary beneficiary. The primary effect of farm subsidies has been to subsidize the most affluent farmers who enjoy incomes far above the national average.

Though under fire from economists and lacking any clear social justification, farm subsidies have remained a significant item of government spending. One possibility for this surprising fact is that farmers have enjoyed significant political leverage, and it is that possibility which will now be explored.

Notes

1. For a statement of the Government's objectives, read the speech by the Minister of

18

Agriculture, Heathcoat Amory, in Hansard, *House of Commons Debates,* **567,** 1956–57, esp. cols. 816–818.

2. The most convenient source for farm subsidies are the White Papers, *Annual Review and Determination of Guarantees,* HMSO, London (published annually).

3. From *Annual Review and Determination of Guarantees,* White Papers, HMSO, London, 1972.

4. Richard W. Howarth, *Agricultural Support in Western Europe,* Institute for Economic Affairs, Research Monograph 25, London, 1971.

5. W. M. Corden, *The Theory of Protection,* Clarendon Press, Oxford, 1971, esp. p. 28.

6. The figure is calculated by the author using the formula:

$$E = \frac{t_2 - t_1[1 - V(1 + t_2)]}{V - (1 - V)t_2 + t_1}$$

where *E is effective protection,*
   V is the ratio of the value added by an industry to the value of its sales,
   t_1 is the tariff protecting an industry or its equivalent in subsidies, and
   t_2 is the tariff on that industry's inputs.

7. J. Ashton, 'Agriculture and the public interest' in J. Ashton and S. J. Rogers (Eds.), *Economic Change and Agriculture,* Oliver and Boyd, Edinburgh, 1967.

8. Figures are taken from the MAFF's *Farm Incomes in England and Wales,* HMSO, London (published annually).

Chapter 2

British Farmers; Minority Power?

For many years farmers have been a small, and declining, proportion of the British population. No group has been more conscious of these facts than British farmers. The most casual observer at meetings of local branches of the National Farmers' Union can build up a vivid impression of how beleaguered farmers feel themselves. As the British farmer sees it, British politicians win elections by competing for the votes of city dwellers who know little and care less about farmers' problems.

Political scientists will be less certain than farmers that being a minority is necessarily a disadvantage. Even democratic political systems do not always guarantee that general, public, or even majority interests are always followed, and there has been some debate about the characteristics of political systems which benefit minorities.

One of the most obvious advantages which members of small blocs of voters enjoy is that, because they are few, politicians can afford to try to buy their favours.[1] Paying out significant subsidies to $2\frac{1}{2}$ per cent of the population is very much less costly than giving benefits of a similar magnitude to 51 per cent, which is not to say, of course, that politicians do not try. (Thus both owner occupiers and council house tenants, 85 per cent of householders, are subsidized in Britain.) Moreover, majorities can be created out of coalitions of minorities as well as by a grouping which is itself more than half the electorate. The ideal situation to be in, as a minority, in a two-party system is one in which each party can count on the support of large blocs of voters, but is short of a majority. In such a situation, politicians have a huge incentive to bid for the support of minorities which are relatively unattached to either party. Have British farmers enjoyed such an advantage?

Several academic commentators have attempted to estimate the number of Parliamentary constituencies in which farmers are sufficiently numerous to decide

19

the outcome of elections. It is not necessary, of course, for farmers to constitute more than half the electorate to decide the outcome of an election. If farmers normally support a Conservative MP in a constituency, and are as numerous as the Conservatives' majority, they could cause the defeat of the MP by switching their support to the party which customarily comes second. Majorities are not always large in Parliamentary elections, and even if only 1 per cent of the electorate are farmers, they may still exceed an MP's margin of victory. If an MP thinks that he normally enjoys the support of farmers, he might well be worried by their defection.

In how many constituencies were, in fact, farmers in a position to decide the outcome of the election? The answer, of course, varies from year to year, not only as the number of farmers but size of MPs' majorities fluctuated. Beynon and Harison,[2] studying the situation after the 1959 Election, calculated that there were fifty-nine constituencies in which the number of farmers and their wives was greater than the majority enjoyed by the MP. Richard Howarth[3] found that after the 1966 Election the number had increased to sixty, reflecting not an increase in the number of farmers but the smaller majorities enjoyed by the MPs than in 1959.

How likely were farmers, however, to switch their votes as a bloc? The traditional picture of voting behaviour in Britain would suggest that it is very unlikely that farmers switch their votes *en bloc*, even if one party seemed to neglect their interests. Deep party loyalties based on class are the stable basis for electoral divisions in Britain, and not transitory issues. Indeed, which issues would farmers respond to? Farmers are citizens affected by taxes, the cost of living, strikes and such foreign policy issues as entry into the European Economic Community, as well as farm policy. Farm policy alone would surely not cause all farmers to switch their votes.

However, recent research on voting behaviour in Britain has placed greater emphasis on the volatility of the British electorate. One recent study discovered that only 67 per cent of the electorate voted for the same party in both the February and October Elections of 1974.[4] Our greater awareness of the volatility of the electorate may suggest less scepticism about the potential impact of a 'farm voter' than was expressed by the authors of previous studies. Though neither Beynon and Harison nor Richard Howarth thought that the 'farm vote' was particularly important in deciding the outcomes of General Elections, all conceded that there were twenty constituencies in which a swing of 30 per cent of farmers' votes away from the winning party would wipe out its majority.

A net change of twenty seats in Parliament between the parties could have had a major effect. It would, for example, have changed the outcomes of the 1950, 1951, 1955, 1964, and February and October 1974 General Elections. Moreover, as there is no nationwide survey which shows how farmers vote, any dogmatic assertion that farmers are irrevocably committed to the Conservatives can be based only on well-informed guesses. We lack the evidence to be sure that had one party refused to compete for the farm vote there would have been no effect on farmers' voting behaviour. We do have evidence, however, to show that a net change of one-third in farmers' voting behaviour could have affected the national balance between the parties significantly.

Perceptions of the importance of the farm vote

Fortunately, it is not necessary to give a definitive assessment of the importance of the 'farm vote'. Much more significant was how important politicians *thought* the farm vote was.

One of the most obvious features in the pattern of government decisions announced after the *Annual Review and Determination of Guarantees* has been for farmers to do unusually well in Election years. It is not that the increases in subsidies planned in Election years were always large, but, even when they were small, they marked the end of attempts to limit farm subsidies. Thus farm subsidies were increased by only £3 million in 1959. This, however, was a significant improvement from the farmers' viewpoint compared with the reduction of £19 million in the previous year. Even more dramatically, in 1964 the Conservatives increased subsidies by £31 million, a large increase after three years' restraint.

Table 2　Estimates of increases in subsidies to agriculture at time of review[5]

Year	Estimated cost of changes (£ millions)
1957	+14
1958	−19
1959*	+ 3
1960	− 9
1961	+14
1962	−11
1963	0
1964*	+31
1965	+10
1966*	+23
1967	+25
1968	+52·5
1969	+10
1970*	+35

* Election years

Commentators have been quick to draw the lesson. In 1964, *The Economist*, always critical of farm subsidies, argued that: 'It would be foolish to be too surprised that the government has given away so much to the farmers in the annual price review; this is an election year ... politicians seem incapable of asking whether the agricultural vote is worth catching at all.'[6] In 1966, *The Times* noted that the Government and the farmers' unions had reached agreement on the level of farm subsidies and that the previous occasions when this had happened were the other Election years of 1959 and 1964. As *The Times* noted, it is 'funny how these things work out'.[7]

Are such interpretations overly cynical? There is some reason to suppose that they are not. Civil servants and Cabinet ministers with experience of the annual bargaining over the level of farm subsidies freely admit that the 'farm vote' was a major influence on their deliberations. Both the political correspondent of *The Times*[8] and Lord Home's official biographer[9] agree that in 1964 he stepped in over the head of his Minister of Agriculture, Sir Christopher Soames, to ensure that subsidies were set at a level acceptable to the National Farmers' Union. As we have seen, a large increase resulted. Harold Wilson, when Prime Minister, also overruled his Ministry of Agriculture to offer the farmers' unions a more generous increase in an election year. In 1966, after talks between the farmers' unions and the Ministry had broken down, Wilson met with the President of the National Farmers' Union and made a more generous offer. The reason Wilson gives in his autobiography was that 'I was anxious that a breakdown in talks should not become ... an election issue'—[10] surely an outstanding euphemism.

It does, in fact, seem clear that during the 1960s the Conservatives grossly overestimated farmers' electoral importance. In 1962, the Parliamentary Correspondent of *The Times* reported that:

It is about eighteen months since a Minister here and there and one or two party managers were first heard trying out the idea in voices pitched no higher than a whisper behind the back of their hands that the day had now passed when the farming interest had an electoral distribution and power capable of breaking a Conservative Ministry.[11]

But he felt constrained to add immediately that the idea had not been accepted; '... the theory lives on. Nor does it merely live; sometimes it has the ring of established doctrine.' Andrew Roth, a seasoned observer of the Parliamentary scene, reports that in the early 1960s, Conservative backbenchers feared that were their party to alienate the farmers, it would lose seventy to eighty seats.[12]

Though such fears were obviously exaggerated, it is possible to see how they arose. The Conservatives do, after all, represent a large number of rural constituencies. In 1966, the Conservatives represented thirty-one of the forty constituencies in which more than 15 per cent of the workforce was employed in farming. Of the sixty constituencies Howarth identified as having a larger farm vote than half the victors' majority, forty were held by Conservatives, whereas Labour held only eleven. (The Liberals were the most dependent on rural seats; nine of their MPs represented constituencies in which their majority was less than the number of farmers.) Obviously, a heavy loss of the farm vote could have been disastrous.

There was, as we have seen, no hard evidence to show that such losses were impossible. Indeed, as our understanding of the reasons for why people as they do were, until recently, so imperfectly understood, even in academic circles, certain key episodes were taken by Conservatives as proof of the dangers of alienating the farmers. In 1958, for example, the Conservatives unexpectedly lost a by-election to the Liberals in Torrington. There were many reasons for the result. The previous MP had been a National Liberal, not a pure Conservative, and had the advantages of traditional links between his family and the constituency. The Government was unpopular throughout the country and had lost several by-elections. The victory was the first of a postwar series the Liberals were to enjoy between General Elections, each raising hopes (or fears) of a 'Liberal Revival' which never materialized at the following General Election.

Yet commentators almost unanimously explained the Conservatives' defeat by the Government's announcement of cuts in subsidies for agricultural products important to the constituency. *The Daily Telegraph* noted the 'unusual if high-minded indifference of the government in issuing in mid campaign a locally unpopular price review'.[13] *The Times* reported that when the defeated Conservative candidate appeared on the balcony when the result of the election was announced, he was greeted with a shout of 'You let the farmers down'.[14] *The Manchester Guardian* had anticipated trouble for the Conservatives as soon as the decisions on farm subsidies were announced, not merely in Torrington but 'in the large number of marginal seats held in rural areas'.[15] Such explanations would have an obvious effect on Conservative MPs.

It is more difficult to explain the Labour party's interest in the farm vote. It is true that there were, as we have seen, some rural Labour constituencies, particularly in Wales. There were, in addition, three highly marginal and very rural constituencies in East Anglia in which Labour always had a real chance of winning. Yet it seems odd that, from such slender facts, such extravagant hopes grew. In 1958, for example, R. H. S. Crossman told a Labour party conference discussing agriculture that 'it may well be through this (agricultural) policy statement more than any other that we shall achieve the twenty or thirty seats we require' (for victory).[16] Speakers at Labour party conferences associated with the National Union of Agricultural and Allied Workers (NUAAW) solemnly assured conferences that 'people in the countryside are once again looking to Labour for a new deal' or that 'the policy outlined . . . will win the countryside for Labour'.[17] As might perhaps be guessed, these policy statements promised measures such as an increase in domestic production, special help for small farmers, and cheap credit for agriculture, measures which would appeal to 'the farm vote'. The 1970 Labour Manifesto, like its predecessors, promised that: 'Our policies will continue to be devised to benefit the farmer as well as the consumer.'[18]

It is hard to discover any theoretical underpinning to the Labour Party's hopes for a new breakthrough. Philip Williams, a student of British elections as well as a distinguished authority on French politics, noted at the time that in the 1950 Election agricultural areas had swung less against Labour than had the suburbs. He argued that the 'Conservative Party may, indeed, slowly be changing, electorally speaking, from a country party with residential accretions to a spa and suburb party with a rural tail—*and a tail which can be cut off*' (emphasis added).[19] Yet Williams argued, too, that the Labour Party General Secretary, Morgan Phillips, had shown 'extraordinary optimism' about rural constituencies 'for which there is (and was) no basis'.

In the last analysis, Labour's quest for the farm vote is explained by three factors. These are the logic implicit in a two-party system, the Labour party's quest for new blocs of voters, and simple miscalculation. The pressures on a party in a two-party system to change policies in order to achieve a majority are obvious. A party with 49 per cent of the seats in Parliament and an ideologically pure manifesto achieves nothing; a party which compromises slightly and wins a majority can do much. There were particular pressures on the Labour party to seek out blocs of voters to add to its natural constituency, for, by 1950, Labour seemed to many to have got as far as it could by relying on the industrial areas alone. Williams argued that: 'Industrial England alone, it is now obvious, can give the Labour Party office but not power; and if the stalemate is to be broken, other groups must be won over.' The belief among Labour party strategists that farmers were a group that could be won over was almost certainly a mistake. It was not, however, a non-rational policy.

Just how strong an effect the supposed necessities of electoral strategy can have be gauged by looking at the Liberals. It has often been claimed that the Liberals, as a party unlikely to form a government, can act as a party of principle, not expediency. Yet because of the importance of rural constituencies to the Liberals, they have had to be sensitive to electoral realities in farm politics. Thus, though claiming to be the party of free trade, the Liberals' agricultural policy was often, during the 1960s, the most protectionist of all the parties. Indeed, the Liberals often seemed to be almost unaware of the contradiction and able, therefore, as *The Times* once noted, to say 'that they support protection for the farmer, but also free trade and all that it implies'.[20]

The cultural context

Not every group can hope to be the beneficiaries of party competition for their votes. Criminals, speculators, and racial minorities are obvious examples of groups whose support politicians seek only at the risk of losing votes elsewhere. Farmers enjoy the great advantage of having few 'natural enemies', so long as the cost of farm subsidies is not oppressive for the city dweller.

The political genius of the method of subsidizing agriculture in Britain prior to membership of the EEC was that it was inconspicuous. Only in a limited number of cases where subsidies were generated through marketing boards—milk being the obvious example—did an increase in subsidies produce an immediate increase in charges to the consumer. For most commodities, higher subsidies were just another charge on the Exchequer. Any link between increasing subsidies and raising taxes was both tenuous and hidden. In the context of such a policy, the natural fondness of the British for farmers was dominant. Opinion polls showed both ready acceptance of farm subsidies and even far greater tolerance of disruptive militant tactics by farmers than was accorded similar behaviour by groups such as students. Even when reminded of their existence, few members of the public wanted to cut government expenditure on farm subsidies.[21]

Conservatives have always claimed to be close to the countryside and their rhetoric reflects this. In 1948, R. A. Butler gave full expression to these emotions:

In saving the agriculture, we are saving more than our own economy. We are saving a way of life in which the features are kindliness, freedom, and above all, wisdom. These are the qualities of the countryman and countrywoman. They are instinct with Conservative policy, they are vital to our existence.[22]

Though the Conservatives in Parliament have become, in terms of their composition, more a party of the City of London and less one of the countryside, Butler's words would find an echo to this day.

The Labour party does not have the same tradition of viewing the countryside as so idyllic. The party's institutional links with agriculture are predominantly through the National Union of Agricultural and Allied Workers (NUAAW), which represents men who have experienced the rough end of rural life. Robert Blythe, in his celebrated portrait of English village life, *Akenfield*, quotes the views of one local organizer on 'the good old days':

I don't want to see the old days back. Every bad thing gets to sound pleasant when time has passed. But it wasn't pleasant then, and that's a fact. Everywhere you looked there was this graft to keep things going. Working at the graft sapped people of their strength to live their lives decently. ... It used to be 'get here' or 'get there'—that is how farmers spoke to their workers.[23]

Yet Labour has shown no hostility to farmers and, indeed, has historically done as much as the Conservatives to help them. As we have seen, the peacetime commitment to agriculture was made by Labour, and Labour governments have made some of the largest postwar increases in farm subsidies. This is partly explained by the pressures of electoral competition which have been described. There is, however, a strand in Labour party thinking which has helped farmers. Both the Left and the Right of the Labour party have a disdain for the market system. The Left of the party has, of course, seen the market system as the antithesis of the socialist society it seeks to create. The Right of the party has more pragmatic objections. The Fabian may not view a free market with the same moral vehemence as the Tribunite, but he is sure that government intervention produces not only a more just but also a more efficient society.

Not surprisingly, therefore, Labour governments have done much to promote closer administrative relations with industry. The 1964–70 Labour Government introduced special organizations—Economic Development Committees—to facilitate contacts between management, unions, and the Government, and, in addition, a special unit—the Industrial Reorganization Corporation—to promote mergers. Whether or not these measures promoted economic efficiency is debatable, but it is obvious that their purpose was not directly related to creating socialism or increasing equality. Interventionism is seen as the way to a more efficient society, and the Labour party feels that as it is more willing to accept intervention than the Conservatives, it falls to it to solve practical problems long neglected by those with an ideological objection to government action.

It was very much this tradition of pragmatic problem solving which Tom Williams used to explain his commitment to the farmers' cause during his time as

Minister of Agriculture. For Williams, the countryside under free enterprise constituted a problem, and he searched for a solution: 'we had tackled a problem which had defeated both Liberals and the Conservatives. . . .'[24]

William's solution to the problem was, of course, a close relationship between government and farming. Each year, the Ministry of Agriculture sat down with a responsible employees' association, the National Farmers' Union, to discuss not only farm incomes but production patterns, investment, and general trends in the industry. This was, effectively, a model for the partnership of government and industry that the Labour Government of 1964–70 tried to create with its National Plan. The reason why the Government had such influence over the industry so early was, of course, that it was the industry's paymaster. This close relationship gave agricultural subsidies a certain immunity from criticism. Agricultural subsidies were the means through which farming became the model of the administered economy in which government would greatly influence industry's major decisions. As the 'administered economy' became the Labour party's favoured solution to Britain's economic problems, criticism of agricultural subsidies became more difficult. Though Labour lacks the Conservatives' emotional commitment to the countryside, it has been, therefore, as little disposed to criticize the system.

Capitalizing on political advantages

Political advantages are, like every other, either squandered or exploited. Politicians within both the Conservative and Labour parties who identify with agriculture have taken steps to ensure that farmers' political advantages are not wasted.

Both the Labour and Conservative Parliamentary committees maintain special standing committees of backbenchers on agriculture. Though both parties' committees run similar programmes of talks by experts on agriculture and officials of agricultural interest groups on matters of current interest, there is little doubt that the Conservatives' committee, reflecting the larger number of Conservative MPs with either a personal or constituency interest in farming and the party's emotional commitment to agriculture, is much the more effective (see Table 3). Clearly, the Conservatives have both more potential members of their committee and a more interested audience in the House than Labour.

It is easy to belittle the backbench committees. Membership of both committees is entirely voluntary. In the case of the Conservative committee, anyone who is a member of the Parliamentary party can attend and even vote for its officers. There is no guarantee that a Conservative MP who participates in one meeting will attend the next, while the Labour party's committee struggles to find members. 'If you take an interest in the car industry, that's acceptable, but if it's agriculture, you're playing for votes' commented one of the members of Labour's committee bitterly. Harold MacMillan's dismissive description of backbench committees, 'adult education classes', may seem to fit either committee. It is, however, underestimating their importance.

A backbench committee which focuses on the work of one ministry, such as the Ministry of Agriculture, is, if the party is in power, its 'natural' constituency. Detailed knowledge of the work, problems, and structure of government ministries among MPs is notoriously low. When the subject is, like agriculture, of little general interest, a minister's backbench committee is the only group of MPs who take a regular, serious interest in his work. As ministers' reputations and prospects for promotion are greatly influenced by the general feeling at Westminster about the quality of their performance, they do well to pay attention to the party's backbench committee that focuses on their ministry. It is that committee which, more than anyone outside the Cabinet, sets the tone in the Lobbies, in the National Press, in the Members' bars, and in conversations with the Whips with comments that 'Smith is making a hash of it (or doing a good job) at Agriculture'.

Ministers of Agriculture of both parties have, therefore, encouraged regular contacts with their backbenchers' agriculture committes in general and their officers in particular. Few men outside the Ministry or the National Farmers' Union have as much opportunity to influence a Conservative Government's

Table 3   Number of MPs with a personal or constituency interest in Agriculture, 1970

	Conservative	Labour	Liberal
Occupational/personal links*	79	10	1
Constituency interest†	31	6	3

* Owning a farm, describing oneself wholly or partly as a farmer or farm manager, or being so listed by A. Roth, *The Business Background of MPs,* Parliamentary Profiles, London, 1970.
† Constituencies held by the parties in 1970 in which more than 15 per cent of the workforce was employed in agriculture.

agriculture policy as the Chairman of the Conservative Backbenchers' Committee on Agriculture. Moreover, there can be no doubt that in both the major Parties, the backbench committees on agriculture have acted as committees *for* agriculture. Dependent on MPs with a personal constituency commitment to farming, the committees have constituted significant pressure on ministers inclined to 'bash the farmers'. It became customary for Conservative ministers to appear to justify themselves before the backbench agriculture committee on the night after they had informed the Commons of the level of subsidies for the coming year. Any minister who had angered the National Farmers' Union could be sure of a rough ride.

A further example of how British MPs can act as a bipartisan pressure group in defence of shared constituency interests was provided by the Select Committee on Agriculture. The Committee was created not for reasons of agricultural politics, but as one of a number created as part of the late Richard Crossman's reforms of Parliamentary procedure. The Committee soon became dominated by MPs who represented rural constituencies, and coincidentally was the most assertive of the Select Committees. The reward for this assertiveness was liquidation at the hands of the Government in 1969. Yet, in three stormy sessions the Select Committee did much to help the farmers' cause. In particular, it held hearings and issued a report supporting the National Farmers' Union's arguments for an expansion of domestic production and higher farm subsidies.[25]

Farmers have benefited from the organized support of surprisingly large numbers of MPs interested in agriculture. Yet it remains doubtful whether these MPs alone have made much impact. The basic laws of British Parliamentary politics apply fully to agriculture overriding constituency interests. Whatever the criticisms voiced in public or in private, no MP in the last thirty years has defied his party's whip in a major vote on agriculture and no government has lost an important vote on an Agriculture Bill. Moreover, even an MP who attends a meeting of his party's Backbench Committee on Agriculture has but a limited knowledge of the industry, and has other constituency duties competing with agriculture for his time and attention. MPs are neither equipped, nor eager, to play a major role in the formulation of agricultural policy.

Conclusion

It is obvious that British farmers, enjoyed real political advantages. The competition between the Conservative and Labour parties for the 'farm vote' was the most important of these. This competition could not have been carried on had helping farmers aroused popular antagonism. However, the British system of agricultural support (described in Chapter 1) made the cost of farm subsidies to the rest of the population relatively inconspicuous, while most people continued to look on farmers with a fondness which reflects the high status of the countryside in British culture. Courting the farm vote did not mean losing the consumer vote. Meanwhile, a surprisingly large number of MPs had some contact with agriculture; within both major parties, enough backbenchers were prepared to staff backbench committees on agriculture to make them viable, an advantage not enjoyed by other industries. Particularly in the case of the Conservative party, the backbench committee could keep a minister on his toes and sensitive to rural opinion, even between elections.

The political advantages enjoyed by farmers provided a constraint on the British Government's freedom of action. Yet such constraints, on their own, may well have proved ineffective. Had the Ministry enjoyed a monopoly of expertise in agricultural policy, it is probable that the political advantages farmers enjoy would have mattered little. MPs, the public, and even farmers could have been convinced that the Government's policy was sensible or even desirable. In fact, of course, the Ministry has not retained a monopoly of expertise, but has shared it with the farmers' unions. Many would consider these unions the farmers' greatest political advantage, while even the sceptic might suppose that they have made the political advantages we have encountered already more effective. How much, in fact, have the farmers' unions added to the other political advantages farmers enjoy?

Notes

1. This point has been argued in relation to farmers by S. J. Rogers, 'Farmers as a pressure group', *New Society*, 5 February, 1970.
2. V. H. Beyron and J. E. Harrison, *The Political Significance of the British Agricultural Vote*, University of Exeter, Department of Economics Report 134, 1962.
3. Richard Howarth, 'The political strength of British agriculture', *Political Studies*, 1969.
4. B. Särlvik, I. Crewe, J. Alt, 'British election study', February–October 1974 panel.
5. From *Annual Review and Determination of Guarantees*, White Papers, HMSO, London, 1956–73.
6. *The Economist*, 21 March, 1964.
7. *The Times*, 17 March, 1966.
8. *The Times*, 19 March, 1964.
9. Kenneth Young, *Sir Alec Douglas Home*, J. M. Dent and Sons, London, 1970, p. 208.
10. Harold Wison, *The Labour Government, 1964–70, A Personal Record*, Weidenfeld and Nicholson and Michael Joseph, London, 1971, pp. 221–222.
11. *The Times*, 9 July, 1962.
12. Andrew Roth, *Heath and the Heathmen*, Routledge and Kegan Paul, London, 1972, p. 154.
13. *The Daily Telegraph*, 20 March, 1958.
14. *The Times*, 29 March, 1958.
15. *The Manchester Guardian*, 21 March, 1958.
16. *Report of the Fifty-eighth Annual Conference of the Labour Party*, Labour Publications, London, 1958, p. 134.
17. Ibid., p. 189.
18. *Now Britain's Strong, Let's Make it Great Again*, The Labour Party, London, 1970, pp. 9–10.
19. P. M. Williams, 'Election analysis', *Socialist Commentary*, 1950.
20. *The Times*, 20 September, 1958.
21. National Opinion Polls, *Political Bulletin*, NOP, London, February and August, 1970.
22. National Union of Conservative and Unionist Associations, *Conference Report, 1948*.
23. Robert Blythe, *Akenfield*, Penguin Books, London, 1972, p. 101.
24. Lord Williams of Barnborough, *Digging for Britain*, Hutchinson, London, 1965, p. 64.
25. The Select Committee on Agriculture, Session 1968–69, *Report Minutes of Evidence*, Appendices and Index.

Chapter 3

Agricultural Interest Groups in Britain

Agriculture is one of Britain's most subsidized industries. The major agricultural interest group, the National Farmers' Union (NFU), is widely regarded as Britain's most efficient. The presumption that this is more than a chance correlation is strengthened by the additional and apparently overwhelming advantages the NFU enjoys, such as its recruitment of a massive proportion of its potential membership, the absence of any threat from rivals, and close relations with the Government Department—the Ministry of Agriculture, Fisheries, and Food—whose work affects its members most.

Though the National Farmers' Union of England and Wales dominates British agricultural politics, it is, as its title implies, only part of a confederation of farmers' unions covering the United Kingdom. Separate unions exist for Scotland and Ulster, unions which, given the structural differences between English, Scottish, and Ulser agriculture, have slightly different priorities to the NFU of England and Wales and have different ministries as patrons. Hill farming, for example, is more important in Scotland and Wales than in England, and ties are to the Scottish Office and the Home Office, the Department responsible for Ulster before direct rule. Size and financial strength ensure that the English and Welsh NFU is far more than *primus inter pares*. In the late 1960s, the headquarters of the NFU of England and Wales was spending over £1 million per annum; the headquarters of the Scottish Farmers' Union was spending under £50,000.[1] The result is a difference not only in the scope but in the technical and political quality of the work done by the NFU of England and Wales, a difference which is well known in government circles.

Membership

The fundamental reason why the NFU of England and Wales can spend so much is the size of its membership. Though the Union does not publish figures, unpublished documents reveal that it has a membership of some 150,000, equivalent to 80 per cent of the full-time farmers in England and Wales today.[2] To organize such a high proportion of any industry would be an achievement; to succeed in organizing an industry renowned for individualism and characterized by geographical isolation and enormous geographical or social differences is striking. The small hill farmer of Wales, keeping sheep on less than 100 acres of poor land and earning some £1,500 per annum, has been joined in common cause with the grain baron of East Anglia, owning perhaps 3,000 acres of land worth up to £3 million. Comparison with the United States, where only 30 per cent of full-time farmers have been organized into several conflicting nationwide pressure groups, or with the factionalism of French farming politics are instructive.

No doubt much of the NFU's success reflects the industry and efficiency of its officials. Social scientists, however, look for more general explanations.

The pioneer of applying theories borrowed from economics to political science, Mancur Olson, has argued that only individualized benefits provide a rational motive for joining a pressure group.[3] If the NFU succeeds in raising farm subsidies, Olson would argue, every farmer will benefit, irrespective of whether or not he belongs to the NFU. Why, then, should he bother to pay the subscription? Indeed, even if a farmer believes that the success of the NFU is dependent on its success in recruiting a high proportion of farmers, joining is still irrational, for each farmer who decides to join is but one individual among many, and has no guarantee or sound reason to suppose that his solitary example will encourage many others to join too. Only individualized benefits restricted to members, benefits such as concessionary insurance rates, provide a rational motive for joining.

There is certainly some evidence to suggest that Olson's arguments apply to the NFU. The NFU has its own insurance company, the NFU Mutual, and its handbook of services for members, *What Our Union Does For Us*, notes that the Union provides legal guidance on literally thousands of matters each year, and gives advice on both national and local taxation issues. Yet Olson's theory is more elegant than convincing. As Barry notes, the provision of selective benefits of at least equal value has not produced as many members for interest groups in the United States.[4] At the very least, Olson would have to explain why, inspite of the provision of greater welfare facilities by the State, British farmers are particularly attracted by selective benefits. There are other problems in applying Olson's theory. It is far from clear that the NFU Mutual offers farmers better or cheaper insurance than they could obtain elsewhere; their patronage may reflect more farmers' loyalty to their Union than a reason for joining it. Finally, the NFU presents itself to its members, or potential members, not as a supplier of individual benefits but as the agent for representing farmers' collective interests to government, firms laying pipelines, and others whose activities affect a large number of farmers. It is, of course, possible that Olson could sell membership in the NFU better than the NFU does itself, but it would seem unlikely.

Indeed, it is even unlikely that the success of the NFU can be explained in terms of its own characteristics. As Samuel Beer has noted,[5] all interest groups in Britain recruit an unusually high proportion of their potential members. The success of the NFU is but one example of a more general feature of British life—the importance of interest groups. Several authorities have found the explanation for this in the British political culture. Beer himself drew attention to the 'widespread acceptance of functional representation in British political culture', while Eckstein,[6] in his study of the British Medical Association, noted a streak of 'persistent corporatism' in the British mentality.

Though the writers who emphasize political culture do us a service in drawing attention to the widespread success of interest groups in Britain, the scarcely provide an explanation. As both Barrington Moore and Brian Barry note,[7] there is a considerable circularity to arguments based on political culture. British interest groups, it is argued, recruit a high proportion of potential members because the British political culture values joining interest groups; we know that the British political culture commends joining interest groups because so many Britons do. Values within the political culture are used to explain the very behaviour from which their existence is inferred.

Nettl, in contrast, laid particular stress on the role of government in fostering interest groups. Indeed, he argued that 'the whole point about representation is that it is largely government sponsored—or at least government encouraged'.[8] In view of the particularly close relations between the NFU and government, which we shall encounter later, Nettl's explanation has an obvious appeal. The Ministry of Agriculture has followed a deliberate policy of giving the NFU a privileged, quasi-monopoly role in representing farmers. When a splinter group, the Farmers' Union of Wales (inspired by both nationalism and a belief that the NFU neglected the interests of the small hill farmer) emerged in the 1950s, the Ministry of Agriculture refused it a role in crucial discussions which set subsidies for the year ahead. (We shall refer further to the Farmers' Union of Wales below.) The very system of subsidies used until Britain entered the EEC facilitated unity in the farming community as subsidies were paid out of Exchequer funds. The problem which occurred in the United States of government help for one type of farmer (e.g. feed grains producers) raising costs for another sort of farmer (e.g. cattle farmers) was avoided. Only for 'final products' such as milk sold to consumers did British governments create subsidies by managing the market with monopolistic marketing boards.

Moreover, Nettl's explanation is given plausibility by the obvious advantages to the Ministry of Agriculture of the NFU's position. Instead of choosing between conflicting advice from squabbling interest groups, the Ministry is given a co-ordinated picture of the industry's needs by the NFU. When government has been particularly closely involved with the industry, as when it supervised farmers to ensure high standards and output during the war, the NFU provided a pool of knowledgeable local people to enforce the Ministry's policy.

Yet plausible though Nettl's theory is, it does not explain adequately the NFU's historical position. The Union achieved a membership of 100,000 in 1925, and thereafter completely dominated English agricultural politics in spite of the fact that its relationship with the Ministry had yet to jell. Indeed, before the Second World War, the NFU concentrated more on sponsoring MPs than fostering close links with Whitehall. Though Nettl's theory may explain a surge in the Union's membership in the 1940s, it does not apply to the Union's earlier dominance. The reasons for this lie deeper, partially outside rural England.

It is a widely held view that employers' associations in Britain have developed as a response to the unusually early and widespread growth of trade unions in Britain.[9] Even agriculture was not unaffected by the rise of unionism; by the middle of 1914, the National Union of Agricultural Workers had only 360 branches in England and Wales, with a membership of 15,000.[10] There had even been successful strikes in Lancashire (around Ormskirk) and agitation in Norfolk and Northamptonshire. Farmworkers were able to make significant improvements in their wages during the labour shortages of the First World War, and when farmers cut wages after the war a prolonged struggle ensued in East Anglia, culminating in the unsuccessful strike of 1923.

Though most of rural England continued quietly in its hierarchical social ways, these were in fact the years in which the NFU developed. Founded in 1908, the NFU had 15,000 members in 1910, 50,000 in 1918, and it passed the 100,000 mark in 1925.[11] Apart from any apprehension over the unionizing of farmworkers, the NFU benefited from a general fear of the widespread growth of militant mass unionism and the concomitant growth of employers' associations. Long accustomed to being a minority in an ever more industrialized society, the British farmer now faced the danger of being the only unorganized interest. British governments had shown their indifference to agriculture during its recession of the late nineteenth century. Now agriculture was further threatened by the formation of non-agricultural interest groups. It was on such fears that the Union played in its early recruiting literature:

The question we propose to ask you is whether you think you are safe at a time when every trade is combining AGAINST EVERY OTHER in remaining outside you own Farmers' Union. Against every other mind you. Every trade is combined against yours. Dare you risk isolation?[12]

Thus it was the strength of groups representing other sectors of the population, ultimately traceable to the development of trades unions, which gave British farmers the incentive to organize. British farmers' unity is traceable to the class consciousness of the British working class.

The hegemony of the National Farmers' Union

Whereas the NFU is an obvious success, other agricultural interest groups suffer from conspicuous weaknesses. The Country Landowners' Association (CLA) was, until recently, more a social club for the country gentry than a modern interest group, organizing a highly successful Game Fair but having little effect on farm policy. Though the CLA is changing, it has identified consciously with the interests of large landowners, and is thus too specialized to challenge the NFU's dominance in questions of general agricultural policy. The National Union of Agricultural and Allied Workers (NUAAW) has always been weak. The reasons for this weakness are entirely obvious. Farmworkers are highly dispersed, with few farmers employing more than a handful of men. Many farmworkers are related to their employer. Even for those who are not, English rural society is, with a few exceptions such as East Anglia, conservative and hierarchical. Moreover, farmworkers, with few alternative forms of employment and often dependent on their employers for housing, have been politically susceptible to intimidation by employers. The result has been that the Union has succeeded in recruiting less than a quarter of its potential membership.

Both the CLA and the NUAAW have wisely avoided competing with the NFU. When the Select Committee on Agriculture took evidence from the two organizations, both disclaimed any wish to play a major role in policymaking. The NUAAW rather deferentially suggested that issues such as the level of subsidies, which in fact, determine the structure and future for the industry in which its members work, was a matter for their employers alone.[13] Only when prompted by the NFU during one of its periodic major campaigns for higher subsidies do the CLA or NUAAW issue statements on general agricultural policy.

The NFU has found splinter groups more troublesome. The most formidable of these has been the Farmers' Union of Wales (FUW), inspired both by nationalism and feelings of neglect among small farmers.[14] Founded in 1955, the FUW's membership has never exceeded that of the NFU in Wales, and may contain non-farmers such as Nonconformist ministers attracted by motives as diverse as nationalism and cheap insurance. Nevertheless, the FUW's claims for recognition from the MAFF have been a constant worry to the NFU.

In another part of the 'Celtic fringe', the South West, the NFU has come under constant attack for being insufficiently militant. Local leaders, of whom the most prominent was Wallace Day, pressed hard for the NFU to organize not only market boycotts but 'direct action' such as blocking roads and disrupting traffic.

The NFU, like a monopolist forestalling the entry of a competitor into its field by marginally cutting its prices, has been able to deal with such challenges by offering minor concessions to its critics. The Welsh malcontents' challenge to the NFU was met by the formation of a Welsh Council, a purely symbolic gesture. The NFU's own enquiry into its structure and management concluded that 'the underlying and only valid reason for the Welsh Council and Conference is political'.[15] The Council did very little, but it did what it did in Wales, and the FUW's claims that the NFU was interested only in England were weakened. Similarly, when in 1970 grass roots pressure for militant action became irresistible, the Executive stole the militants' clothes and called a market boycott. Though *The Economist* noted the NFU leaders' 'nippiness in getting out a part plan chock full of extravagant demands', it also saw that their main motive was 'to wipe the eyes of the county action committees springing up all over the place'.[16] The market boycott was called at a time when it caused the least effect on prices and little embarrassment to the Government. The Union's symbolic display of militancy absorbed the pressure from the militants without compromising its general policy of close, statesmanlike relations with government. As the giant which dominates its field, the NFU has proved its ability to smother nationalist or militant critics by embracing them.

The NFU and government

It is a commonplace to remark that British pressure groups have ready access to government departments which are of particular relevance to their members. Studies of the links between pressure groups and government in Britain stress not only the practical advantages for government which flow from this (such as the supply of information and the avoidance of political trouble if the interest group 'consents')[17] but also that interest groups have a right to be consulted. Failure to consult with interests before government policy is announced is taken as *prima facie* proof of maladministration.[18]

That the NFU should have regular contacts with the Ministry of Agriculture is, to anyone with knowledge of British government, wholly predictable. There is a widespread feeling in academic and government circles, however, that the relationship between the NFU and the Ministry of Agriculture is far closer than is normal. This feeling rests on several factors. The most obvious is that, prior to Britain's entry into the EEC, farm subsidies were set after a long series of meetings between the NFU and the Ministry of Agriculture, meetings which were officially no more than consultations but which looked to many more like negotiations. Moreover, many people suspect that the Ministry of Agriculture has defined its role as spokesman *for* agriculture, encouraging partnership with the NFU.

The truth of these claims will be discussed in the next chapter. However, whether or not the NFU's relationship with the Ministry of Agriculture is unusual, it is certainly close. During the Select Committee on Agriculture's hearings on the conduct of Britain's application to join the EEC, several MPs made a strong effort to establish that the NFU had been insufficiently consulted. The Union's President, Sir Gwilym Williams, would have no part of such criticism. He agreed that there had been no conference with the Ministry on the British application to join the EEC, but explained that the Union's links with the Ministry made one superfluous.

Sir Gwilym suggested that:

It may be that there is a special relationship here. We are *constantly* in touch with the Ministry *at all levels* on one problem or another, and many times in the course of conversation, a particular problem *vis a vis* the Common Market may have come up over the years (italics added).

Pressed further to criticize the Ministry, Sir Gwilym replied:

No conference, we do not deal that way with the Department.[19]

The political influence that this relationship gives the NFU is a question for the next chapter. It is obvious, however, that the NFU's close relationship with government is an enormous advantage to the Union as an organization. Government has made it clear that any farmer who wishes to talk or negotiate with it about agricultural policy must do so through the farmers' unions. The unions have, in effect, been granted what is known in trade union circles as a closed shop.

Everything so far might lead us to take an ever higher view of the power of British farmers than we did in the previous chapter. To the advantages of the overestimation of the 'farm vote' by politicians and a large, well-organized lobby in Parliament can be added that of having a large, successful interest group with close ties to government. Yet it is wise to pause before assuming that the NFU is unambiguously a supplement to farmers' political advantages. The impact of the NFU cannot be assessed without considering the nature of the Union, its own policymaking process and, of course, the impact of government on the only established voice of British agriculture.

The NFU: who governs?

Organizations differ in the freedom of action they allow their leaders. In some organizations, such as British trades unions with powerful shop stewards, leaders must always be looking over their shoulders to see if their followers are with them. It is more commonly thought, however, that pressure groups and other voluntary organizations consist of an indifferent mass membership and an active, interested elite. The ready acceptance of the view that voluntary organizations are governed by an elite owes much to the scholarship of Michels, who generalized his finding that an elite controlled even social democratic parties into an 'Iron Law of Oligarchy'; whatever the formal commitment to democracy in an organization's constitution, control by an elite is inevitable. The apathy and technical incompetence of ordinary members defeats formally participatory arrangements.

The NFU appears to fit Michels's law. It is formally a pyramidic but democratic organization. Local branches elect delegates to county farmers' unions, which in turn send delegates to the Council of the NFU, which elects the President and other national officers. An Annual General Meeting provides further opportunities for the county branch activist to participate at the national level. Unfortunately, this chain designed to provide a link between members of the Union and even their highest officers, and which the Union argues makes it 'democratic in the extreme',[20] is broken at key points. At the local level, an official NFU report found that the local branch was not fulfilling its theoretical functions. Indeed, 'its survival seems to be little more than a time-hallowed convention'.[21] Because of a shortage of sufficient volunteers to fill posts, activists had to fill several, forming an involuntary elite.

Moreover, the farmer who takes a major part in NFU affairs is not sociologically typical. A study of the Cheshire county branch of the NFU showed that though its activists were not the social elite of the county, they were farmers with holdings at least twice the size of the average farm in the county.[22] The problem is even more severe at the national level. Not only must the member of the national Council attend its monthly meetings but is also expected to sit on one of Council's specialist committees and attend county and local branch meetings. If he becomes chairman of one of Council's committees, he will find himself travelling to London at least once a week. The NFU's Cowen Report on its structure noted that: 'Council duties must seriously diminish his [a farmer's] ability to supervise and take part in the work on his farm which is his livelihood.'[23] Only the richer farmer can afford this loss: a survey by the NFU's own journal, the *British Farmer*, showed that no chairman of a Council committee had a holding of less than 200 acres, substantial by British standards.[24]

Even farmers who do find it possible to belong to Council are trapped between its claims on their time and those of their farms. As unpaid amateurs, they are too short of information and time and are too numerous to formulate policy. The initiative passes to their elected and appointed full-time officials. Council may express anger, discontent, or approval; it cannot formulate policy. Only once since the war has a President of the NFU been removed because Council disapproved of his style or policies, in spite of a rule that a President seeking re-election should obtain 85 per cent of the vote. Even he, Sir Gwilym Williams, was replaced by his Vice-President, with little observable effect on policy.

The effect of government on the NFU

The 'natural' trend within the NFU has been, therefore, towards concentration of power in the hands of the President and his permanent officials. The Union's relationship with government has added a further powerful impetus to this, however. The fact is that there have been, until recently, certain unwritten rules which British pressure groups had to obey if they hoped to enjoy a close partnership with government. The chief of these were that those consulted should respect confidences, that they should have technical expertise, that they should refrain from political activity which might embarrass the Government during discussions, that their proposals should be 'reasonable' or moderate, and that the organization should produce a spokesman who had clear authority to speak on its behalf. A pressure group which did not conform to this code might still be consulted formally. It would not, however, enjoy the same opportunity to hear, and have the opportunity to shape, the Government's own opinions in their formative stages.

This code immediately strengthened the position of its leaders *vis à vis* its members. The secrecy, or 'confidence', which the Government requires as a condition for frank consultation strikes an immediate blow at the authority of its Council. The Ministry of Agriculture will not allow the NFU's representatives to take one of its proposals to a vote or even debate in the Union's Council. The Union's position must be stated and formed by its officers. Council cannot mandate its officers without the Ministry of Agriculture becoming intransigent; its officers cannot seek guidance from Council without, in the Ministry's view, breaking its confidence.

The Ministry's requirement that a pressure group that wishes to be taken seriously should have a clearly accepted spokesman also strengthens the position of the NFU's President. When the NFU first became closely involved in setting agricultural subsidies in the 1940s, the chairman of Council's specialist committees were involved in discussions with the Government. The frank presentation of differences in interests between the commodities the different chairmen represented antagonized the Ministry of Agriculture and weakened the position of the NFU. Committee chairmen were soon banished from all major discussions with the Government affecting farmers as a whole, and were left only minor, specialist activities. The President, assisted by the highest permanent officials, took an exclusive responsibility for major discussions with the Government.

Thus, partly because of the pressures so often found in voluntary organizations and partly because of those which result from its close relationship with government, power in the NFU has been concentrated in the hands of its office-holders. The NFU's enquiry into its structure, the Cowen Report, noted that:

... the major decisions of policy are not instigated by Council or even by the General Purposes Committee but from a quite small group centred on the office holders ... it [Council] has delegated the policy making function to the Office Holders it appoints annually ... Council is, in fact, very largely consultative.[25]

Other commentators have endorsed this view.[26]

The relationship with government has not only influenced the location of power within the NFU but has also helped determine the sort of person who exercises it. The style of the Union's leadership has been technocratic; even the elected leaders of the Union who must, of necessity, possess political skills, emphasize their technical competence. Among the permanent staff at the NFU's Knightsbridge headquarters, the atmosphere is reminiscent of a shadow but slightly more luxurious Ministry of Agriculture. Apart from the everyday contact with the Ministry, the highly trained staff produce praiseworthy technical papers and sober analyses of the effects of British or EEC policies presented in the style of government White Papers. Involvement in electoral politics is almost inconceivable.

This technocratic atmosphere makes it difficult to assess the political attitudes of the NFU. A technical approach may preclude radicalism, but does the NFU reflect the overwhelmingly Conservative affiliation of its members? There is often suspicion in Labour circles that the NFU is more likely to criticize a Labour than a Conservative Government, but such attitudes seem ill-founded. The worst relations between a President of the NFU and a Minister of Agriculture were undoubtedly between Sir Harold Woolley and Sir Christopher Soames. Indeed, the most serious allegations of bias against the leadership of the NFU suggests that it has been too friendly to the Labour party. In the mid 1960s, there were serious disagreements between the leadership of the Union and the Conservatives about the best method of subsidizing agriculture. Thereafter, committed Conservatives suspected that the NFU's leadership was trying to throw its members' votes to Labour. A columnist in a leading farm newspaper wrote:

When I look through the N.F.U.'s formidable list of suggested questions for (Parliamentary) candidates, I was made to feel that Mr. Wilson (the Labour Prime Minister) might well have had a hand in their drafting. Two questions accuse the Tories of twisting facts, a dozen go along with Labour, not in so many words but in step for all that. Is the Union's hierarchy saying 'Vote Labour and be secure?'[27]

The columnist struck a responsive chord with several correspondents, one of whom commented that 'this final action has left no doubt in the minds of farmers that the Union is saying "Preserve the *status quo* with Labour. The Conservative policy puts your livelihood at risk".'[28]

The leadership did, in fact, believe precisely that. The Union's leaders felt that the Conservatives, who were anxious to abolish subsidies to farmers from the Exchequer and wished instead to subsidize farmers through higher prices, were not providing farmers with adequate security. It is significant, therefore, not that the NFU's questions to candidates were biased towards Labour but that its support for Labour's agricultural policies, which were more or less identical with the Union's, was so muted. The explanation lies in the fact that a British pressure group which aimed for as close involvement in policymaking as did the NFU was not 'allowed' by the Whitehall code of practice to play electoral politics, in spite of the Union's sympathy for the policies of the party in power. Surprisingly, considering the numerous political advantages farmers enjoy, the NFU operates in an almost a-political fashion.

Criticisms of the leadership

It is not unusual for presidents of the NFU to be accused of insufficient militancy and too great a desire to cooperate with the Government. Sir Gwilym Williams was removed from office, according to the *Farmer and Stockbreeder*, because he was 'too fair-minded, quite and patient an operator for these thrusting, strident and impatient times'.[29] The current President of the NFU, Sir Henry Plumb, though firmly in control, has been criticized, too. *The Financial Times*'s agriculture correspondent, John Charrington, noted that: 'His negotiating style is criticized as being too inclined to compromise by some of the members ... [Plumb] rejects disruptive protest when inconvenience can be caused. He is much more a man for thorough and persistent negotiation.'[30]

Criticisms of the styles of individual presidents can be broadened into criticisms of the institution. There is, as we have seen, evidence to suggest that the Union is dominated by farmers who have larger than average farms and higher than average farm incomes. As men with an enormous stake in farming, with holdings of immense value, they are not the type to engage in militant action. The difficulties small farmers face in participating extensively in the affairs of the Union (or their natural unwillingness to do so) make the NFU a mechanism for dampening agrarian protest. The farmers who live on the margin of bankruptcy, who will be driven out of business, into a new occupation, way of life, and possibly from their homes if subsidies and prices are not high enough, are not the men who decide the NFU's tactics. The Union's policy is shaped by men who can afford to be more moderate.

At the highest levels of the Union, power has passed to technically competent permanent officials and elected officers who live in the *ambiance* of Whitehall. The way the Union does business has been deeply influenced by its close contact with Whitehall. The style of its publications and its negotiators has come to resemble that of the Civil Service. This style may be liked or disliked; more important is the impact of the unwritten 'laws' the relationship with the civil service imposes. These were, it may be recalled, to pursue 'reasonable' goals through well-informed argument in private and confidential meetings while abjuring open involvement in politics. The Union's critics contend that abjuring political involvement means that valuable political weapons, such as the willingness of politicians to compete for the farm vote, have been left to rust. The NFU has been 'coopted'; it channels rural discontent away from electoral politics or direct action and into a form Whitehall can handle.

The Union's leaders have a reply to such criticsms. It is that the supposed political advantages of farmers were limited or illusory. Frequent threats to unleash the farm vote, for example, would have encouraged politicians to make a more realistic appraisal of its importance. The NFU, on the other hand, is certain that it has had a real effect on government policy, moving it in a direction beneficial to farmers through quiet, patient, and well-informed discussion. By avoiding the use of political threats, farmers' significant but limited political advantages have not been put to the test and, through proven failure, discredited.

Whether or not the Union's leaders, with their reliance on partnership with government, or its critics with their calls for more militant political and economic action, have been the wiser can be proved only after assessing the advantages for the farmer which the policymaking process, in which the Union plays such a major role, provides. It is that policymaking process which is assessed in the next chapter. However, while assessing that policy process it is well to bear in mind the fact that it is the character of the NFU which enables farming policy in Britain to be formulated after informed rational discussion and not militant, demagogic argument. While mobilizing Britain's farmers to present their case cogently, the NFU has avoided, through the dominance of a moderate elite, the politics of confrontation and has made possible a civilized dialogue with government. Both the structure of the Union and the partnership in policymaking which government has offered its leaders have ensured that the political advantages farmers enjoy are rarely, if ever, deployed. However, the nature of that policymaking process is such, as we shall now see, that farmers have not been without influence.

Notes

1. National Farmers' Union of England and Wales, *Report on the Organisation and Management of the National Farmers' Union*, December, 1971, p. 8; National Farmers' Union of Scotland, *Annual Reports*.
2. T. J. Cowen, *Survey and Report on the Structure and Administration of County Branches*, NFU Unpublished Report, p. 48 (hereafter, Cowen Report).
3. Mancur Olson, *The Logic of Collective Action*, Harvard University Press, Cambridge, 1965.

4. Brian Barry, *Sociologists, Economists and Democracy*, Collier MacMillan, London, 1970, p. 29.
5. Samuel Beer, 'Pressure groups and parties in Britain', *APSR*, **50** (1956).
6. Harry Eckstein, *Pressure Group Politics, The Case of the BMA*, George Allen and Unwin, London, 1960, p. 24.
7. Barry, op. cit.; Barrington Moore, Jr., *The Social Origins of Dictatorship and Democracy*, Alan Lane, The Penguin Press, London 1967.
8. J. P. Nettl, 'Consensus or elite domination: The case of business', *Political Studies*, **13** 1965.
9. H. Gespal (with I. Beardwell and F. Woodcock), *Employers' Organisations and Industrial Relations*, Commission on Industrial Relations, Study 1, HMSO, London, 1972, p. 7.
10. Reg Groves, *Sharpen the Sickle, The History of the Farm Workers' Union*, Porcupine Press, London, p. 136 ff.
11. Unpublished cyclostyle history supplied by the NFU.
12. Quoted in 'Self and storing', p. 41.
13. Select Committee on Agriculture, Session 1968–69, *Minutes of Evidence*, p. 1062, and the NUAAW's memo to the Committee therein.
14. See Alan Butt Philip, *The Political and Sociological Significance of Welsh Nationalism Since 1945*, Unpublished Oxford D. Phil.
15. Cowen Report, op. cit., p. 91.
16. *The Economist*, 31 January, 1970.
17. S. E. Finer, *Anonymous Empire*, Pall Mall Press, London, 1962, pp. 19–21; Eckstein, op. cit., esp. p. 43 ff; Samuel H. Beer, *Modern British Politics*, Faber and Faber, London, 1965, esp. pp. 231, 321, 325.
18. Beer, op. cit., p. 30; H. D. Stewart, *British Pressure Groups, Their Role in Relation to the House of Commons*, Oxford University Press, London and Oxford, 1958, esp. Chap. 1.
19. Report from the Select Committee on Agriculture, Session 1966–67, *Minutes of Evidence*, Vol. II, pp. 1037–1039.
20. NFU of England and Wales, *The Role of a Farmers' Union*, Undated cyclostyle.
21. Cowen Report, op. cit., p. 25.
22. P. L. H. Walters, *Farming Politics in Cheshire, A Study of the Cheshire County Branch of the National Farmers' Union*, Unpublished Ph.D. Thesis, University of Manchester, 1970.
23. Cowen Report, op. cit., p. 60.
24. A monthly series in *The British Farmer* starting in June, 1960.
24. Cowen Report, op. cit., p. 45.
26. See, for example, the views of the agricultural correspondent of *The Times*, 18 April, 1966.
27. 'Blythe', *Farmer and Stockbreeder*, 29 March, 1966.
28. Ibid., Letters, 5 March, 1966.
29. *Farmer and Stockbreeder*, 3 February, 1970.
30. *The Financial Times*, 14 September, 1974.

Chapter 4

The Policy Process in Britain

As political scientists are fond of remarking, procedures are rarely, if ever, neutral. The way in which a decision is taken has an important impact on what decision is made. Nothing, in the view of its critics, provides a better example of this than the way in which British governments decided on the appropriate level for agricultural subsidies in the *Annual Review and Determination of Guarantees*. The Annual Review often has been described as a neogitation between farmers' unions pressing for more money and a Ministry of Agriculture, Fisheries, and Food (MAFF) which identifies with their cause. The NFU has fostered the illusion that it is the Government's equal partner in the Review. It issues a counter 'White Paper' to the Government's; it announces with due gravity whether it 'agrees' (approves with) or 'disagrees' (disapproves with) the Review; and the Union's President calls a press conference to express his views the same day as the Minister announces his decisions.

The secrecy in which the Annual Review takes place and the privileged position accorded the farmers' unions have prompted fears that the taxpayers' or consumers' interests are neglected. One Left-wing Labour MP, Stanley Orme, expressed quite widespread anxiety when he referred to the Review as an 'annual outpouring of money ... done in a closed way between the Ministry' (of Agriculture).[1] What, however, has been the reality of the Review as opposed to the rhetoric? Has the policymaking process been as biased towards farmers as Orme suggests?

The development of the Review

Though, as we have remarked before, it is far from unusual for British interest groups to be consulted by the Government, farmers' interest groups are somewhat unusually accorded this right by law. The Agriculture Act of 1947, the basic piece

42

of agricultural subsidy legislation, orders the Government while setting subsidies to consult 'such bodies of persons who appear to them to represent the interests of producers in the agricultural industry'.[2]

Why should the promise to consult farmers be enshrined in law? The answer is to be found in wartime circumstances. During both the First and Second World Wars, when German submarines menaced Allied shipping, the supply of food to Britain was a major problem. Quite naturally, from the start of the Second World War, the British Government tried to maximize domestic food production, and also found it necessary to control the distribution of food. The Government therefore decided to buy the entire output of British agriculture at prices considerably in excess of those prevailing in peacetime.[3] Unfortunately, production was not encouraged by a dispute in 1940 between the farmers, the Ministry of Agriculture, the Ministry of Food, and the Treasury over the appropriate price for their produce. Though the farmers, supported by the Ministry of Agriculture, lost the battle, the War Cabinet, anxious to avoid such future disputes, ordered that in future changes in farm prices, or farmers' costs, should be discussed with farmers' representatives.[4] This was a simple version of the Annual Review which has survived to this day. As the Labour Minister of Agriculture, Tom Williams, remarked in introducing the postwar Agriculture Act, it merely confirmed procedures which had been 'in operation during the past few years'.[5]

In the years that followed, many changes occurred. As part of their campaign 'to set the people free', the Conservatives ended rationing, merged the Ministry of Food with the Ministry of Agriculture, and decided that the Government would no longer buy British agricultural produce. Farmers would not be left to a free market, however. Deficiency payments, described in Chapter 1, would guarantee farmers that the Government would pay them the difference between the market and a 'fair' price set at the Annual Review. A concurrent development was the growth of sophisticated analysis for use at the Annual Review. The NFU built up an economic staff capable of taking on, in argument, the Civil Service, while the Ministry of Agriculture itself increased the variety of statistics available to evaluate the situation and prospects of British farming. Both sides involved the agricultural economics departments of British universities as neutral agents who would conduct a sample survey of British farms to alert policy-makers to any regional or crop variations in the state of agriculture which aggregate figures might hide.

Indeed, by the early 1960s, it was customary to distinguish two distinct parts to the Annual Review.[6] The first of these was an annual examination of the state of the industry. From November to February, economists from the NFU and the MAFF would meet to discuss the state of the industry, sifting through a mass of information in order to achieve an agreed diagnosis. In February, more senior people from both sides would be brought in to settle any remaining differences. After this, the second part of the Annual Review would start, in which an attempt would be made to settle what ought to be done. Thus the Annual Review tried to maintain an 'is-ought' distinction between analysis and prescription which would have pleased David Hume.

The intense factual preparation for the Annual Review was, however, a major influence on its outcome. It was difficult for the Government to agree that agriculture was suffering from a depression without offering to do anything to improve the situation. A more severe limitation on the Government's freedom of action was the Agriculture Act of 1957.[7] Under this Act, the Government was obliged to maintain agricultural subsidies in general at not less than $97\frac{1}{2}$ per cent of the level in the previous year. Even this reduction could be made only to the degree that there had not been an offsetting increase in 'relevant costs'. Moreover, the Government lost the freedom to switch subsidies between commodities at will; subsidies for each commodity could not be less than 96 per cent of the level in the previous year.

It is not altogether clear why the Minister responsible for the 1957 Act, Heathcoat Amory so tied his successor's hands. Amory's policy was to reverse the worrying trend for agricultural subsidies to grow inexorably and to force the industry into greater self-reliance. This policy brought sharp clashes with the NFU and rural unpopularity typified by the loss of the Torrington by-election, described in Chapter 2. The Agriculture Act was quite possibly a concession to political pressure. To disarm his critics, Amory promised in law that any reductions in farm subsidies would be gradual. It is also possible, however, that Amory was primarily concerned, like the Wartime Government, to avoid a loss of confidence in the industry, with a consequent reduction in modernizing investment and a fall in output. Whichever was the dominant influence, Amory's bequest to future Ministers of Agriculture was a promise enshrined in law that any change of policy would be incremental.

By the late 1950s, the institutional and legal framework of the Annual Review has been established. Typically of British government, its roots lay in wartime convenience rather than conscious planning, and its characteristics had gradually evolved rather than being carefully designed. The Annual Review had a legal basis, but had been shaped primarily by precedents set to meet the convenience of the farmers' unions and the Government.

In spite of this, the Annual Review has had enthusiastic friends and defenders. The very way in which the Government took a regular, integrated view of the industry and its needs contrasted well with the disconnected, and often contradictory, concessions made to different commodity producers in other countries. The attempt to provide a rational basis for policy through the accumulation of an agreed analysis of the condition and prospects of the industry seemed, as we have seen, a precursor to 'indicative planning', which was such a vogue at the time. Indeed, there were even those who could see in the Review a 'third way'—an alternative to both capitalism and free enterprise. The Government through its disbursement of grants and subsidies set the direction in which the industry would develop; leaving production in the hands of private entrepreneurial farmers avoided the inefficiencies of state-owned or collectivized agriculture.

Critics of agricultural subsidies have suspected that they are sustained by the Review itself. They suspect that the MAFF is committed to the cause of the British farmer and that, though the Annual Review has given farmers a good hearing, it has not provided any real check on them. Interests which conflict with agriculture have not been given 'equal time'. Are such arguments justified?

British executive politics: *ex uno plures?*

Any suggestion that the British MAFF is a tool of the farmers' unions is probably simplistic. There have been deep disagreements between the farmers' unions and the Ministry at Price Reviews and a former Permanent Secretary even claimed that the Ministry officials have an instinctive tendency to distrust the claims or arguments of the NFU. Officials of the Ministry have been eager to deny that they are too concerned with the farmers' viewpoint. Top officials of the MAFF assured the Select Committee on Agriculture that they do take consumers' interests into account,[8] and do bear in mind 'wider considerations and ... have regard to appropriate limitations on public expenditure'.[9] Beyond this lies the general features of the top British Civil Service, its shared background and training, and its belief that there exists, no matter how difficult to define, some general or public interest which it should serve. As is so often remarked, the British civil servant is under no institutional pressure (as is his American counterpart) to surrender to sectional interests. Indeed, the reverse may be true; stubborn defence of a general government policy in a department's work may bring added prestige.

Yet cutting across the ideals of the Civil Service are certain organizational pressures. In the first place, the close relationship with the NFU cannot but have an effect. As we have seen, the Ministry is in almost hourly contact with the NFU. It is only natural that a community of shared beliefs and attitudes should develop between the officials of the two organizations in such close contact. Moreover, until recently, agriculture, not food, was the natural preoccupation of top Ministry officials. Before the explosion of food prices in the early 1970s, the 'Food' part of the Ministry's title stood mainly for the inspection of places such as slaughterhouses to assure the maintenance of reasonable standards of hygiene. Finally, but most important, is the acceptance of a form of neo-pluralism by civil servants within the Ministry. They argue in private that the ramifications of any change in policy are too great for any one ministry to appreciate. 'We cannot worry about everything, so we leave some factors to other Ministries to worry about', one civil servant summarized their attitude. 'The duty of the M.A.F.F. is to present the arguments for help for farming. Other Ministries will soon bring forth criticisms based on trade policy implications for public expenditure.' Another civil servant explicitly compared the Ministry's role to that of an advocate in a British or American court. He should, without illegality or conscious dishonesty, present his client's (the farmers') case capably, trusting that wisdom and truth will emerge from a clash of opinion and evidence. There is no obligation, however, to point to facts damaging to one's client. More circumspect in public, another official of the MAFF told the Select Committee on Agriculture that: 'If the farmers' unions have a strong view on any subject, it is the duty of the Department to report it to other Ministers ...'[10]

There are grounds, therefore, to suppose that the MAFF identifies with the cause of agriculture. It is essential, however, to appreciate the extent to which the MAFF's identification with the farmers' cause rests upon a *general* belief among the British Civil Service that every ministry has certain abiding friends and perpetual interests to protect. The MAFF is not a deviant from a norm of Whitehall detachment, but is merely a ministry whose main clientele is particularly easy to identify. Thus the Department of Education and Science (DES) not only governs education but acts as advocate of a certain conception of it within the policy machine. Even, or perhaps particularly, when ministers discuss the allocation of resources between ministries, and so in a sense reveal the collective values of their government, they fight for their sectional interest. Antony Crosland saw it as 'the primary duty of a Minister to be successful with the Treasury' and thought it 'quite right' that his officials should 'judge him by how successful he is'.[11] In their most valuable description of the British budgetary process, Heclo and Wildavsky emphasize the role of the minister as advocate for this department's programmes. Failure to fight for resources for his department's work will undermine his prestige within the ministry and even with his Cabinet colleagues: 'The spending minister who does not put up a fight loses authority for ever.'[12]

The widespread acceptance of the view that the civil servants and politicians, of whichever party, have an identifiable set of attitudes and interests to represent has important consequences for the MAFF. It is a fact that agricultural policy, perhaps more than most, cannot be contained within its own framework. Some of the points where it impinges on the work of other ministries are clear. For example, the Treasury's reluctance to provide more funds for agricultural subsidies would surprise no one acquainted with the lore of British government. What may be less obvious is the number of hostile, predatory ministries watching over any increase in subsidies the MAFF is planning.

The MAFF's predators

The role of the Treasury in supervizing the work of other ministries and bringing out the values of politicians by probing their willingness to find new projects is well known.[13] The Treasury has developed an eagle eye for expensive changes in farm subsidies, and it defines its role as that of dispassionate critic. No longer does the Treasury approach the budgets of other ministries with the hope of saving candle-ends but, at least in theory, this restraint is designed to free its attention for more important features of a budget, pointing out the major implications for government expenditure of changes in its policies.

The Treasury's attitude to agricultural subsidies exemplifies its general role. It commits a Principal to work full time on agriculture supported by an Under-Secretary spending a quarter of his time on the subject. They do not gather information independently, but:

... see a great deal of the information the Ministry of Agriculture have got. I see their statistics, I discuss with them their views about any abnormalities there may have been in the previous year, their view about what will happen to production in the year ... and I apply the best judgement I can to what would be the effects of particular changes.[14]

Yet using the information supplied by the MAFF, the Treasury can reach very different conclusions. To the Treasury, the MAFF is too close to its subject to see all the implications. A spokesman for the Treasury argued this view to a Commons Committee:

Let me put it this way. The Department which is in very close contact with the industry is naturally, I think, inclined to adopt a certain amount of the industry's arguments, the industry's special pleading, the argument of the industry's special case and so forth. The second line Department standing back, still knowing a good deal about it like the Treasury can be more sceptical and perhaps see a little more of the wood and a little less of the trees.[15]

One of the Treasury's most formidable allies in opposing increases in farm subsidies has been the Board (now Department) of Trade. What, it might fairly be asked, does the Board of Trade have to do with agricultural policy? The answer lies in Britain's traditional pattern of trade. If Britain is to sell manufactures to a country, it must be prepared to buy produce from it. There is, in fact, an observed relationship between the willingness of a country to buy from Britain and the amount it sells to Britain. The Board of Trade was the Department entrusted with increasing British exports and negotiating trade agreements. This has conditioned the Board of Trade to view every policy in terms of its effects on more liberal trade policy and British exports:

... we are, at the Board of Trade, the custodians of certain national interests and we should try to represent these ... they are the conduct of our trade relations with other countries, in particular the industrial aspects of our international trade.[16]

The conflict between such attitudes and increased farm subsidies is clear. While the Board of Trade worked for increased trade, the case for agricultural subsidies rested on arguments for the desirability of greater self-sufficiency. While the Board of Trade was planning closer trading relations with, say, Argentina, the Ministry of Agriculture and the farmers' unions were planning to replace imports of meat from Argentina with domestic production. A clash between the two ministries was inevitable and, indeed, desirable, as they represented important conflicting ideas and interests in trade policy.

The Treasury and Board of Trade were formidable adversaries for the farming interest, and they could count on further support from more marginally involved ministries. The Foreign and Commonwealth Office (FCO), for example, was unwilling to see Britain's trading partners antagonized by an expansion of British agriculture at the expense of imports (though the FCO attached a higher priority to membership of the EEC). The Department of Economic Affairs (DEA), during its brief, unhappy lifetime, was also likely to be unsympathetic to the farmers' cause, as it saw farming as a source of resources (labour in particular) ripe for 'redeployment'.

The critics' chance

It is not really surprising that the Treasury or Board of Trade should be unsympathetic to farm subsidies. The striking feature of the British policy process, however, has been the degree to which such suspicious ministries actually participate in making agricultural policy. At every stage of the Annual Review, the Ministry of Agriculture acted as intermediary between the farmers' unions and a system of interdepartmental contacts which brings the non-agricultural ministries into play. The links between the MAFF and the 'anti-farm subsidy' ministries rest formally on their membership at both the official and ministerial level of interdepartmental committes charged with formulating farm policy. Yet, just as with the links between the farmers' unions and the MAFF, interdepartmental contacts are too close to be limited to formal committee meetings. One member of the MAFF told the Select Committee on Agriculture that other departments 'keep in touch very closely. We discuss what we are going to say at the next session (with the farmers' unions) or what they (the unions) said at the last session.' Nor are other departments confined to a passive role in such contacts: '... they can suggest "You can say this" or "You can say that" or "That line of argument is very dangerous" and so on.'[17] So close are the contacts that an official of the MAFF told MPs that: 'In most of these things, we are so close to the Treasury that it is not quite so easy to determine from where the initiative actually comes.'[18]

The major rule which governs this policymaking process is that the MAFF should not in any way commit the Government without the approval of other departments and their ministers. If the Ministry of Agriculture proposed to change policy, 'let us say the potato guarantee arrangements', on either its own initiative or at the request of the farmers' unions, it would be obliged to make its case to a meeting of the 'Annual Review Team', the 'standing committee' of ministries interested in agricultural policy.[19] If agreement was not reached, the dispute would be referred to the Agricultural Policy Committee of Cabinet Ministers. Both the official and ministerial committees consisted of representatives of the three ministries administering agricultural policy, the MAFF, the Scottish Office, and the Home Office, opposed by the Treasury, the Board of Trade, and FCO. Presiding over a conflict, no less avoidable for taking place annually, was a 'neutral' chairman such as the Chancellor of the Duchy of Lancaster. Yet in spite of the disagreement which characterized the committee and the division between those who put farmers first and those who did not, the MAFF could not move without its assent. As a civil servant told a Parliamentary committee, 'The official representatives of the department cannot say to the farmers "Yes, we will accept that proposition" unless they know that the Chancellor and the other Ministers concerned will accept that.'[20]

The negotiations which take place between the MAFF and the farmers' unions have attracted much attention. Yet the negotiations between the ministries interested in agriculture and the ministries representing fundamental conflicting interests in agricultural policy are more important. Popularizers of agricultural politics have stressed the dangers of the close contacts between the farmers' unions and the Ministry of Agriculture. It is not possible, however, that the Ministry has been too circumscribed in making policy by the close oversight of 'anti-farmer' departments such as the Treasury or Board of Trade?

The Annual Review: opportunity or constraint?

It would be impossible to argue that the Annual Review involved a surrender of financial control in agricultural policy to the farmers' unions. British governments have, in fact, 'held the line' on farm subsidies. The cost to the Government of agricultural subsidies from the early 1960s (1962–63) to the end of the decade was held near the levels of the late 1950s, as we saw in Chapter 2.

The percentage of civil expenditure claimed by farm subsidies fell from 9·32 per cent in 1961–62 to 3·82 per cent in 1966–67.[21] Though such figures ignore the major transfer of the costs of protecting the farmer from the taxpayer to the consumer, a trend described in Chapter 1, they still challenge any notion that farmers have unbridled control over farm policy.

It might still seem that the Government took a major risk. Farmers, well represented in Parliament and constantly being offered the favours of the political parties, were, like other interests, given the chance to present their case to the Government. Farmers were, however, given something more by the Annual Review, namely an annual, ritualized occasion to pronounce on the Government's farm policy. Governments can usually obfuscate or delay in any dispute with an interest. A pressure group, they can suggest, has misunderstood the drift of policy or should await further developments which may provide a pleasant surprise. The Annual Review, on the other hand, simplifies and dramatizes providing farmers' unions with the opportunity to pronounce authoritatively on government policy. Surely this opportunity must have added to the political advantages farmers enjoyed, described in Chapter 2?

The reasons why the Annual Review did not, in fact, strengthen farmers' political hand are ultimately reducable to the secrecy of the Review. One of the main rules imposed by Whitehall on pressure groups that want close relations with it is confidentiality. Throughout the Annual Review, the representatives of the farmers' unions, it will be remembered, were not allowed to consult freely with their Council. Still less were they allowed to mount a campaign in Parliament or the country. Only when the Review had been announced to the Commons and the Government could impose party discipline if challenged by a vote could the farmers' unions deploy their political advantages, and by then it was too late. The best efforts of the NFU not withstanding, no government has ever reopened an Annual Review. Indeed, Ministers of Agriculture have been able to use the Annual Review as a political shield. Because discussions are in train with the NFU, any political pressure is improper. Thus Peart refused to receive Labour MPs representing rural constituencies until the Review was over and announced.

This is not to argue that the Review has been of value to farmers. It is quite possible that the NFU are entirely correct in their claims that, in the case of one Review, their technical arguments have won the farmers tens of millions of pounds. Persuasion can achieve results, even with governments. The NFU has been well equipped to produce arguments to show that if the Government is to achieve general objectives (e.g. balancing imports and exports), the farmer must be given more help. It is, however, to argue that the cost of this opportunity for technical persuasion has been a loss of political power.

The bias of procedures

Thus far, the Annual Review has seemed an almost ideal policymaking process. Admirers of rationality will admire the assembling of as many facts as possible on the state of the industry. Pluralists will be pleased not only by the position accorded the NFU in decision-making but by the range of interests represented by other government departments. There is, however, a conspicuous failing of the Review which provided farmers with a real advantage. Though the Review provided great opportunities for critical challenges to *changes* in farm policy, it did little to provide opportunities for critical appraisals of *existing* policies. This was due to two factors, the first of which was the rather special commitment of the MAFF to the farmers' cause and the second a belief that departments should be left some autonomy.

The MAFF, we have argued, has not been captured by the farmers' unions, but is, nevertheless, committed to the farmers' cause. It would be asking far too much to expect the MAFF to be critical of the agricultural subsidy policies which are its *raison d'être*. It would be reasonable, but incorrect, to assume that the ministries which are critical of increases in farm subsidies are likely to make cogent comments on existing policies. Gentlemen in the Civil Service do not interfere too deeply in other ministries' affairs. Thus a Treasury official could deny to a Commons' Committee that his department would ever press for a revision of policy:

Q. Bearing in mind the tremendous cost of support this year would the Treasury ever say to the Ministry of Agriculture 'The cost of support is getting so great, it is not about time you devised some different system of supporting agriculture.'
A. No, I do not think we would ever say that. I do not think it would be our function to say that.[22]

If it is not the Treasury's function 'to say that', whose is it? The Ministry of Agriculture itself has proved unlikely to be sceptical about its own work, and other departments have shared the Treasury's inhibitions. In short, the traditional Whitehall machine has been geared to the analysis of changing, not continuing, policy.

Yet the politicians have proved no more sceptical. The continuing willingness of both Labour and Conservative Cabinets to question the existing value of farm subsidies is partly attributable to their vague, ill-defined, and possibly ill-founded fears of 'the farm vote'. It is due, too, to the character of the Cabinet. It is easy to suppose that members of the Cabinet view the allocation of funds between ministries as a 'zero sum game' in which money not spent on agriculture, for example, thereby becomes available for education and science. Whatever the rationality of such an approach, it is not, apparently, how the Cabinet works. The attitude seems to be more that ministers in charge of spending departments should hang together lest they hang separately. If the Minister of Agriculture is in dispute with the Chancellor, the wise Secretary of State for Education and Science will not rush to the Chancellor's aid. One day he, too, will have a dispute with the Treasury, and will not want gratuitously made enemies sitting around the Cabinet table. Only when an essential interest of his or her own department is at stake will a minister challenge another department's work. As a Treasury official commented sourly to Heclo and Wildavsky, 'Ministers live by supporting each other. Dog doesn't eat dog.'[23]

During the 1960s and 1970s, there has been increasing concern over the inability of British government to review critically continuing policies in general. Agricultural policy has seemed at worst typical and at best unusual, in that the Annual Review did provide some scrutiny of the work of the MAFF on a regular basis. The concern over the capacity of British government for policy review has led to several attempts at reform. From the early 1960s, the Public Expenditure Survey Committee (PESC) has attempted to make ministers more conscious of trends in government spending, the opportunity cost of spending money on one project rather than another, and the potential incongruity with ministers' values of what the Government will be doing if policy is not changed. The Heath Government created a Central Policy Review Staff (CPRS) specifically to analyse existing policies free from the entrenched attitudes of departments responsible for their implementation.

So far, none of these reforms have impinged deeply on agricultural subsidy policy. Heclo and Wildavsky report that the annual surveys of expenditure take little account of agriculture. Thus the PESC exercise, for example, involves no real analysis of expenditure on agriculture: '. . . conditions are so uncertain that there is no real attempt at forecasting . . . P.E.S.C. does not try to anticipate the annual price reviews or market prices; it merely projects the level of support agreed at the last price review.'[24] That is little more than guessing.

The CPRS did not exist in the period covered by this book (up to 1970). However, in 1975 the CPRS did undertake a project on agricultural subsidies. The original purpose of the study was to consider whether the present level of agricultural subsidies was too high or too low. The very limited resources the CPRS devoted to the subject (one full-time member) and fears that asking such a fundamental question would seem 'unrealistic', caused the CPRS to limit its analysis to the desirability of the current distribution of farm subsidies in the light of increases in the cost of food, energy, and chemical fertilizers. Even here, punches were pulled. For example, proposals on beef subsidies were watered down at the request of the MAFF before the document went before ministers. Members of the CPRS are themselves sceptical whether, without a minister to represent them, their mild recommendations will have any impact on decision-making in the future. In short, not even the CPRS has plugged the gap in British policy analysis.

This failure to provide an effective means of evaluating policy has produced a paradoxical situation. Comparatively small changes in policy and the cost of sub-sidies has been subjected to the most searching analysis. Yet fundamental questions about the desirability of existing subsidies have not been considered nearly as seriously. The basic features of policy have continued without major challenge. Even changes in the method used to subsidize British agriculture have sprung not from the agricultural policymaking process itself, but have been im-posed on the Ministry by pressures from outside the agricultural community. The most radical shift, the adoption of the Common Agricultural Policy, is occurring in spite of the MAFF's objections because of Britain's entry into the EEC. The shift away from deficiency payments in the early 1960s came because the Treasury would not meet an ever-growing bill, while the very adoption of defi-ciency payments in the early 1950s reflected the Conservative's imposition on agriculture of their desire to 'set the people free' and reduce government in-terference in economic life. The agricultural policy process itself has not produced innovation. On the contrary, its characteristic has been inertia. It is that inertia which has been the chief explanation for the subsidizing of British agriculture.

Notes

1. Hansard, *House of Commons Debates,* **709,** col. 1646.
2. 10 and 11 George VI, Public General Acts and Measures of 1947, Chap. 48.
3. A. H. Murray, *History of the Second World War, Agriculture,* HMSO and Longmans, London, 1955.
4. Ibid., pp. 166–167.
5. Hansard, *House of Commons Debates,* **432,** col. 630.
6. Sir John Winnifrith, KCB, *The Ministry of Agriculture, Fisheries and Food,* George Allen and Unwin, London, 1962, p. 47.
7. 5 and 6 Elizabeth II, Public General Acts and Measures, Chap. 57, 1957.
8. Sir Basil Engholm (Permanent Secretary, MAFF), evidence to the Select Committee on Agriculture, *Minutes of Evidence,* Session 1968–69, p. 610.
9. Mitchell (MAFF), evidence to the Select Committee on Agriculture, *Minutes of Evidence,* Session 1968–69, p. 672.
10. Ibid., p. 676.
11. Maurice Kogen, Antony Crosland, and Edward Boyle (Eds.), *The Politics of Educa-tion,* Penguin, London, 1971, p. 167.
12. Hugh Heclo and Aron Wildavsky, *The Private Government of Public Money,* MacMillan, London, 1974, p. 136.
13. Samuel Beer, *Treasury Control, The Co-Ordination of Financial and Economic Policy in Britain,* Oxford University Press, Oxford, 1956, provides the classic statement.
14. Evidence to the Select Committee on Agriculture, Session 1968–69, *Minutes of Evidence,* p. 773.
15. Ibid., p. 780.
16. Evidence to the Select Committee on Agriculture, Session 1968–69, *Minutes of Evidence,* p. 890.
17. Select Committee on the Estimates, Sub-committee D, Session 1957–58, *Minutes of Evidence, Treasury Control,* p. 1091.
18. Ibid., p. 1101.
19. Ibid., pp. 1055, 1057.
20. Ibid., p. 1064.

21. Select Committee on Agriculture, *Report*, Session 1968–69.
22. Select Committee on Agriculture, Session 1968–69, *Minutes of Evidence*, p. 768.
23. Heclo and Wildavsky, op. cit., p. 186.
24. Ibid., p. 224.

PART II

Chapter 5

Policy in America; Change without Reform

The American approach to 'the farm problem' since the 1930s has been predicated on the assumption that the farm problem consisted of overproduction and the low prices which farmers consequently received for their produce. The answer, quite naturally, has been defined as government action to raise prices and, in order to achieve higher prices, to restrict production.

The reasons why this approach became established are easily understood. Whereas industry prospered during the 1920s in America, farming (as in Britain) suffered a slump from soon after the First World War. Farm income, which had been $7,107 million in 1920, fell to $5,841 million by 1928. Thus the Great Depression inflicted further suffering on farmers already living in a recession. By 1933, grain prices were at 44 per cent of the 1910–14 level, while cotton and cotton seed were at 47 per cent of the average in those four years. Farm income, which had fallen with farm prices through the 1920s, fell by two-thirds between the late 1920s and the early 1930s.[1]

If anyone asked, therefore, what was the nature of the farm problem in the United States, the answer seemed obvious. Prices were too low, and, it might be added by the comparatively sophisticated, they were too low because too much was being offered for sale. It seemed obvious that the answer was to keep prices up by keeping production down, or by the government buying up surplus stocks, or by a combination of these techniques. During the 1920s, most farmers pressed for the McNary-Haugen plan, under which the government was to buy up domestic surpluses and dump them on foreign markets. But it was not until 1933, when the Democrats controlled both the Congress and the Presidency, that effective action was taken and the Agricultural Adjustment Act of 1933 passed. The two Agriculture Acts of the New Deal (the second was passed in 1938) are absolutely central to an understanding of agricultural politics since 1956.[2] Though much amended, they remained on the statute book throughout the period covered by this study.

Both Acts followed much the same strategy. Output was restricted in those commodities where farmers voted for production limitations in a special referendum. In return, farmers received a 'fair' price from a quasi-governmental body, the Commodity Credit Corporation (CCC). This fair price was defined in terms of the ratio of farm prices and incomes to other prices and incomes in the last peacetime, golden era of American farming, 1910–14. The figure this formula produced, following the great rural political rallying cry of the 1920s, was known as 'parity'. It was to remain a central part of American farm policy for many years thereafter. The major differences between the two New Deal Agriculture Acts were merely in the way they were financed and how they were justified. After the Supreme Court invalidated the Agricultural Adjustment Act of 1933 in 1936 (*United States versus Butler et al., Receivers of the Hoosac Mills Corporation*—29 US 1) on the grounds that it was an improper exercise of the taxing power and an invasion of the rights of the states, the farm programmes were financed not by taxes on processors but by payments from the US Treasury. The basic strategy remained unaltered and was, indeed, set firmly for the next generation.

The procedure the Acts established was as follows. The Department of Agriculture calculated the amount of agricultural produce that the United States needed. The Department then calculated what acreage would produce this quantity. Licenses to produce on fixed numbers of acres, or 'acreage allotments', were then allocated to individual farmers by state and local committees elected by farmers themselves. The allotments granted were, *in toto*, supposed to produce the national production the Secretary had planned. Farmers who wished to receive government subsidies (nominally granted as 'loans' by the CCC, as the farmer had one year to sell his produce privately if the market price rose above the subsidy level before consigning ownership to the CCC) had to comply with their acreage allotment. If a farmer exceeded his 'allotment' he became ineligible for government assistance. Moreover, government assistance was granted only to growers of a commodity who had produced it for several years.

All this seemed a reasonable sensible answer to the proximate problem—rapidly falling farm prices and incomes. But it was not a sensible answer to the problem of how to deal with an agricultural industry whose main characteristic was to become rapid technological change. Some measure of the dramatic change in the character of farming can be obtained from Table 4.[3]

In the context of this dramatic change, freezing the ratio of farm to non-farm prices at the ratio prevailing in 1910–14 was as sensible as freezing the ratio of the prices of the early, handmade motor cars to the prices of all other goods in the same period. Policy-makers in the New Deal had a good excuse, of course, for they were aware that the technological evolution made it possible to move perhaps one-third of farmers off the land and into other industries.[4] Their problem, however, was that in the midst of the mass unemployment of the 1930s anyone who left farming was likely to end up in a dole queue. The size of the farm population had to be frozen in spite of technological advances, to keep farm families employed. Unfortunately, by adopting rigid formulae in legislation, the New Deal

Table 4

Crop	Average yield per acre (bushels)	
	1945	1964
Wheat	17·0	26·2
Corn	32·7	62·1
Grain sorghums	15·2	41·1

policy-makers left a commitment to a stable agricultural population which was to survive into more prosperous times. The New Deal approach was, in addition, fossilized in the minds of most Democrats; the answer to 'the farm problem' was government action to keep prices up to some outdated figure.

Not only was the shape of American agricultural policy to stand intact but the New Deal also forged a powerful alliance to stand by farm legislation. This coalition included not only Representatives and Senators from rural areas which benefited significantly from farm legislation (particularly the South) but also the more liberal Democrats from urban areas. A typical example of an urban liberal who stood behind farm legislation was Mayor LaGuardia of New York. He helped persuade city Representatives to vote for farm subsidy laws in exchange for the help of the American Farm Bureau Federation (AFBF) in rounding up rural votes for urban relief. But LaGuardia's commitment to farm subsidies was not just logrolling; he genuinely believed that farmers were part of the depressed minority liberals ought to help. 'It is,' he told Congress, 'the exploited masses that now require the attention of this Congress, and in this great army of exploited masses is to be included the farmer.'[5]

Were the New Deal farm laws so liberal in their effects? Because they paid subsidies by increasing prices per unit of output, the farm subsidy laws benefited mainly the rich farmer who produced the most. At the same time, the farm subsidy laws encouraged inefficiency. Poor farmers, particularly share-croppers, were often displaced as their landlords cut output.[6] Not only were too many resources kept in farming, but they were kept in the wrong sort of farming. The 'basic' commodities (the Southern commodities such as rice, cotton, tobacco, peanuts, and a few Midwestern commodities such as wheat) were very much more subsidized than others, such as beef. Farmers were encouraged to produce unwanted commodities and thereby discouraged from growing commodities for which markets existed. Moreover, as acreage allotments for a commodity were offered only to farmers who had grown it in the past, farmers who could grow it more efficiently on fresh land or by new techniques were deprived of subsidies. (Thus the movement of cotton into California and out of the Confederacy was greatly inhibited.) But the only politicians who were prepared to voice criticisms of the New Deal farm policies were Republicans motivated mainly by a distaste for New Deal, interventionist policies. Their criticisms merely served to increase the loyalty of urban Democrats to farm subsidy laws, which did not benefit their constituents but which seemed part of the progressive struggle against *laissez-faire* economics.

The attempt to freeze farm prices when technology was changing rapidly was bound to produce surpluses. Just when they started to appear, however, in the late 1930s, the Second World War started, food became a major strategic resource, and farmers took full advantage of the fact.[7] By 1944, Congress had been persuaded to push guaranteed prices up to 100 per cent of parity. Farmers also gained advantageous special treatment such as exemptions from minimum wage laws and military service. Everyone knew that, were farm subsidies to be continued at their wartime rates after the cessation of hostilities, massive surpluses would appear. Like their British colleagues, American farmers had received a promise, enshrined in law, that farm subsidies would not be reduced until 31 December, 1948. What then? The answer was to be a drawing of battle lines which set *laissez-faire* Republicans against interventionist Democrats.

Postwar policy trends

It was only gradually that the clear differences between Republican and Democratic farm policy opened, however. Though Truman (the first former dirt farmer President since Ulysses S. Grant) was, as he recorded in his memoires,[8] fully committed to an interventionist farm policy, his first Secretary of Agriculture, Clinton Anderson, was not. Anderson, like most Senators and farm interest groups (but not the House), believed that farm subsidies fixed at a high rate should be superceded by a sliding scale of subsidies designed to balance supply and demand, thus averting huge surpluses. But the Presidential elections of 1948 were to shatter this widespread consensus.

As the 1948 campaign began, Truman attempted to restore relations with Roosevelt's supporters, such as farmers, even though he seemed doomed to defeat. Anderson resigned in July and was replaced by Charles Brannan, an interventionist US Department of Agriculture official and friend of the pro-Democrat National Farmers' Union (NFU) President, James Patton. As the election neared, farm prices weakened, reviving depression fears. Truman blamed the drift in prices on a too-restrictive charter for the CCC passed by the Republican Congress, though with no objection from Truman. Truman's only other request to Congress for legislation had been for the passage of the International Wheat Agreement, but he attacked the 'do nothing Congress' for planting 'a pitchfork in the farmers' back'. Truman's political achievement was to revive fears among farmers that Republicans would abandon them to a free market. 'His surprise victory was often attributed to this success with the farm vote. Had he (Dewey) swept the Middle West as all the experts forecast, he would have soon won the presidency.'[9] But as well as holding Minnesota, Missouri, and Illinois, Truman won back Iowa, Wisconsin, and Ohio which Roosevelt had lost to Dewey in 1944—losing only Michigan. Truman's success in Ohio, Iowa, and Wisconsin was at least partly due to the farm vote, but his successes elsewhere were explained too by commentators such as the *US News and World Report* as a reaction to Dewey's apparent threat to reduce farm subsidies which caused farmers to return to the Democrats.[10]

The New Democratic Congress and the Democratic President extended supports at 90 per cent of parity to 1950. However, Secretary Brannan was anxious to find a permanent solution to the problem of maintaining farm incomes which would not produce surpluses. Brannan realized that his proposals would be contentious, but was encouraged by Truman to proceed. The result, the Brannan Plan.[11] is of critical importance in the history of postwar American agriculture, for its rejection was the rejection of that method of subsidizing agriculture (direct payments) which economists agree is the best (or least harmful) way to subsidize the industry. The Brannan Plan would have avoided many of the faults of the existing farm laws. By substituting government payments for artificially high market prices, it would have encouraged consumption. Above all, while the traditional programmes hindered exports (vital to American agriculture) by driving up the market prices while limiting American, but not world, production, the Brannan Plan would have allowed American commodities to compete freely on world markets. Finally, as direct payments are financed by direct taxation, usually thought to be mildly progressive, the cost of subsidizing agriculture would have been more equitably distributed than under the traditional programmes, which bore most heavily on the poor.[12]

Initial reaction to the plan was favourable and Republicans, trying to recapture the farm vote, feared it would tie the farmers permanently to the Democrats. In the end, however, the Brannan Plan foundered on the opposition of an amazing coalition.[13] The Republicans opposed the measure partly for party reasons. Conservatives opposed it as government largesse which would inevitably (to keep budgetary cost down) lead to further federal controls and thus 'socialize' agriculture. Tranditional rural supporters of farm programmes opposed Brannan's plans to substitute a ten-year average of incomes support for parity and feared that there would be great difficulties in securing the annual appropriations needed for the Bill. Conservatives, including many Southerners, feared that the plan would help the smaller producer disproportionately, particularly as the plan included a limitation on the size of direct government payments any one farmer could receive while relying less on the 'loans' and quotas which had served the large-scale producer so well. Urban liberals, however, opposed the plan because most of the subsidies would still go to the richest farmers.

Brannan, then, left the 'farm problem' unsolved. But he had the distinction, if such it is, of initiating the pattern of postwar policymaking. One after the other, his successors would present Congress with clear alternative solutions to the farm problem. And Congress would continue to fail to make the necessary choice between hard alternatives, but would make minor, confusing changes in the New Deal laws.

The Eisenhower years

Eisenhower's election campaign seemed to promise few reforms. Anxious not to repeat Dewey's mistake in the 1948 campaign, Eisenhower pledged himself to maintain existing farm laws in the traditional candidate's speech to the National Ploughing Contest, that year held in Kasson, Missouri. This pledge concealed, however, a determination not to maintain subsidies at their present rates, but to return farming to a freer market. Eisenhower's plan for agriculture was to reduce controls while avoiding surpluses by letting farm prices sink. The claim that this policy was maintaining existing laws was strictly correct, for the basic New Deal legislation, until amended by temporary wartime concessions to farmers, did give the Secretary wide powers to vary parity rates. It was not, however, what Eisenhower's audience had in mind by maintaining existing laws.

Any doubts in the minds of farmers about Eisenhower's determination to return them to a free market should have been shattered by his choice for the Secretaryship of Agriculture, Ezra Taft Benson, a tough, uncompromising and opinionated Mormon. Benson was a fervent advocate of capitalism tainted as little as was possible by government. Benson's memoires[14] give a picture of a man who believed to a much greater extent than most politicians that this policies were morally as well as technically the only acceptable approach. He describes himself as a 'conservative conservative; Goldwater represented by basic philosophy much more closely than either Nixon or Rockefeller', and his belief in capitalism was repeatedly emphasized: 'The blessings of abundance that we now possess have come down to us through our economic system that rests on three pillars . . . free enterprise . . . private property . . . a market economy.'[15]

Benson's belief, as expressed in his writings[16] and his testimony to congressional committees,[17] was that the proper role for the government in agriculture was merely to minize the effects of chance, and hopefully infrequent, disasters. It followed that the American government was too closely involved in farming. Production controls and planning were abhorrent to Benson. Subsidies were equally objectionable, and clearly could not be sustained anyway without production controls. The Secretary wished to abolish controls and push subsidies down to 90 per cent of average market prices, so that they would not be needed in normal times.

Benson had some interim plans to help farmers by leasing land to the US Department of Agriculture and keeping it out of production. However, his long-term objective was, in short, to end farm subsidies for good. Benson clearly accepted that his policies were found to reduce the number of farmers. Indeed, a fall in the farm population became one of his objectives. Elderly farmers were to be helped to retire, while retraining programmes, those favourite progressive gestures of American politicians, were to be provided for their younger colleagues. When Jefferson had seen the farmer as the repository of virtue, Benson saw no virtue in any way of life which did not generate enough profit on which to live.

In spite of, or because of, Benson's didactic intolerant style, he achieved little. His legislative triumphs, the Agriculture Acts of 1954 and 1958, were more symbolic victories than real, in spite of the tough fights to get them enacted. The 1954 Act gave the Secretary only minute powers to reduce subsidy rates from 90 to 82·5 per cent of parity. The 1958 Act, which Benson rammed through a Democratic Congress, expanded this range down to 65 per cent for cotton, and corn and rice. In contrast, mandatory price supports were also extended to oats, rye, barley, and grain sorghums 'at a fair and reasonable price in relation to corn'.

The Wool Act, under which producers received deficiency payments which Benson regarded as 'socialistic' (though operated by a Conservative Government in Britain), was renewed. In return, production controls were relaxed.

Yet if Benson achieved little, he achieved it with great noise. Not surprisingly, when farm incomes dropped, farmers blamed it on Benson. The 1950s were not particularly prosperous times for American farmers. Whereas the disposable incomes of Americans almost doubled from $1,331 per capita in 1947–49 to $2,017 in 1960, farm per capita incomes lagged behind, rising from $886 to $1,195 in the same period. Even this improvement in per capita farm incomes was achieved only by a reduction in the farm population; aggregate farm incomes actually fell from $15,699 to $11,526 million.[18]

Even when farmers did not blame Benson for the weakness of farm commodity prices, they resented his determination not to help them more during this difficult period. Farmers enjoyed the rare distinction among voting groups of favouring Eisenhower less in 1956 than in 1952.[19] Not surprisingly, therefore, in 1958 Congressional rural Republicans made determined efforts to force the resignation of Benson and then to make clear to their voters that they did not share his views.

The Congressional Republicans were not very successful in this, and heavy Republican losses in the 1958 midterm elections were often linked to Benson's unpopularity. The Democratic party, working closely with the NFU, gained strength in areas such as the Dakotas, Wisconsin, and Minnesota, which had been safe Republican territory. (The election to Congress of George McGovern from South Dakota was a typical example.) In retrospect, this may have been part of a broader pattern of redrawing American party lines along clearer ideological lines. Rural liberals who had voted for LaFollette in the 1920s and who had joined the Non-Partisan League were transferring their allegiance to the Democrats in the 1950s. At the time, the message seemed simpler. A newly elected Democratic Representative from Wisconsin, Flyn, explained to the House Agriculture Committee in 1959:

The bulk of farmers in my district are Republican. I am a Democrat. ... We became a state in 1848 and since that time there has been but one Democrat from my state coming to Congress. That was in 1892. ... I believe that I am here strictly because the farmers in my state revolted.[20]

Yet though Benson's policies were politically costly, they were not successful in solving the farm problem. Benson could argue with some justice that this was the result of congressional obstruction. Congress could barely be persuaded to give Benson his narrow victories, and maintained many loopholes, such as a requirement that the national wheat acreage allotments should not be cut, in spite of massive wheat surpluses. Congress also declined to fund Benson's plan to rent land and take it out of production. Technological innovation reduced the real costs of production faster than Benson could persuade Congress to allow him to cut subsidies.

The real bankruptcy of Benson's policies seemed, however, that while farm income fell, surpluses of farm commodities rose. By the end of the 1950s, officials of the US Department of Agriculture felt that another good harvest would finish them. Grain filled proper stores and rotted in old liberty ships as the government spent $1 million per day on storage fees. Nor could more be given away to poor countries without reducing the prices that American exporters received. Benson's policy of returning agriculture to the free market seemingly produced low prices, surpluses, and rural discontent. Politicians could be pardoned for viewing it with suspicion.

The Kennedy and Johnson years

Benson's plan to return agriculture to the free market was one approach. An alternative argument, which found favour among Democrats, was that the only thing wrong with the farm laws was that production controls were not sufficiently stringent. The solution, therefore, was to keep subsidies up, while keeping output down. Legal controls would override market forces. Farmers were soon to show that they found this approach no more congenial than Benson's.

President Kennedy devoted much of his time during the 1960 campaign to the farm problem. In part this was because (as when Roosevelt was running for President), the agricultural situation with low prices and great surpluses was so bad that it was an issue to which any Presidential candidate had to address himself. Neustadt in his *Presidential Power*,[21] written at the time, listed the farm problem as one of the great issues to be resolved in the 1960s. Yet the attention the candidates gave to farm policy indicated something more—their high regard for the farm vote.

The Democrats' gains among farmers in 1956 and 1958 filled them with hopes that they could make massive inroads into the rural Republican vote in 1960. No one worked harder to capture the farm vote than Kennedy. Whereas prior to 1956 Kennedy's Senate votes had helped Benson, after 1956 he consciously reversed his position in a bid to win delegates at the Convention and rural votes in the Election. Robert Novak commented during the campaign in the *Wall Street Journal:*

The furious quest for the farm vote by rival candidates constitutes the greatest charade of this Presidential campaign. Judging from the effort expanded by both Democrat John F. Kennedy and Republican Richard M. Nixon in forging new programmes and selling them to the farmer, it would seem this was the key to the White House door. Senator Kennedy calls the farm programme the most pressing domestic issue of the day; so far Vice President Nixon has spent more time talking about farm policy than any single other domestic topic.[22]

Kennedy had made his plans for capturing the farm vote after consultations with Midwestern Senators and Governors in early August. His final proposals were, according to the tradition cemented by Truman in 1948, announced in a speech to the National Ploughing Contest, that year held at Sioux Falls, South Dakota.[23] The aim of Kennedy's policy was full parity but, he argued, it had to be achieved without a mushrooming of surpluses or government expenditure.

Kennedy's problem was how to reconcile high prices with a reduction in surpluses and government costs. His solution was 'supply management'—careful, tight controls over production to balance it with demand at prices which would give farmers a reasonable income.

What were the sources of his policy? Kennedy did not really find his policy within the Congressional party. The belief in supply management had been current in Democratic circles since the New Deal, but had been fostered recently by a pressure group, the liberal NFU. Like Roosevelt before him, Kennedy turned to a professor for the details of his policy—Willard Cochrane, a professor of agricultural economics from Minnesota. To implement this policy, however, Kennedy appointed as Secretary of Agriculture the former governor of Minnesota, Orville Freeman. Freeman had been drawn already to supply management as the only viable way to increase farm income. In 1960, Freeman had presented a survey to the House Agriculture Committee,[24] which showed the prevalence of low incomes among Minnesota farmers. To improve the situation, he suggested a package of policies called *Managed Abundance in Food and Agriculture*. The main proposal was 'provision of those tools by which farmers can realistically gear production to these expanded demands'. As the last phrase indicates, Freeman balanced the rather negative supply control with plans to expand the distribution of food to low-income groups at home and abroad, the maintenance of reserves to cover emergencies, and the improvements of conservation practices. The objective was that shared by the NFU—'a fair income for the American family farm'. Freeman justified supply management in what was to be a standard Democratic argument; agriculture has the same right to withhold excessive supplies as has industry and, through collective bargaining, labour.

Kennedy took office, then, with clear ideas on how to solve the farm problem. He did not, after all, owe his election to the farm vote. Indeed, perhaps because of the religious issue, Kennedy did not make the gains among farmers he had hoped. *Wallace's Farmer* noted in December that Kennedy was disappointed at not attracting more of the farm vote and his 'love affairs with farmers is all but on the rocks'. Both Senator Humphrey, and Hadwiger and Talbot in their study of the Kennedy farm laws, argued that farmers did give Kennedy victory margins in Minnesota, Missouri, and Wisconsin,[25] but Kennedy's personal belief that he owed no special debt to farmers strengthened his resolve to cut the cost of farm programmes. Though, as temporary measures, loan rates on basic commodities were increased and an emergency Act (the Feed Grain Act of 1961) was rushed through to provide for payments to divert acreages from corn, the Department started to draft legislation for supply management.

Freeman realized that he would have extreme difficulty in getting specific proposals for the supply management of each commodity through Congress. He asked, therefore, for a broad delegation of power from Congress to the Secretary and a committee representing producers of that commodity. When the Secretary considered a programme was necessary he would invite the proposals of a committee representing producers of the commodity concerned. The committees would be chosen partly by nominations from farm organizations and partly by elections from the local farmer committees, which administered programmes for the Department's Agricultural Stabilisation and Conservation Service. The Secretary would formulate a programme based on these consultations. The programme would then have to be approved by the President, Congress, and two-thirds of the producers before it became operational.

These provisions were demolished by Congress, however. The Senate Committee reported mild provision for purely advisory consultation with farm organizations.[26] The House Committee was more direct. 'The committee through HR 8230 seeks to achieve unity on farm policy. . . . Therefore the committee has revised the administration's bill introduced as HR 6400 to remove controversial provisions. . . .'[27]

As the House report also indicated, much of the opposition to the Freeman proposals was based on a defence of congressional prerogatives. Neither House nor Senate Agriculture Committee would accept that Congress should be limited to approving or rejecting programmes having no right to amend them. The Republicans found this constitutional objection a handy peg on which to hang their opposition to all physical controls. But as the opposition of the Democrats on the Committee indicates, Freeman had raised serious problems in his Bill. If the drafting of programmes was taken from the congressional committees, then the chances of their rejection by the House as a whole would probably increase, for one of the main tasks of a committee is gauging what Congress will take. Freeman provided no way for Congress to reconcile conflicts of interest which would arise between different commodities—a major part of its work. And there was a widespread feeling that, particularly in the first year, the Secretary would have many opportunities to pick committee men to advise him who would do his will. The Congress would, if such suspicions were well founded, have handed over policymaking to the Executive alone. Members of the agriculture committees, who invariably come from rural areas, could never hand over to the Executive sole responsibility for an issue on which they feel such pressure from their constituents. The failure of the 1961 Bill forced Freeman to seek approval of specific supply management proposals from Congress.

These were embodied in his proposals for the Food and Agriculture Act of 1962. Kennedy put forward the Administration's requests in a message to Congress on 31 January, 1962. They were for the most stringent controls ever on feed grains, wheat, and dairy products. Existing legislation, known as PL 480, would continue to use surpluses for foreign aid, while grants would be offered to individuals and communities to divert cropland to recreational uses to reduce the acreage under production. The Administration had, however, to apply extreme pressure to get the Bill (HR 11222) of the House Agriculture Committee. This was because three Southern Democrats from areas which produced cattle but not feed grains opposed the feed grain provisions of the Bill which would have increased prices of feed grain.[28] Chairman Cooley despairingly adjourned the Committee after three futile attempts to have it report out the Bill, for the three Southern Democrats allied with the Republicans commanded a majority of one on the Committee. Finally, President Kennedy swung the one vote necessary by personally lobbying one of the Southern Democrats, Harold B. McSween of

Louisiana.[29] McSween remained opposed to the Bill, but agreed to allow the House to vote on it.

After a stormy passage through the Senate and amendment in Committee, the major provisions of the Bill were defeated in the House. The Administration and House Committee leadership used the Senate majority to restore them in Conference, and the House finally swallowed the Bill by 202 votes to 197.

The Act as passed provided that feed grains would continue to operate under the costly 1961 'emergency' legislation under which the Government paid producers to cut output below the acreage to which they were entitled. As the sections of the Act covering dairy produce had been deleted, and cotton never included, the test case for supply management was to be wheat (though existing controls on tobacco, rice, cotton, etc., continued). The Secretary would decide on a national allotment to balance supply and demand, and set price supports at 65 to 90 per cent of parity. But if producers rejected the plan, then support would be slashed to 50 per cent of party (which was very low) and government stocks would have been sold off at only 105 per cent of this price. As this would have caused market prices to slump, the intention was to force wheat producers to choose between strict controls and ruin.

Would wheat producers hesitate faced with such a choice? There were good grounds for believing that wheat farmers would vote for controls. Wheat farmers had been much more reliable supporters of controls than had feed grain producers, and if prices fell to 50 per cent of parity it would obviously be ruinous. But was the choice so clear? The Administration had insisted that it was determined to have strict controls for feed grains, yet, on 31 January, 1963, Kennedy yielded to Congressional opposition and requested an extension of the emergency feed grain legislation, arguing that: 'The emergency and temporary feed grain legislation of 1961 and 1962 has worked well.' Under the emergency feed grain legislation farmers received 25 to 65 cents a bushel in return for reducing their feed grain acreage. However, wheat farmers were still expected to reduce acreage without direct payment. Kennedy argued that:

Failure to approve the wheat programme will leave the wheat farmer without either supply management or effective price supports at the mercy of unlimited production and unlimited prices. I do not believe that anyone who understands the choice would prefer a return to the depression conditions that preceded the initiation of price supports a generation ago. *New legislation for wheat is neither necessary nor feasible this year.*[30]

If less than two-thirds of producers voted for restrictions, would President and Congress have the political will to deny wheat farmers legislation which would be as favourable as that now granted to feed grain producers? The AFBF, campaigning hard for a 'No' vote, could not persuade farmers that they should accept its extreme *laissez-faire* views. But the AFBF could point to how feed grains had obtained more favourable legislation with less tough controls by opposing the supply management plans in spite of threats from Congress and the Administration that by 1964 feed grains would receive minimal price supports. The AFBF argued that farmers could afford to vote 'No' because, in spite of their threats,

Congress would soon provide a more attractive programme if the referendum failed.[31] The programme fared disastrously in the referendum. Not only did it fail to attract the support of two-thirds of producers but a majority (52·2 per cent) voted 'No'. States where it was expected to do well such as the Dakotas, Wisconsin, and Minnesota approved the programme but by less than the two-thirds required nationally for the adoption. Halfway through his first term, Kennedy's policy was in wreckage and it was not surprising that Washington was full of rumours that Freeman would resign.

Thirty years after their adoption, the New Deal farm policies continued to operate in spite of their inefficiency, wasteful surpluses, and tendency to favour large-scale producers. A further attempt at systematic reform had ended.

The temptation to pull the house down in ruins around the heads of recalcitrant farmers must have been strong. But 1964 was an election year, and the Administration wanted neither the President nor his congressional allies to seek re-election in the midst of a farm depression. President Johnson was sure that he did not, and ordered Freeman to produce a Bill covering wheat that could pass Congress before the election.[32] Democratic Senators first elected in 1958 were expected to be vulnerable. Not surprisingly, those such as Hart (Michigan), Hartke (Indiana), McCarthy (Minnesota), McGee (Wyoming), and Young (Ohio) who had wheat farming constituents were particularly keen to have fresh legislation. Unfortunately, there were many Congressional words uttered in 1962 that would have to be swallowed before any fresh wheat legislation passed. The Chairman of the House Agriculture Committee, Harold Cooley (Democrat, North Carolina), introducing the 1962 Bill had said: 'It makes no sense for me for the government to provide price supports for the unlimited production of anything.'[33] The Chairman of the Senate Agriculture Committee, Alan J. Ellender (Democrat, Louisana), had been even more explicit: 'It is wrong for a farmer to expect his government to provide him with price supports when he is not willing to adjust himself to acreage controls.'[34]

Fortunately for the Democrats, a cotton Bill was working its way through Congress in late 1962 (HR 6196). Cotton clearly could not be fitted into the supply management approach. Restricting the production and raising the price of American cotton would mainly have benefited foreign growers. At the same time, existing programmes of acreage restrictions and high price supports made American textiles uncompetitive. Foreign textile mills could buy cotton on the international market much cheaper than Americans could buy on the domestic market, partly because the United States paid an export subsidy of 8·5 cents per pound. On 4 December, 1963, the House passed a Bill to subsidize textile mills to compensate them for the high prices of domestic cotton that the farm programmes produced. The Bill also, and more importantly, provided for direct payments to cotton growers to compensate them for the lowering of price support levels. When the Bill reached the Senate, Senator George McGovern attached a wheat section under which participants would receive price supports and payments through marketing certificates for land diversion, whereas non-compliers would receive neither. A proposal to delete the wheat provision was defeated by margin sufficiently narrow (42 votes to 46) to show wheat farmers how close they had come to having no programme. When the Bill returned to the House, Members were spared the embarrassment of eating words uttered in 1962 by a rare procedural motion (H Res. 665) which completed action on the Bill without it being debated. The Resolution was carried by 211 votes to 203 and the House thus never debated the wheat section. The passage of the resolution was attributed to the direct intervention of President Johnson with Democratic Congressmen, the linking of the Wheat–Cotton Bill vote on H Res. 665) with a vote on the Food Stamp Bill (HR 10222)—a measure which Northern Democrats wanted and on which Southern support was shaky—and the traditional strategy in agricultural politics of linking the political fortunes of a Southern commodity (cotton) with that of a Midwestern commodity (wheat). The Democrats were once more able to make farm policy an issue in the 1964 Elections, and Goldwater obliged by suggesting that if elected he would abolish the federal farm programmes.[35]

By the end of 1964, the attempt to reform fundamentally farm subsidy legislation had been abandoned. Even the Administration had forgotten the coherent approach which Kennedy had embraced in 1960. There had been, however, significant changes. The Government had moved away from straightforward price supports for cotton, wheat, and feed grains. Price supports for these commodities continued at a slightly lower level and farmers received compensating payments direct from the government. These payments bought the cooperation of farmers in reducing their acreage, cooperation which Freeman and Kennedy had insisted farmers must give in return for the subsidies they already received. Whereas Kennedy had been determined to reduce the Exchequer cost, agriculture became dependent on direct payments from government to an unprecedent degree. However, as direct payments were accompanied by lower market prices, the CCC achieved a major reduction in surplus stocks, aided by crop failures in foreign countries (notably India).

The Food and Agriculture Act of 1965 (HR 9611) was in many ways a consolidating Act, tidying and improving the separate hurried measures which had established these changes for cotton, wheat, and feed grains. A cropland retirement clause marked the acceptance by the Democrats of a long-term land diversion programme which they had so fiercely condemned under Benson. The original proposals of the Administration had been to put much of the burden of farm support on the consumer. However, the Bureau of the Budget had favoured substituting direct government payments in order to bring the cost of farm programmes into the open. After heavy lobbying by trade interests and the AFL–CIO against financing farm programmes by special charges on processors which were then passed on to consumers (as in the 1964 wheat programme), the Administration accepted the principle of financing farm subsidies from general taxation. Cotton price supports were pitched low (at 90 per cent of the world market price), but producers were eligible for both acreage diversion payments and direct payments at 9·42 cents a pound. Lower prices would, it was argued, reduce surpluses and help the domestic textile industry. Cotton would be made more competitive with artificial fibres. Wheat producers, too, were helped not by increasing the value of marketing certificates (which millers were forced to buy from the farmer at a set rate) but by direct payments from the government. The feed grain programme was continued, as were the wool, dairy, and rice schemes. The House leadership closely linked the vote on the Act to a vote to repeal Section 14b of the Taft Hartley Act (long opposed by labour unions), which allowed states to pass 'right to work' laws. The tactic was regarded as successful, keeping many rural Democrats, particularly from the South, behind the vote on the Taft Hartley Act (HR 77) and urban Democrats behind the Food and Agriculture Act.

Much of the opposition to switching to direct government payments, especially for cotton, came from Southern Congressmen and tactical and ideological reasons. Cotton in the South was produced by predominantly large-scale producers, and the region was very vulnerable therefore to limits on total payments to any one farmer, which, as we have seen, had been proposed at least as far back as the Brannan Plan. Two Southern Members of the House Agriculture Committee, Abernethy of Mississippi and Gathings of Arkansas, entered a separate report (HR 9811, dissent by Representatives Abernethy and Gathings) which warned of the dangers that subsidies from the Treasury which had to be voted annually were less reliable than the old method of subsidizing farmers by manipulating prices.

Not all cotton-state Senators opposed the plan (Talmadge of Georgia, for example, had long favoured direct payments), but the direct government payments to farmers were a painful necessity to conservative Southerners who sympathized with the views of Senators Ellender (Democrat, Louisanna) and Eastland (Democrat, Mississippi) who argued not only the tactical point that 'There would be a limitation based on payments to any one farmer' but that 'it is inherently wrong that a farmer should receive a large percentage of his income from the Treasury of the United States'.[36]

The Southerners were absolutely right to expect attempts to put a limitation on payments. Repeated attempts were made by Representatives Paul Findley of Illinois and Conte of Massachusetts to add riders to Appropriations Bills limiting payments. Though both were Republicans and though Findley was a conservative on economic issues and, therefore, opposed to the farm programmes on principle, Findley and Conte could pick up substantial support from urban Democrats by using this tactic. Voting for payment limitation was an easy way for urban liberals to retaliate for the party indiscipline of the Southern conservative Democrats. Large payments to plantation owners such as Senator Eastland (were something that Northern liberals instinctively opposed. Payment limitation also split Southern Democrats from Midwestern Democrats, for the rural liberals from the Dakotas, Wisconsin, Minnesota, etc., welcomed payment limitation as a curb on the expansion of corporate farming at the expense of the family farmer. Findley was thus able to use payment limitation to disrupt not only the Democratic urban/rural alliance but also the Democrats Midwestern/Southern rural alliance. Indeed, had an effective payment limitation been adopted, this might have caused cotton-state Congressmen to oppose all farm programmes posing a major threat to their future, thus achieving Findley's ultimate objective. By 1969 Conte and

Findley had sufficient support to attach a payment limitation clause to the Agriculture Appropriations Bill by a roll-call vote of 225 to 142, in spite of the opposition of the Administration, the Republican House leadership, and the Democratic House leadership. The Senate heavily defeated (53 votes to 34) payment limitations and the House leaders appointed conferees who, with only two exceptions, were known to oppose payment limitation. Payment limitation was deleted in the Conference Report and the House narrowly accepted this voting by 181 to 177 to order conferees to keep in payment limitation and by 214 votes to 172 to recommit the entire Conference Report.

Congress had not surprisingly tired of agricultural legislation in 1965. The unusually large Administration majority in that Congress had therefore given the 1965 Act the unusually long period of four years to run. In 1968, Freeman asked for further extension of the 1965 Act, but surprisingly the agriculture committees felt it only proper to wait until the next Administration took office. Had Nixon returned with a fierce Benson-like determination to end farm programmes, this could have been embarrassing. However, Nixon had, as in 1960, eagerly courted the farm vote. He had pledged himself to raise farm income and specifically promised not to endanger this objective by 'calamitous' attempts to revolutionize farm programmes, even though he doubted their long-term suitability.[37]

Nixon's choice as Secretary of Agriculture was a Professor Clifford M. Hardin from Purdue University, the home of Republican *laissez-faire* farm economics. Hardin, however, recognized the realities of obtaining legislation from a Congress controlled by the Democrats. In place of Benson's self-righteous confrontation with Congress, Hardin chose close cooperation. This was possible because the Chairman of the House Agriculture, now Bob Poage (Democrats, Texas) had decided that he could not get a Bill through an urban-oriented Congress without the cooperation of the Administration. In addition to formal hearings, the House Committee held twenty-seven informal and confidential meetings with the Secretary.

The result was the only Agriculture Act since the First World War which was substantially agreed by Republicans and Democrats.[38] The Republicans made two advances which they had long sought: greater use of cropland retirement programmes and relaxation of production controls. The major feature of the Act, however, was the continuation of the policy begun by the Wheat–Cotton Act of relying more on direct government payments and less on artificially raised market prices to subsidize farmers. Advocates of payments limitations were satisfied with a symbolic ceiling of $50,000 per crop per farmer which everyone knew would not work.[39]

The political system had still not, in any real sense, 'solved' the farm problem by 1972, even though the American subsidy system had changed significantly. The system of subsidizing farmers by manipulating the market, a system which had prevailed from the New Deal to 1964, had been modified by greater reliance on direct payments from the government to farmers. A significant proportion of the cost of farm subsidies had thus been transferred from consumers to taxpayers. As in the New Deal era, government policy still aimed at raising prices by discouraging production, a policy which was to look decidedly odd in the next few years. After a generation of government action to restrict production, a crop failure in the Soviet Union and the perverse behaviour of ocean currents off Peru, which caused demand for soya beans to rise and supplies of fish to fail, transformed the outlook for agriculture. An era of scarcity had, totally unexpectedly, crept up on a United States still exulting in its success in reducing surpluses. Yet surpluses, the curse of the 1950s and 1960s, would, it seemed now, have been the blessing of the 1970s.

The effects of farm subsidies; *cui bono?*

The rhetoric of debates on farm subsidies in the United States has been heavily spiced with reference to rural disadvantage. Farmers are poor, operate on low margins, and are constantly living under the threat of bankruptcy. The impression has been created that farm subsidies are a lifeline thrown to the modest family farmer threatened with bankruptcy and absorption by agribusiness. The family farmer is seen as one of the few businessmen left operating in something approaching the perfect market of classical economics but unable, like 'big business' or 'big labour', to regular supply and price. It is the duty of government to help him and thereby redress the balance.

There can be no doubt that the American farm subsidy system has had a major effect on farm incomes. The Legislative Reference Service of the Library of Congress has calculated that had farm subsidies been ended, within three to five years farm incomes would have fallen to half their actual level. Other studies have confirmed their findings.[40]

It is interesting to note that whereas subsidies of all kinds accounted for 50 per cent of farm income in the United States, in Britain Exchequer payments alone (disregarding the effects of marketing boards and import restrictions) accounted for a slightly higher percentage of farm income. Indeed, the average subsidy per farm in Britain in the 1960s (accepting Howarth's estimates) was of the order of $2,352·5 while the equivalent in the United States was about $1,729·1. Such comparisons of average figures can be misleading, however, for subsidies in the United States have been very unevenly distributed. Larry Wipf, an American economist, has shown that the value of protection for producers in the United States has ranged from +158·5 per cent for wheat and +95 per cent for cotton to −11·7 per cent for poultry and egg producers.[41] Schultze has demonstrated that the richest, largest-scale farmers receive much more than the poor farmer; the wealthiest 19·1 per cent receives 63 per cent of farm subsidies. He concludes that:

By their very nature, current farm programs tend to provide benefits—paid for by consumers and taxpayers—primarily to those farmers who produce the bulk of agricultural output. Conversely, the very large number of small farmers . . . are helped relatively little by these programs.[42]

Thus, even compared with Britain, American farm subsidy policies have benefited a small proportion of the rural population. Richard Howarth, a critic of the British subsidy system, has argued that it benefits only 56 per cent of agricultural production; President Eisenhower, a critic of the American system, argued that it subsidized primarily less than 25 per cent of American agricultural output.[43] If both are right, the average British beneficiary of farm subsidies (as opposed to the average farmer) received almost twice the average subsidy per farm, or some $4,705 per annum; his American counterpart received four times the average, or $6,916·4 per annum. The Americans, in brief, provide feather-beds for a few, while the British provide straw pallets for all.

Yet such contrasts between the two countries should not obscure important similarities. In the United States, as in Britain, farm subsidies have been both economically inefficient and socially indefensible, distributing benefits preponderantly to the wealthiest minority of farmers. We have attempted to explain why they have survived nonetheless in Britain; we turn now to the United States, looking first at the importance of agricultural pressure groups there.

Notes

1. Information from House of Representatives, Ninety-second Congress, First Session 1971, Committee on Agriculture, *Food Costs, Farm Prices*, p. 30.
2. D. R. Fusfeld, *The Economic Thought of Franklin D. Roosevelt and the Origins of the New Deal*, Columbia University Press, New York, 1956, p. 197.
3. See also D. Gale Johnson, *World Agriculture in Disarray*, Fontana Collins, London, 1962, Table 4.2.
4. US Congress, House of Representatives, Eightieth Congress, First Session, *Long Range Agricultural Policy—A Study of the Agricultural Adjustment Programmes, 1933–41*, Tables 10, 12, 16, 18, 19, 20; see also Edwin Nourse, Davis, and Black, *Three Years of the Agricultural Adjustment Administration*, Brookings Institution, Washington, 1937.
5. Reprinted in Howard Zinn (Ed.), *New Deal Thought*, Bobbs Merrill, New York, 1966, p. 227.
6. Arthur Schlesinger, Jr., *The Coming of the New Deal*, Houghton Mifflin Co., New York, 1959, p. 77.
7. Allen J. Matusow, *Farm Policies and Politics in the Truman Years*, Harvard Press, Cambridge, Mass., 1967, pp. 10–38.
8. Harry S. Truman, *Years of Trial and Hope, 1944–53*, Hodder and Stoughton, London, 1956, p. 278 ff. 'The old *laissez faire* theorists would tell us that the answer to the farm problem is to cut down on producing units until the fittest survive. But this theory is without humanity, for it means the break up of homes, the destruction of families and the surrender of the family farm to the absentee landlord or corporate owners'.
9. Matusow, op. cit., p. 175.
10. Ibid., p. 185 ff.
11. For an excellent discussion of the politics and economics of the Brannan Plan, see Reo M. Christenson, *The Brannan Plan, Farm Politics and Policy*, University of Michigan Press, Ann Arbor, 1959. See also Matusow, op cit.
12. Some of Brannan's proposals were incorporated in the 1973 Agriculture Act.
13. Christenson, op. cit.
14. Ezra Taft Benson, *Cross Fire; The Eight Years with Eisenhower*, Doubleday and Co., New York, 1962.
15. Ibid., p. 580.

74

16. Ezra Taft Benson, *Freedom to Farm*, Doubleday and Co., New York, 1960.
17. US Congress, 86th Congress, Second Session, House Committee on Agriculture, Hearings, *General Farm Legislation*, 1960.
18. US Congress, House of Representatives, Ninety-second Congress, First Session, Committee on Agriculture, *Food Costs, Farm Prices*, p. 32.
19. V. O. Key, *The Responsible Electorate*, Vintage Books, New York, 1966, p. 87.
20. US Congress, Eighty-sixth Congress, First Session, House Committee on Agriculture, Hearings, *General Farm Legislation, 1959*.
21. R. E. Neustadt, *Presidential Power*, John Wiley and Co., New York, 1960, p. 189.
22. Robert Novak, *Wall Street Journal*, 29 September, 1960.
23. *Wall Street Journal*, 23 September, 1960.
24. US Congress, House of Representatives, Eighty-sixth Congress, Second Session, Committee on Agriculture, Hearings, *General Farm Legislation*, 1960.
25. *Wallace's Farmer*, 3 December, 1960; *New York Times*, 4 December, 1960; Don F. Hadwiger and Ross B. Talbot, *Pressures and Protests, The Kennedy Farm Programme and the Wheat Referendum of 1963*, Chandler, San Francisco, 1965, p. 27.
26. Calendar No. 539, 17 July, 1961, Senate Report to accompany S 1643; Union Calendar No. 293 to accompany HR 8230, House Report.
27. Ibid.
28. Hadwiger and Talbot, op. cit., *passim; Washington Post*, 8 May, 1962.
29. *New York Times*, 11 May, 1962.
30. Quoted Hadwiger and Talbot, op. cit., p. 257.
31. *Washington Post*, 29 January, 1963.
32. *Washington Post*, 18 December, 1963; *Wall Street Journal*, 17 January, 1964.
33. *Congressional Record* (House), Vol. 108, part 8, 19 June, 1962.
34. *Congressional Record* (Senate), Vol. 108, part 7, 21 May, 1962.
35. For Johnson's speeches attacking Goldwater's farm programme as 'heartless prescriptions of economic nonsense' see *Washington Post*, 7 October, 1964, and *Washington Evening Star*, 12 October, 1964.
36. *Congressional Record* (Senate), Vol. 111, part 17, col. 23351, 1965.
37. *Washington Post*, 15 September, 1968.
38. This agreement was short lived; 1973 produced a long and acrimonious wrangle between Republicans and Democrats, Congress and Executive.
39. The point was repeatedly made by advocates of a 20,000 dollar ceiling, such as Findley in the House debate on the Agriculture Act of 1970. See *Congressional Record* (House), Vol. 116, para. 20, 1970.
40. US Senate, Eighty-ninth Congress, First Session, Committee on Agriculture and Forestry, *Farm Programs and Dynamic Forces in Agriculture*, Tables 4 and 5; Luther G. Tweeten, Earl O. Meady, and Leo U. Mayer, *Farm Program Alternatives, Farm Incomes and Public Costs under Alternative Commodity Programs for Feed Grains and Wheat*, CAED Report 18, Iowa State University, 1963; Charles Schultze, *The Distribution of Farm Subsidies, Who Gets the Benefits?*, Brookings Institution Staff Paper, Washington DC, 1971, esp. p. 23.
41. Larry J. Wipf, 'Tariffs, non-tariff distortions and effective protection in U.S. agriculture', *American Journal of Agricultural Economics*, 1971.
42. Schultze, op. cit., p. 30.
43. Special Message to the Congress on Agriculture, 29 January, 1959, *Public Papers of the Presidents*; Dwight D. Eisenhower, US GPO, 1960, p. 147.

Chapter 6

The American Interest Groups

The stereotype notion of omnipotent pressure groups becomes completely untenable once there are groups aligned on both sides. The result of opposing equipotent forces is stalemate. But even taken by themselves, the groups did not appear to have the raw material of great power.[1]

One plausible explanation for the failure of the United States to adopt more sensible agricultural policies is that agricultural interest groups, representing farmers who receive farm subsidies, have proved too powerful. The reason why attempts to reform the farm subsidy laws have run into the sands, according to this argument, is that either Congress, the Executive, or both, have been unwilling to offend these powerful organized interests whose members have profited from both Benson's failure to cut prices and Freeman's failure to control output. How plausible is such an interpretation?

The student of comparative government will also wish to know how similar to the British are the American agricultural interest groups in their structure, history, policy, and mode of operating. How well founded is the conventional wisdom that interest groups are more important in American politics than in British?

Membership: general characteristics

As in the remainder of this chapter many contrasts will be drawn between American agricultural interest groups, it is worth starting with one striking similarity which will become the more puzzling as the chapter progresses. It is that there is no obvious difference, least of all in terms of social class, between the *memberships* of the contending American agricultural interest groups.

Beer's striking comparison of the proportion of farmers who join the British NFU (76 per cent) and who join any agricultural interest group in the United States (30 per cent) has been quoted in Chapter 3. The demise of the marginal farmer in the United States (aided by the indifference of the largest agricultural interest group) has probably improved the average somewhat since, but not nearly enough to make a significant difference to Beer's comment. In the light of Lipset's[2] general finding that the more privileged are more likely to join voluntary organizations than the less privileged (a finding which Schattschneider immortalized in his comment that the pluralist heavenly choir sings with an upper class accent), we should not be surprised to discover the characteristics of the joining farmer. He is affluent. In contrast, Crampton[3] cites evidence to suggest that 86 per cent of the poorest farmers and 70·9 per cent of middle income farmers belong to no organization at all. Rohwer found a similar—and similarly striking—tendency for joiners of agricultural interest groups in Oklahoma to be almost exclusively the more affluent.[4] A survey by the *Des Moines Register* showed that 43·5 per cent of farmers in Iowa and 44·1 per cent in Indiana belong to no farm organization. Again, they are the poorer farmers.[5]

The social similarities of the members of the different agricultural interest groups are considerable, particularly if they are compared with the non-joiner. It is a fact that will become all the more curious as differences between these organizations emerge—that is the members of the more liberal groups who are the slightly richer, not poorer, farmers.[6] In spite of the fact that one of the agricultural interest groups, the Grange, is almost exclusively East coast and another, the National Farmers' Union, almost exclusively Midwestern, any attempt to differentiate the membership of the farm organizations in terms of the crops they produce similarly fails. Crampton[7] in his study of the NFU finds no significant difference between the sort of crop grown by a farmer who joins the liberal NFU or by a farmer who joins the more conservative rival. Indeed, any attempt to explain which organization farmers join in terms of the region they live or the crops they grow founders on the fact that the largest of the American agricultural interest groups, the American Farm Bureau Federation, is established in every region and among the producers of every type of crop.

The American Farm Bureau Federation (AFBF)

The AFBF is by far the largest of the American agricultural interest groups. Though (as will be seen below) there are doubts about the meaning and reliability of its figures, the AFBF claims over two million members in every state but Alaska and 2,824 counties.[8] It is, therefore, the only truly national agricultural interest group in the United States.

Its development

It is remarkable that such a large organization, far from developing spontaneously like the British NFU, should have needed careful fostering by government officials and non-agricultural interests. As a critic has somewhat sharply but not unfairly commented, the AFBF was 'conceived by businessmen, and the first county agents (government paid agricultural advisers), born in a Chamber of Commerce, nurtured on funds from industry and has never completely left its home and parents'.[9] The first farm bureau was created by the local Chamber of Commerce in Binghampton, Broome County, New York, in 1911 (though Campbell, in her history of the AFBF, claims that the first bureau like the modern bureaux was that formed in Pettis County, Missouri, in the same year).[10]

However, it was not until the passing on the Smith Lever Act of 1914 that there was a reason to believe that the farm bureau would become a major force in agricultural politics. The Smith Lever Act provided for federal funds to be used with state money to provide an Agricultural Extension Service. The Service provided a network of county agents who often voluntarily organized farm bureaux to work with them in order to promote better relations with local farmers and greater acceptance of the techniques they were teaching. By 1915 there were sufficient farm bureaux to make state federations viable, and the growth of the organization was further aided by the requirements, imposed by many states, that the county agent form a local farm bureaux.

From the early days, the local bureaux were allowed to collect membership subscriptions. At first these merely supplemented state and federal funds, but they made possible a growing degree of autonomy from the state agricultural colleges, which were the original employers and appointers of the county agent. Encouraged by the county agents to solidify the position of the farmer by organizing, the State Farm Bureau Federations formed a national organization in 1919.

The early history of the AFBF endowed it with a conservative philosophy. The Founding Fathers of the organization were often consciously creating a conservative alternative to radical rural politics which, of course, had swept both the South and Midwest in the 1880s and 1890s. An early President of the Federation's Illinois branch, the Illinois Agricultural Association, warned, 'It is our duty in creating this organization to avoid any policy which will align organised farmers with the radicals of other organisations.'[11] The Federation moved quickly to out-organize the Non-Partisan League in Illinois, not only because of organizational rivalry but because it disliked the League as it was 'socialistic and political in nature'.[12] In spite of ever-standing conflicts with merchants, meat packers, interests opposed to state aid to revitalize rural areas such as the Muscle Shoals Project, and the collapse of commodity markets, the Federation eschewed radicialism and instead worked for 'a better understanding of the farmers' basic difficulties on the part of business and financial leaders'.[13] Moreover, the close links with the Extension Service also encouraged conservatism. As Hardin[14] notes, the Extension Service existed to teach farmers how to improve their lot through better farming practice and sharper marketing. It tended, naturally, to believe that following its teaching was a more efficacious means of raising farm income than political action.

However, the objective circumstances of the interwar years made reliance on self-help an implausible strategy for even determined conservatives. Faced with the crushing slump in commodity prices detailed in the previous chapter, the AFBF turned to politicians for help. Coolidge twice vetoed a plan, embodied in the McNary–Haugen Bill, to raise farm incomes by forcing up domestic prices through intervention buying at home and dumping surpluses abroad. This act of economic statesmanship delivered the AFBF to the Democrats, and the Federation began a close relationship with the Democrats, which was to last over a dozen years, by forming the Independent Agricultural League to help Al Smith. The League's slogan, 'Vote as farmers, not partisans', failed to overcome Smith's defects as a 'wet', and a catholic to boot. However, Hoover's mild essay in mild interventionism, the Farm Board, failed to halt either the decline in commodity prices or to retrieve the AFBF from the Democratic fold. Roosevelt was careful to consult fully with the AFBF before he took office, and the Federation had a major hand in drawing up the New Deal programmes it was to despise later.[15]

The New Deal brought not only prosperity to the membership but, after early alarms, greater success to the organization. Until the New Deal, the Federation had been rather weak in the South. The farmer-elected committees created at county and state level to administer the New Deal programmes posed a threat to the AFBF that an organization which had itself grown out of a government agency was not slow to appreciate. The answer was to organize the South by coopting the key members of the organization that the Agricultural Adjustment Act had created:

Wherever practicable, A.A.A. (Agricultural Adjustment Administration) production control committees were to be invited to serve as organisation committees to organise a farm bureau in their local communities. In many instances it was expected that the chairman of the production control committees would become the president of the county farm bureau and the members of the committee constitute the board of directors of the county farm bureau. They would be asked to serve not in their capacity as committee men but as leaders in whom farmers have confidence.[16]

The degree to which this tactic worked varied from state to state. In some states reliance on the old tactic of working with the Extension Service was the most helpful. A crude violation of the True–Howard agreement (supposedly banning work by the Extension Service for the AFBF attracted much attention in Alabama. The county agent sent out a letter to farmers advising them that their AAA cheques were awaiting them in his office and urging them to join the AFBF.[17] However, in Tennessee and North Carolina, the New Deal agencies were a more effective means of expanding the Federation.[18]

The reliance by the Federation on New Deal agencies to farm bureaux in most of the South helps to explain why Southern state farm bureaux remained loyal to the New Deal agricultural programmes when bureaux more influenced by extension agents defected. It is more significant that by the Second World War the AFBF had used skilfully both the Extension Service and the AAAs to establish a virtually complete national organizational base. Whether or not the Government had deliberately created a conservative farm group can be debated; the 'soundness' of its views, particularly when contrasted with the radicalism of the NFU and other movements of the period, reduced the temptation to disrupt the cosy relationship between the AFBF and the Extension Service.

Contemporary membership

In spite of the decline in the farm population, the membership claimed by the AFBF has risen steadily. The major strength of the AFBF continues, however, to be in the Midwest and South.

Though all regions apart from the West have grown steadily, it is the growth of the South that is particularly impressive. During the 1960s it became the largest single region, overtaking the Midwest by 1967. Though this makes a return to the Southern leadership in favour of interventionist farm laws more likely, Southern candidates for the Presidency of the AFBF have been less able than Midwesterners to draw support from other regions.

Table 5   Number of families claimed as members of the AFBF[19]

Region	1971	1967	1965
South	982,177	783,096	721,607
Midwest	876,137	771,856	771,500
Northeast	67,565	63,722	63,161
West	131,786	134,858	130,552
Total	2,057,665	1,753,532	1,686,820

What do these membership figures mean? The critics of the AFBF would argue that they mean little. In 1967, Congressman Resnick (Democrat, New York) launched an investigation of the AFBF which alleged that, though there was no reason to suppose that the figures for membership were incorrect as totals, they did not indicate how many farmers were members. In fact, Resnick claimed, 50 per cent of the membership were not farmers.[20] Though the Agriculture Committee voted 27 to 1 to disassociate themselves from Resnick's report (an action due as much to the unpopularity of Resnick on the Committee as to the power of the AFBF), Resnick and his staff continued their work. In 1971 Resnick's former aide published the results.[21] The book produced very strong evidence that the AFBF could not be composed purely of farmers. In four states—Illinois, Alabama, Florida, and Indiana—the AFBF claimed more family farm memberships than there are farms. In Cook County, Illinois, which has 1,000 farms, the AFBF claimed 7,000 family memberships. The explanation which Resnick supplies is that the AFBF has attracted many non-farm members who want to enjoy the cheap insurance, tyres, and other discounts that the bureaux supply. As a consequence, 'The Farm Bureau business activities now clearly dominate the organization.'[22]

The AFBF does not deny that its membership services are a considerable incentive to membership. Indeed, its officers argue that as it cannot, even if it wanted to, force farmers to join a closed shop, then it must rely on providing specific benefits to win members. This is a good example of the point which Olson argues. In material terms it is irrational for an individual to join an organization working to secure benefits—such as legislation—which will benefit all irrespective of whether they are members of that organization. Not only does the individual have the option of a free ride, enjoying benefits which he has not worked to secure; he cannot rationally decide that his joining the organization will significantly improve the chances of the organization being successful, for he is one individual among many.[23] Olson actually uses the American farm organization as an empirical example. Only by providing specific individual benefits such as cheap insurance can membership be maintained. The AFBF further argues, however, that in order to provide good services to its members, it has to sell them as widely as possible. Thus non-farmers are invited to join the AFBF so that they can take advantage of the services to members. The important point is to ensure that non-farmers do not dominate the voting in elections, etc. Article 10 (f) of the *Membership Memorandum Agreement* between the AFBF and individual states reads:

AFBF and State Association recognise the need and urgency for an early classification of members by all County Farm Bureaux in order to make certain that the control of the Farm Bureau will all ways remain in the hands of bona fide farmers and ranchers ... The terms 'voting member' and 'non voting' or 'associate member' should be used to designate the two types of membership.[24]

The clause then sets out minimum qualifications for being a voting member—that the voting member should be 'Persons, partnerships, unincorporated associations and corporations actively engaged in the production of agricultural products ... who receive a substantial proportion of their income from such products ...'.

Such a classification is rather vague, but what is more (and this illustrates the decentralization of power not only within the AFBF but within State Farm Bureau Federations) the agreement has not been enforced. It is not possible, therefore, as it should be, to say what proportion of the AFBF members are farmers. Only one-third of the state farm bureaux so far elect delegates under rules which make only farmers eligible to vote. In this minority of states which do separate farmers from non-farming members, the proportion of non-farming members varies from 10 to 45 per cent. As the states which make this division tend to be the stronger, highly organized farm bureaux (e.g. the Illinois Agricultural Association), it is probable that the nationwide percentage of non-farming members should be higher than the average in these successful states. The pressures to offer membership to non-farmers in the less organized states in order to reach a viable level for operating the services is probably greater than in a state such as Illinois, where many farmers are willing to join and the AFBF has a large farm membership and clientele for its services. All that can be said at present, though it is hard to be precise, is that a very significant minority of the AFBF's members are not farmers.

The ideology and policies of the AFBF

What are the normal concerns of interest groups? With the possible exception of trade unions and the definite exception of the National Union of Students, most

British interest groups confine their activities to the concerns of their members as members of a trade or profession, or as farmers or industrialists. The British observer can only be astonished at the range of issues with which the AFBF concerns itself. It is, of course, hard to draw a firm line beyond which an interest group has ceased to foster the immediate interests of its members and is, indeed, playing politics. It is equally hard to deny that the AFBF frequently crosses that line.

In practice all would agree that a declaration that 'we oppose the granting of amnesty to military deserters and draft dodgers'[25] has little immediate relevance to farming. The policy resolutions for the AFBF conference in 1973, for example, were concerned with issues of no direct importance to farm policy, such as a declaration on 'Socialism and Communism':

Tolerance of socialist and communist group practices in our land threatens the American way of life. The welfare state is based on centralisation of power in the federal government and the redistribution of the benefits of our economic system by political means and is akin to socialism and communism. We reaffirm our opposition to all socialistic and communistic systems.

There is to be no 'middle way' either once communism and socialism have been cast aside: 'We believe in the American capitalistic, private, competitive enterprise system in which property is privately owned, privately managed and operated for profit and individual satisfaction.'[26] The AFBF also believes 'that property rights are inseparable from human rights' and that 'One of the greatest dangers threatening our republic and our system of private competitive enterprise is the apathy of the American people and apparent lack of responsibility on the part of the individual citizen allowing the socialisation of America. . . .'[27] These quotations from the AFBF's published policy statements give a little of the flavour of the Federation.

The AFBF's policy declarations provide a veritable compendium of issues which have excited American conservatives since the last war. Its *bêtes noires* include the Warren Court and its liberal decisions; its favourite causes include 'aid for the people of South Vietnam in their defence of freedom'. Demands for reductions in government spending and taxation, increased autonomy for the Federal Reserve Board, the closed shop, and implacable opposition to higher minimum wages find regular places in its policy declarations. At times, the Federation's statements seem close to a parody of the American right. It believes that child labour laws have reached the point where they 'encourage idleness and juvenile delinquency' (1969) while Farm Bureau policy statements for 1973 claim that:

. . . maintaining the headquarters (of the United Nations) here is no longer in the best interests of our country. Many member nations are using the United Nations for espionage, for distributing communist propaganda, for promoting socialistic reform and for infiltrating many of the youth organisations on college and university campuses. The U.N. is being used as a platform for ridicule and vindictiveness against our free enterprise system and constitutional government . . . .

The AFBF and agriculture

It is very much to the credit of the AFBF that it applies its fearsomely conservative and *laissez-faire* principles to farm policy, even though this is contrary to the material interests of its members. Since the late 1940s, the Federation has urged the Government to abandon the interventionist farm policies which, as we noted in the last chapter, have doubled American farmers' incomes. The Federation argues that it has nothing against farmers enjoying high incomes but that 'this objective can best be achieved by preserving the market price system'. Existing farm subsidy programmes, be they based on 'acreage bases, acreage allotments, marketing quotas (or) compensatory payments', should be ended 'as rapidly as possible'. The Federation believes that the federal farm programmes have been self-defeating; to the extent that they have raised prices, they have lowered consumption, and to the degree that they have curtailed production, they merely increased the opportunities for America's foreign competitors. The Federation's only compromise has been to accept for 'three or maybe five years' a government programme to reduce production by renting land and keeping it out of use. Yet, even here, the Federation shows its devotion to agriculture as a business, not a way of life, by advocating the renting of whole farms, an approach condemned by other as undermining rural communitities and speeding depopulation of the countryside. Once the Government has disengaged itself from existing policies, the Federation would confine it to ironing out drastic and short-term fluctuations in price.

Quite natually, in the light of such beliefs, the Federation's national leaders have opposed every postwar proposal from the Democrats designed to solve the farm problem through government intervention. Predictably, the Federation's President, Charles Shuman, condemned the Kennedy Administration's plan to solve the farm problem by controlling production as 'the road to a licensed and regimented agriculture. . . . Government planning, control and coercion on a scale that has no precedent'. Less predictably, the Federation also opposed energetically the move which took place during the 1960s to subsidize agriculture through direct payments from the Government which do not require physical controls over production. The Federation's opposition was rooted in its *laissez-faire* beliefs. Government payments make farmers' incomes dependent on political, rather than market, decision, and that, to borrow a phrase from one of the Federation's intellectual mentors, is the road to serfdom.

The representativeness of the AFBF

Not surprisingly, the advocacy of a policy by the AFBF which would cost its members a great deal of money has caused many people to wonder if the AFBF represent either the interests or the wishes of its members. Representative Cooley (Democrat, North Carolina), a former Chairman of the Agriculture Committee, was prone to doleful commentaries on the decline of the AFBF:

One half of the nation's farms are in the South. We have numerous farms. I must say, and

I confess to the House, that the position and activities of the A.F.B.F. and particularly its Washington headquarters has been a mystery to me since the late Ed. O'Neal (President during the New Deal) the greatest farm organisation statesman of our time, retired as a farm Bureau President some fifteen years ago.[28]

The Washington office did not, he argued, represent feeling in the counties and states.

Cooley's belief that the AFBF national leadership was unrepresentative enabled him to hurl defiance at AFBF lobbyists. 'You are speaking for my farmers', Cooley told President Shuman once, 'but you are not having any effect on me.'[29] Tom Foley, then Chairman of the important Livestock and Feed Grains Subcommittee and new Chairman of the whole Committee (Democrat, Washington), commented in a House Committee hearing that the AFBF's

... national policies do not often find reflection in local agricultural areas and in our own areas there are substantial and important wheat arising areas which have heavy Farm Bureau membership. These individual Farm Bureaux have not taken the positions of hostility to these (farm) programmes that has been reflected on the national level and the fact ... of 96 per cent (of wheat producers) sign up (for a programme of production limitation) in the State of Washington is very good evidence that this programme is extremely popular with operators in wheat areas generally.[30]

Foley returned to his theme in hearings held by his Subcommittee: 'I do not know how we are to evaluate presentations that come before us from the Farm Bureau when members have so many constituents who do not agree with these presentations'. Kleppe (Republican, North Dakota) agreed that it was puzzling:

Somehow or other the Farm Bureau members that I know in North Dakota, I think I can honestly say, feel as I do that we are very very skeptical of this (the A.F.B.F.'s proposals) ... we do sense a tremendous difference in the attitude of individual members of the Farm Bureau from the position taken by the American Farm Bureau.[31]

The Republican (as well as the Democratic) Counsel to the Senate Agricultural and Forestry Committee claimed that in 1973 only Illinois and Indiana of the state farm bureaux had advocated the same policies as had the national leadership.[32]

The impression of disunity has been strengthened by several state farm bureaux lobbying with varying degrees of openness for government programmes. Kleppe told the House in 1970 that 'members of the Farm Bureau from my State came down and asked me to support the Bill'[33] which the AFBF opposed. Sometimes a Northern state's farm bureau has taken a stand against the national leadership. In 1960, for example, the Illinois Agricultural Association (IAA), the most *laissez-faire* group of all, was overwhelmed by a rank-and file revolt. The rebels met to plan strategy at Dekald, Illinois. They were urged on by a letter of support from Earl Smith (former Vice-President of the AFBF, President of the Illinois Agricultural Association 1926–45): 'I have little if any patience with the philosophy that doing nothing to curtail surplus production and letting prices fall to ruinous levels is the cure.' The meeting adopted a resolution calling not only for government prgrammes but for mandatory rather than voluntary controls.[34] After the IAA had adopted the rebel programme three members presented it to the House Committee on Agriculture,[35] to the obvious delight of the Democrats. In 1959, Coad of Iowa told the hapless Shuman as he appeared before the House Agriculture Committee:

This last fall and every fall I go around to various counties. In almost every county a delegation from your organisation comes to call on me. For fifteen minutes they give me the policy of the A.F.B.F and after they then say, 'That is the official position of the A.F.B.F. Now we want to tell you what we think.'[36]

Southern farm bureaux have been the main critics of the AFBF's policies and openly voice their criticisms to Congress. In 1958, the Louisiana State Farm Bureau President welcomes 'charity' as long as there were not stringent controls. The President of the South Carolina Farm Bureau said his members 'were sympathetic to I believe what Mr. Poage discussed, the proposition of parity'.[37] In 1968 P. R. Smith, testifying both as President of the Southern Cotton Growers Inc. *and* Vice-President of the Georgia Farm Bureau argued that 'the best course would be to extend the Food Agriculture Act of 1965 including the present cotton programme'. He went on to demand the repeal of all cropland retirement programmes so beloved by the AFBF. 'Such programmes decimate the farm population, create ghost towns and dump rural people on the relief roles of the cities.' Congressman Speed O. Long of Louisiana, testifying on behalf of the Louisana State Farm Bureau, told the same committee that there should be tighter national production allotments—an idea which was anathema to the national leadership.[38]

Morrison and Warner[39] suggest that support for AFBF policies at the grass roots is not very strong. Their survey of Michigan and Wisconsin farmers in 1965 showed that a difference of only -5.7 per cent existed between the proportion of AFBF members favouring supports and non-AFBF farmers who favoured supports. Significantly, the differences between farmers in the AFBF and these who were not were much less clear than the differences between affiliated Republicans and Democrats. In spite of the AFBF's support for Benson's politics, a 1957 opinion poll by *Wallace's Farmer* showed 57 per cent disapproving, 31 per cent 'don't know', and only 12 per cent approving of the Secretary's performance.[40] Bartell found that only 34 per cent of AFBF members in Michigan said they approved of AFBF policies 'very much' or 'quite a bit'—a lower proportion than he found in other farm organizations. Forty-six per cent of both National Farmers' Organization (NFO) and AFBF members agreed with the statement that 'strong government programmes are necessary to boost farm income', though AFBF members tended to be more opposed (56 per cent compared with 35 per cent) to *mandatory* programmes.[41]

The record shows that for upland cotton, extra long stable cotton, rice, wheat from 1941 to 1963, peanuts, and tobacco except in 1939, growers have voted in US Department of Agriculture referenda in favour of mandatory controls and against a free market by a sizeable margin.[42] American farmers have been more prepared to accept government help, even if it involves regulation, than their Federation.

The leadership's style

The British are accustomed to pressure group leaders who pose as statesmen, or at least civil servants. Anxious to convey the impression that they are technically expert men amenable to compromise, British pressure group leaders mix easily with the civil servants with whom most of their work is done. In particular, leaders of British pressure groups, be they from trades unions, employers' associations, or the NFU, stress their willingness or eagerness to work with any government, irrespective of its political complexion.

The style of pressure group leaders in the United States is radically different, and nothing illustrates this contrast better than the AFBF. Since the last war, its leaders, though very pleasant individually, have been sharp-tongued, highly political, and moralistic in their activities.

Like most pressure group leaders, the Federation's leaders claim that their policies are set by democratically elected conventions, a claim which will be discussed later. All pressure group leaders have some discretion, however, in determining strategy and which aspects of their organization's policy statements they will emphasize. British pressure group leaders commonly use this discretion to moderate the more extreme resolutions adopted by their conventions and to bury quietly any resolutions adopted by their organization which are not germane to its main purpose. Certain British unions, such as the Amalgamated Union of Engineering Workers, are committed by their constitutions to the nationalization without compensation of their industry; their leaders spend remarkably little time pursuing that goal. In contrast, the AFBF's leaders magnify the extremism of its policy declarations and eagerly pursue the Federation's declarations on general politics far removed from farm policy.

No one encapsulated the uncompromising and moralistic style of the Federation better than Charles Shuman, President from 1954 to 1968. Under his leadership, the Federation refused to produce compromise proposals which had any chance of acceptance by the Democratic majority in Congress, and turned every disagreement of detail into one of principle. Shuman saw the clash between the interventionist policies of the Democrats and the *laissez-faire* approach of the Federation as a moral, not merely political, disagreement. He told the Federation's 1968 Convention that:

Economic laws are as closely related to moral and natural laws. They are as surely God given as are the great truths which have been recorded and demonstrated in the Bible. There is a law of supply and demand which constitutes an economic truth as well as a basic moral law.

Support for farm subsidies merely exemplified a deeper problem for Shuman: 'The depth of our moral decay is indicated by the greedy clamour from individual citizens, state administrators and local community leaders for more federal spending.' Shuman was not alone among the leadership in this moralizing. It seemed appropriate to the character of the Federation when its top administrator, Secretary-Treasurer Roger Flemming, concluded his 1964 report with a quotation from the Right-wing preacher, Norman Vincent Peale, 'This world is full of hope and joy, but it is also beset by evil, immorality and sin. You can't say "yes" to these things, or even "maybe", you have to say "no" and you have to make it stick.'[43]

Democracy and the AFBF

We have seen that there is considerable evidence to suggest that the AFBF's members do not share their leaders' dogmatic attachment to policies which, if implemented, would have halved their income. We might expect, therefore, that the leadership would moderate its policies to stay in office. Yet, as we have seen, this does not happen. How, then, does the leadership survive?

Apathy is probably the major explanation. Many members are attracted to the AFBF not by its policies but by the services it provides; even the others, as in Britain, are unwilling to attend meetings or run for office. Two consequences follow. First, those who do attend meetings tend to be a small minority (usually less than 10 per cent of the membership) with extreme views. Even the conservative Republican Senator Young (North Dakota) claimed that the Federation's local branches had been taken over by the John Birch Society.[44] Second, the absence of spontaneous involvement by the membership makes it easier for the leadership to manipulate them. State and local leaders may deserve praise for their efforts to boost attendance at meetings, but they have sent some very questionable material out explaining issues to the membership. During the Federation's campaign against the Kennedy Administration's proposals to boost farm incomes by controlling production more closely, the national headquarters sent out kits to involve the membership and explain the issues to them. The kits solemnly explained that the Kennedy proposals were policies typical of communist countries, a claim of doubtful truth or relevance but of some considerable emotional power.

Indeed, this example of the use of a communist smear tactic to discredit a proposal on farm policy advanced by one of the doughtiest Cold War Administrations serves to illustrate another basis for the power of the leadership and the value to it of its apparently irrational style. The Federation's strength is at its greatest in areas of the United States (the Southern Midwest and the South) which are deeply conservative. The leadership's involvement in Right-wing crusades of no relevance to farm policy may seem comic to the liberal social scientist; it almost certainly wins approval in Illinois or Georgia. Moreover, to the degree that farmers identify interventionist farm policies as measures which boost their incomes, they favour them; to the degree that the national leadership can link the Agriculture Acts to such emotionally charged themes as 'big government', 'federal interference', or 'socialistic policies', the membership will be critical.

A different sort of apathy strengthens the national leadership *vis-à-vis* the state organizations. One of the more puzzling features of the Federation is the absence of visible politics or controversy. This reflects neither consensus nor intimidation but indifference. In fact, power, understood as the ability to compel compliance, is extensively developed within the Federation. This is reflected in the provisions the constitution makes for 'dissenting'. Under this procedure, a state (or, within a state, a county) may inform the national organization that it cannot accept a particular policy. Attempts are then made to change the mind of the state, but if these fail, the constitution is clear on their right to persist in their views. Yet the remarkable fact is that very few such 'dissents' have been recorded. Indeed, the last such rejection of the fundamental policies of the Federation occurred in the late 1940s when Southern states refused to accept the switch from supporting to opposing interventionist farm policies. The reason why there are so few 'dissents' is not that national policy is widely accepted but that it is so easily disregarded. So easy is it for a state farm bureau to follow quietly its own policy that there is no incentive to fight bruising battles at the national level. The President of an important Southern farm bureau argued in an interview with me that a formal dissent was an unpleasant business rather like a family row. He preferred to lobby his state's Congressional delegation in a way which often conflicted with national policy without going through the 'dissent' procedure. Indeed, at that very moment while the Federation nationally was opposing the Agriculture Act of 1973, he was working for its adoption. The unwillingness to bother fighting battles within the Federation has reached such ludicrous limits that state delegations have sat mute through voice votes on proposals with which they disagree. So little attempt is made to reconcile conflicting views that disagreements are not even formally recorded.

The effectiveness of the AFBF

A prominent British writer on American politics, Maurice Vile, voiced a common misconception when he wrote of the AFBF that 'its support is necessary for the success of any legislation relating to agriculture and the Federation can, if it wishes, turn enormous pressure on in Washington'.[45] Part of the view that Vile reports is demonstrably false; every single important Agriculture Bill enacted by the Democrats has been opposed by the Federation. Before passing judgement on the overall effectiveness of the Federation, it is worth recalling the different bases for pressure group power which political scientists commonly distinguish. These are the symbolic role of a group as spokesman for an element in society, its ability to supply the consent of an interest in society to proposals which affect them, its ability to supply information about either technical problems or the feelings of those affected by a proposal, and possibly an ability to influence its members' votes in elections.

The Federation clearly lacks any of these potential strengths. Politicians not only do not believe that it speaks for American farmers in general (for any such claim is challenged by the very existence of other farm interest groups) but they do not believe it represents its own members faithfully. Congressmen and Senators in the United States attach great importance to staying in touch with their electorate and are, of necessity, much better than British MPs at assessing the reaction of constituents. As we have seen, Congressmen have detected significant differences between what their constituents want and what the AFBF says they want. The weakness of the Federation is, in fact, a matter of some regret to policy-makers in both Congress and the Executive. Guidance would be very much appreciated on what sort of farm legislation would be acceptable to all the many different types of farmer there are in the United States. If the Federation could speak authoritatively as the one truly nationwide farm organization, it would command serious attention. Unfortunately, far from being able to speak for all American farmers, the Federation's national farm policies do not even command the support of all its constituent states, or, to phrase the point more technically, the Federation fails to aggregate interests supposedly represented within it. It is clear, too, that the Federation has damaged its chances of claiming technical expertise by adopting a highly political role. It employs almost no technical experts on farming or economics, a significant contrast with the British NFU. Moreover, by campaigning for Right-wing, non-farm issues, it has destroyed its credibility with liberal politicians even though urban liberals might have been amenable to its criticisms of farm subsidies. Finally, the Federation has made no impact on electoral politics. Political scientists have long accepted V. O. Key's dictum that: 'When pressure group leaders threaten reprisals at the polls, as one unwisely does every now and then, they are usually pointing an empty gun at the legislator. . . .'[46] The gap between the Federation's leadership and membership is an obvious handicap in trying to swing farm votes. Typically, the Federation tried, but failed. One of the few Republican friends of farm subsidies, H. Carl Anderson, advised the Senate Agriculture Committee that: 'I wouldn't take to heart too much the viewpoint of the Farm Bureau. . . . They fought and tried to lick me in the last ten years in every primary and I would send their men down to defeat.'[47] In short, the potentially most powerful farm pressure group has rendered itself ineffective. What can be said of its rivals, effectiveness and, particularly, its arch enemy, the National Farmers' Union?

The National Farmers' Union

Early history

The NFU is, in fact, the second oldest of the American agricultural interest groups; only the Grange has operated continuously for longer. The remarkable feature of the NFU is that whereas it started in the South, it is now almost entirely based in the Northern Midwest, with only Texas, Oklahoma, and Arkansas of the Southern states having a significant membership. (See Figure 1, kindly supplied by the NFU.) Total membership fluctuates around 250,000 today, with recessions usually encouraging membership. The first farmers' union was founded in Raines County, Texas, in 1902, and the first President of the NFU was a Georgian, Chalres S. Barrett.[48] Why the membership declined so disastrously after the First World War is something of a mystery. The folk history of the NFU is that it has

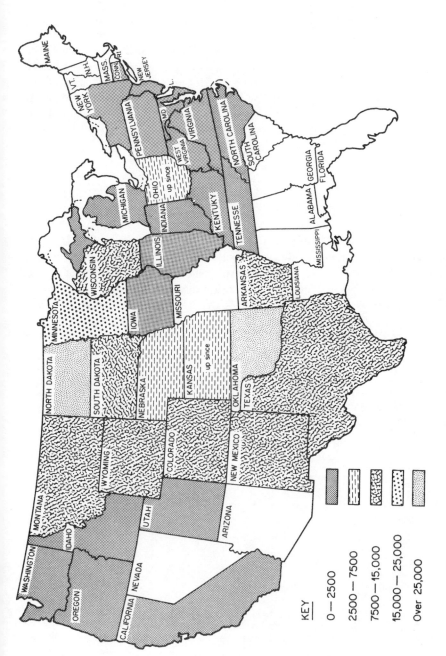

KEY

0 — 2500

2500 — 7500

7500 — 15,000

15,000 — 25,000

Over 25,000

Figure 1 Farmers' union membership. (Kindly supplied by the National Farmers' Union)

based its growth on developing cooperatives. (By 1920 the number of cooperatives had grown from 1,000 to 11,000.) The failure of the NFU is explained by a tendency of these cooperatives to break away from the NFU, which, the folklore continues, was encouraged by disagreements over the NFU's support for the United States to join the League of Nations. The NFU languished, eclipsed by the AFBF, until the New Deal, when it utilized government grants in many areas such as the Dakotas to start grain elevators and other facilities. These facilities were limited to members. Thus the NFU was reborn by providing services partially financed, as Olson notes, under New Deal Legislation. As in the case of the AFBF, the government had helped to foster an interest group, though less consciously than in the case of the AFBF.

The ideology of the NFU

The NFU is as determinedly liberal as the AFBF is conservative. It is interesting to look at which Senators the NFU thought had the best records in the 92nd Congress (not counting absences of Senators on key votes). All of them are Democrats; nearly all are highly rated by the liberal Americans for Democratic action. Magnuson (Democrat, Washington) would have scored 100 per cent had not he allowed his state's interest in aircraft construction to cause him to vote counter to NFU wishes to halt the building of the Supersonic Transport. Gravel (Alaska), Inouge (Hawaii), Symington (Missouri), Mansfield (Montana), Williams (New Jersey), and Jordan (North Carolina)—all Democrats—were all rated very

Table 6   NFU box score of 92nd Congress, First Session

Senators with 100% pro-NFU record	Rating by Americans for Democratic action 1970	Party	State
Fulbright	66	D	Arkansas
Cranston	91	D	California
Tunney	60	D	California
Ribicoff	94	D	Connecticut
Church	75	D	Idaho
Stevenson	Na	D	Illinois
Hartke	72	D	Indiana
Hughes	97	D	Iowa
Kennedy	84	D	Massachusetts
Humphrey	Na	D	Minnesota
Mondale	97	D	Minnesota
Eagleston	91	D	Missouri
Metcalf	72	D	Montana
McIntyre	50	D	New Hampshire
Montoya	63	D	New Mexico
Burdick	84	D	North Dakota
McGovern	84	D	South Dakota
Nelson	97	D	Wisconsin
Proxmire	78	D	Wisconsin

highly by the NFU. Almost half the Democratic Senators thus earned its endorsement, but not a single Republican.

Like the AFBF, but from a sharply contrasting position, the NFU evaluated legislators by how they vote on issues of little direct relevance to farming. Issues which appear in its *Washington Newsletter*'s boxscore have included, of late, the SST, the Vietnam War, Appalachian Development, extending the work of the Office of Economic Opportunity, increasing social security payments, and easing the rules governing their eligibility for benefit. The NFU has taken the liberal line on every issue. It is not surprising, therefore, that no Republican gets a '100 per cent correct' rating from the NFU on his roll-call voting. The NFU is a fully paid-up member of the Democratic party's liberal wing. Where there is a state with a high NFU membership and a Senator from both parties, the Democrat receives a much higher rating than the Republican from the NFU. Thus McGovern outstrips Mundt in South Dakota; Young trails Burdick in North Dakota. Party, not region, is the key variable in predicting the NFU's evaluation of a legislator.

Like the AFBF, the NFU's attitude to agricultural programmes is consistent with its general outlook. As benefits a liberal group, it believes in bringing in the government to redress the imbalance of the market-place. It is passionately devoted to defence of the family farm (though of course in the wheat belt a family farm can be very large indeed) and, unlike the AFBF, believes that farming is a way of life, not just an industry. The 1972 Policy Statement of the NFU makes their attitude clear:

The United States in 1972 has a 'mixed' economy in which the free market has been modified and circumvented in various ways by corporate structures for businesses, by tariffs and import restrictions, by laws for fair trade pricing and fair competition, by exclusive franchises and an assured return on investment for the utilities, by restriction of entry into certain trades and professions, and by collective bargaining for workers. The independent family farmers stand virtually alone as a textbook example of free competition in the United States economy. We reaffirm the N.F.U.'s position that Federal governmental programmes and policies are essential to protect family farmers against the hazards of the market place where almost everyone else except the farmer is protected. The power of public policy must be used to sustain the independent farmer in an economy which is otherwise strongly organised—in which most other production is planned, most marketings rationed and most prices and profits are administered.[49]

The NFU would work, the statement continued, to achieve 'full parity prices for all producers who wish to be included, government determination of what quantities should be produced, direct payments, and supply management by legal controls'. The NFU also favours limiting payments, partly to try to keep the very large-scale producer (agribusiness) out and partly to placate urban critics of the farm programmes.

Just as opposition to government intervention has carried the AFBF into perpetual opposition to the Democrats and alliance with the Republicans, so belief in government intervention has made the NFU the perpetual ally of the Democrats and opponent of Republican administrations. The NFU spent much effort in the 1950s in helping Democrats attack Benson.[50] It played a major role in shaping the thinking of the Kennedy Administration in its early days and proved to be a more consistent supporter of the Administration's policy of a stringent production controls than the President himself. The Union sent its legislative Director to whole-heartedly endorse the Administration's proposals in 1961[51] and its President, Patton, testified in favour of the 1962 Act. The Union campaigned unsuccessfully for the Administration's proposals for production controls for wheat in the 1963 referendum.[52] After the defeat of supply management in that referendum, the NFU remained loyal to the principle, though the Administration offered legislation in 1964 and 1965 which offered farmers financial inducements instead. Nevertheless, the NFU did not allow this difference to interfere with its loyalty to the Democrats, and in 1968 asked Congress to extend the life of the 1965 Agriculture Act before the anticipated Republican victory in the Presidential Elections.[53] In fear of the policies that Nixon would follow, the NFU formed a coalition with nearly all farm groups other than the AFBF which narrowly failed to get its programme through Congress. The NFU has, therefore, enjoyed close relations with Democratic Administrations. Particularly in the early days of an Administration, before the need for Congressional compromise became decisive, the NFU has exercised a considerable influence on the thinking of Democratic appointees to the Department of Agriculture. It has been almost entirely ignored by Republican administrations.

Like most American pressure groups, the NFU focuses its work on Congressmen who it knows already are sympathetic. Naturally, working steadily with these Congressmen promotes good relations. But the links between the NFU and the Democrats are more solidly based than on mere sentiment. Indeed, there are grounds to believe that the NFU has, in effect, become part of the Democratic party apparatus, or, where the party has been very weak, has substituted for it.

Talbot outlines a role for the NFU in North Dakota[54] of providing an electoral machine for Democratic candidates which is reminiscent of the role that Greenstone finds labour unions playing where the Democratic machine is weak.[55] Indeed, Talbot argues, the North Dakota Democratic party is to a great extent the creation of the NFU. North Dakota had been a one-party state until 1956. Liberals had operated within the Republican party, though from 1916 they had filed lists of primary candidates under the banner of the Non-Partisan League (NPL). The NFU itself had gained strength in North Dakota during the New Deal period, using government grants to provide services such as grain elevators. By the end of the 1930s, the NFU clearly had great influence in local politics. But in 1947 Bills were introduced into the state legislature which, the Farmers' Union felt, were direct attacks upon it. The Bills would have weakened the control of the Union over service companies it owned (e.g. for insurance) and would have taken away the tax advantages of cooperatives. The Union established a political wing whose objective is 'to mobilise the voting strength inherent in the Farmers' Union behind Progressive candidates and in open opposition to those who would use the power of State Government to destroy us'. A coalition was formed with labour unions and the NPL and a joint ticket of Ervin Schumaker (farmers' unions), Usher L. Burdick (Non-Partisan League), and Agnes Gleean was unsuccessfully promoted for the 1948 Elections for Governor and the two at large US Representatives. Relations between the NFU and the NPL were not close, and the NFU leadership, particularly President Talbot, were attracted to the campaign of Henry Wallace.

In 1950, Talbot took the NFU into the Democratic party which was then still very weak. NFU officers gained many places in Democratic party state and local committees. The Union worked hard for Stevenson and Sparkman in 1952, Talbot touring the state and introducing Truman on tours of the Midwest. Though the Union was still active in the 1954 Convention of the still weak Democratic party, it rather machiavellianly transferred its attention back to the Non-Partisan League in 1954, working hard to elect delegates and committee members. In January, 1955, the NFU played an important role in creating an insurgent group within the NPL which took control of the board and merged the NPL with the Democratic party. This was the true foundation of Democratic strength in the state, which was able to exploit the dissatisfaction with Benson and elect Burdick's son in a special election in 1960 for the US Senate. The ties have been close ever since. Thus, inspite of widespread agreement on agricultural policy between the Republican Senator Young and the NFU, the NFU gives him only a rating of 43 out of 100, whereas Burdick in the same year (1970) was rated 87.[56]

Where the NFU does not play as prominent a part in politics as it does in North Dakota, it still helps the Democrats through the supply of 'information' to its members. Throughout the 1972 Election period, in its newsletters and handouts it consistently focused on issues which brought little credit to the Republicans. There was a special handout on the wheat deal scandal and another on *The Dead and Dying Programs of Rural America*—on the alleged neglect of rural America by the Nixon Administration. In addition to the close personal relations between NFU Presidents and leading Democrats, there is an interchange of personnel between Democratic Administrations and the NFU. Truman's former Secretary of Agriculture, Brannan, is now General Counsel to the NFU, the Director of Legislative Service in the 1950s of the NFU, John Baker, was appointed head of the ASCS by Kennedy, and three other NFU employees were given major Department of Agriculture posts.[57] In the 1968 primary struggles both Eugene McCarthy and Hubert Humphrey attached much importance to obtaining the support of the NFU. The NFU has tried to establish a rural counterpart to COPE (the Rural Political Education Committee), but with limited success. NFU officials claim that their most valuable work for candidates has to be done through the Union's regular organization and this limits how partisan they can be. Much of their effort to help liberals is, therefore, directed into voter registration drives.

It is particularly important to note the very close relations between the NFU AFL–CIO. Their Washington lobbyists frequently work together. Neither can deliver congressional votes at will, but each has access to different types of Congressmen. The NFU has a much better chance of reaching the liberals from, say, the Dakotas, to convince them that Taft–Hartley ought to be repealed than has the AFL–CIO. On the other hand, the AFL–CIO is more sympathetically received by urban liberals and can present therefore the case for farm programmes to urban Democrats more successfully than the NFU. The relationships with the AFL–CIO is given particular importance because the AFL–CIO is the surrogate for consumers. Until the rise of Ralph Nader and the consumer movement, the unions were the only group that could claim to speak for the consumers of the United States. When the AFL–CIO told Congressmen at the request of the NFU that it approved of farm legislation, it was telling the urban Congressmen that the Bill was not contrary to the interests of his consumers. If the AFL–CIO had not reassured the urban Congressmen, it is much more likely that they would have paid critical attention to the farm programme. The NFU and AFL–CIO alliance could not always prevent urban Congressmen opposing farm Bills, but the fact that the unions said that a programme was acceptable would often lull urban Democrats into apathetic support.

Why is the NFU so liberal? Many would deny that it is genuinely liberal. Its critics argue that farmers join the NFU for the same reason that they join the AFBF (i.e. to take advantage of services). The Iowa NFU doubled its membership within a month after Blue Cross/Blue Shield approved a special plan for NFU members. Indeed, the states where the map on page 89 shows the NFU to be strongest are states with a history of Republicanism. Some might argue that the NFU's liberalism, like the AFBF's conservatism, reflects merely the capture of a pressure group by an unrepresentative elite. Others, particularly AFBF officials, have another, equally unflattering explanation for the Union's liberalism. They argue that the NFU is liberal on non-farm issues because it is advocating government agricultural policies which cost a lot of money. It therefore joins a coalition of big spenders led by AFL–CIO.

There can be no doubt about the extent of the NFU's liberal commitment, which was noted above. In an excellent study of the NFU, which deserves to be better known, Crampton[58] argues that the NFU can be understood not merely as a campaign for government money but as a moral and highly politically committed force. Crampton has accurately summarized its outlook as 'the sense of disadvantage'. As the first NFU President argued:

You ought to sit at the first table, but you don't. Your clothes should be as good as any man wears, but they are not. Your house should be as well furnished and as comfortable as any man's house. But it is not. You should have the comforts and pleasures others enjoy. But you don't. You and your family should be able to go to resort and rest as others do. But you don't.[59]

In addition, Crampton notes three other strands in the Union's history—pacifism, cooperativism, and the family farm ideal. The farmer is as much a victim of the economic system—the financier, the distributors, the railroads—as is the worker. A former official of the NFU recollects rural life in the great depression:

I knew the long hours, the aching muscles, the worry over the price of wheat, of grasshoppers, rust, freight rates and storage rates. I knew of the mortgages that had sucked the life out of more than two-thirds of the farmers who had worked hard themselves and their families. And I knew there was something wrong when the people who tilled the land lived as we did.[60]

The farmer needs a better deal and not only higher prices:

It is high time we junk the idea that farmer prosperity is based on prices alone. . . . Parity means equality in all things—in incomes, in schools, in roads, in markets, in parks and playgrounds, in recreation. That's true parity.[61]

The pacifism of the NFU, which can be traced back to a pledge in 1914 to work for 'harmony and good will among all mankind' is not the mark of obscurantism as has been claimed sometimes. President Patton led the Union from a call for non-involvement in the Second World War in 1940 to support for military aid for the countries 'bearing the brunt of military battles against the menace to our civilisation' and then to outright support for war as soon as Pearl Harbor happened.[62] Indeed, in the postwar period the NFU has been more truly international than the liberal academics who disparage the tradition it embodies. For example, the Union supported the Korean War after great soul-searching only because the United Nations supposedly led the allies. And the Union preferred technical assistance for development to the bombs and napalm of the Vietnam War.

The Union's liberalism is surprising to those brought up on an academic tradition that disparages the rural protest movements of the United States. Claims by Lipset[63] and Shils[64] that the ideological and social base of McCarthyism were identical with that of populism make the NFU seem an oddity, a progressive pressure group representing areas which according to Lipset are hotbeds of 'racism, supernationalism, anticosmopolitanism, McCarthyism, Fascism'. However, more recent scholarship, notably by Rogin,[65] solves the problem by showing that Lipset and others ought never to have created it. Rural liberalism he argues, has been an enduring tradition in the Midwest, and the failing of Lipset and others is that they failed to notice that the rural progressives had changed their party by the time of McCarthy. Rural progressives, who had voted as Republicans for LaFollette, were *not* voting for McCarthy; they were voting against him as Democrats! Sundquist,[66] too, supports this interpretation. The NFU, therefore is a liberal pressure group representing an enduring liberal tradition in the prairie states.

Structure of the NFU

The NFU is controlled more centrally than the AFBF. State farmers' unions are created by the national leadership when the national board of directors considers that they are strong enough; if the membership falls below a level set by the NFU leadership, the state charter is revoked, and the national leadership may by majority vote impose direct rule. Regular membership is defined nationally and is tightly limited to those who obtain most of their income from some sort of farming. The issue of state versus national rights seems never to have arisen as clearly in the NFU as in the AFBF. The South has swallowed the liberal policies of the NFU surprisingly easily—including pro-civil rights platforms. On economic liberal issues, the border farmers' unions have been enthusiastic, and Oklahoma and Arkansas have put more effort into 'Greenthumb' (a farm programme operated for the Office of Economic Opportunity by the NFU) than the other state unions.[67] Participation rates are no higher in the NFU than in the AFBF, and national officials will readily suggest that members join 'just for the insurance'.[68] The Union has been dominated by its Presidents, notably James Patton. Patton served as President from 1940 to 1966, and naturally he came for many to embody the NFU. The *Washington Post* described his style as 'hell for leather agrarian reform'.[69] His successor, Tony Dechant, is philosophically identical, but much suaver and more technocratic.

The political influence of the NFU

It might be supposed that the NFU, by being as determinedly liberal over a wide range of issues as the AFBF has been conservative, has been equally ineffective. Such a conclusion would be too severe. Though, like the Federation, the NFU has been associated closely with one political party, at least it has been the majority party in Congress, the Democrats. Thus the Union has had friends in power since the Republicans lost control of Congress in 1954. Though Republican Administrations attach as little importance to the views of the NFU as Democratic do to those of the AFBF, the Farmers' Union has been an important influence on Congress, which has retained a major role in agricultural policymaking. It may well be however that the greatest postwar achievement of the NFU was the adoption of the Full Employment Act of 1946 which, Bailey reports, the Union did much to bring about. If Bailey is right, it is a fitting comment on the Union that its greatest success was outside agricultural policy.

Other interest groups

The Grange

Though comparatively few people may join any pressure group with the idea of working hard to influence policy, the Grange is still somewhat startling. Though the oldest and once most powerful of the farmers' interest groups, the Grange turned away from politics and became predominantly a social club. Grant McConnell noted how early this change took place:

... political issues ... seem out of place in the proceedings of the Grange during the first quarter of the century. The greater love of the organisation was for its ritual, its apostrophes to Ceres, Flora and Demeter and all the harmless mumo-jumbo of its pseudo Masonry.[70]

The transition to 'pseudo Masonry' has turned the Grange into a social organization recruiting people who have little or no connection with agriculture. Thus a

Washington Post reporter found that the Grange fluourished in the capital's sub-urbs where there was not a farmer within miles.[71] The Grange's claim to have 600,000 members is not as impressive as it sounds; indeed, even its congressional friends refer to it sadly as 'the old maid'.

The lack of political muscle which afflicts the Grange at least prevents it suffering from the delusions of political grandeur which occur in the AFBF. The Grange maintains only one full-time lobbyist in Washington, who wisely concen-trates on farm issues. Though the Grane's Convention adopts many policy statements on broad political issues, the Washington office quitely buries them, for the moderate conservatism of the Grange on non-farm issues would conflict with the alliances it frequently forms with the NFU and AFL–CIO on Agriculture Bills. The Grange also pursues its policies gently relying on friendly persuasion, not pressure. The reliance of the Grange on personal contacts and friendships rather than rural membership was fully illustrated by the advice it received from the Chairman of the House Agriculture Committee, Bob Poage (Democrat, Texas), whose Bill the Grange was supporting in 1969:

Poage: Can you get us six (votes) from either party from *Philadelphia or Pittsburgh* who will vote for the continuation of a sound program?
Mr Scott (the Grange): Mr Chairman, through my work in the Legislature of Penn-sylvania ... I have some very good griends who have moved to the Congress and I tell you this much; I will do my best.
Poage: Good. That is what we need. ... That is the only way we are going to pass this bill, get votes. *The only votes you are going to get are some people you know and who have confidence in you (emphasis added).*[72]

It is ironic that though the Grange is so weak politically it has seen much of its agricultural policy pass into law. This is because it tends to occupy the middle ground between the *laissez-faire* policies of the AFBF and the interventionism of the NFU. The 1970 policy statement gives the flavour of the Grange's am-bivalence over farm policy as it is torn between opposing close and detailed government intervention, on the one hand, and avoiding a return to the free market low prices of the prewar years, on the other. The Grange's advice lapses into a judicious ambivalence expressed in a proverbial style worthy of Polonius. Thus:

There is no quick or easy answer; no one solution will provide a solution to the problems. ... The program for each commodity must involve the best use of that combination of economic devices best suited to the particular commodity. When necessary, it is a proper function of government to provide programs through which producers themselves can effectively control, regulate and manage the supply of their commodities. Wherever fea-sible, government control should be avoided.[73]

The Grange might not create American farm policy, but it faithfully reflects the unwillingness to make necessary choices between firm government control and a free market which has plagued the subject.

The National Farmers' Organisation

If the Grange constitutes an example of organizational senility then the National Farmers' Organisation (NFO) constitutes an example of youthful vigour. The NFO was not formed as a political organization; indeed, it was created because farmers had lost faith in the willingness of politicians to safeguard their incomes. The NFO came into being so that farmers could unite and bargain for higher prices. Its members promise to 'withhold' produce if processors or other purchasers offer low prices. In short, the NFO set out to overcome the disadvantages farmers suffer from being individuals selling a small proportion of total output to comparatively few oligopolistic purchasers.

Like most American farm groups, the NFO found it impossible to stay out of politics. This was partly because the NFO was copying a radical Midwestern tradition which had tried to raise Depression prices by a 'farm holiday' or farmers' strike. More important was the Supreme Court's decision that farmers had no right to restrict trade. In language which could have come from Justice Sutherland in the 1930s, Justic Black, speaking for the Court, struck at the NFO's main tactic of organizing boycotts of producers whose prices were unsatisfactory. Whereas the NFO argued that the Capper–Volstead Act exempted farmer cooperatives, Black ruled that the Act 'does not suggest Congressional desire to vest cooperatives with unrestricted power to retrain trade or to achieve monopoly by preying on independent producers, processors or dealers intent on carrying on their business in their own legitimate way'.[74] The NFO set out to provide the Justices with fresh evidence of Congressional intent.

Like the NFU, the NFO found that the best way to pursue its policies was through a close alliance with liberal Democrats. Throughout the 1972 Election campaign, the NFO's journals kept up a constant flow of stories critical of the Nixon Administration, emphasizing corruption and the influence of 'agribusiness' in its farm policies. At the end of 1972, however, something of a backlash occurred. Orin Lee Staley, leader of the Organisation since its formation, was relected with the unprecedented low proportion of 60 per cent of the votes cast. His opponents contended that the NFO had become too political and argued that it should concentrate on being a more technically proficient marketing organization. While Staley remains in office, the Organisation is unlikely to become much less partisan, however.

The role of agricultural interest groups in the United States

The beginning of this chapter raised questions of how influential American agricultural interest groups had been and how like British interest groups. Our conclusions must be that not only are American agricultural groups very different from British ones but they are surprisingly less important.

We have been taught, after all, that American politics is more pragmatic than British, that American parties are weak, and that, therefore, interest groups in American politics are relatively strong. The United States is a society where Key's dictum, quoted in the Introduction, that 'the study of politics must rest on an analysis of the objectives and composition of the interest groups within a society' is supposedly particularly apposite. American interest groups play a Downsian game, selling their funds, organization, and possibly members' votes to the politician who is the highest bidder. Yet the classic model is grossly inaccurate.

The pressure groups we have examined are characterized above all by the breadth and intensity of their ideological commitment. They are not open to bids on farm issues alone. In the case of the AFBF an extensive conservative commitment has carried over into opposing farm policies which raise its members' incomes substantially. Both the NFU and the AFBF are locked into stable ideological coalitions in which they have perpetual friends and enemies at the expense of their abiding interests. Friends except their support; enemies discount their opposition. The legislator regards none of the agricultural interest groups purely as the authentic voice of agriculture, not only because they disagree so but because the squander claims to expertise through committing themselves to campaigns on social security, foreign policy, the Supreme Court, and other issues of doubtful relevance to agriculture.

Moreover, the skilful politician knows not only that American agricultural interest groups have failed to recruit the majority of his farmer constituents but that the leaderships' representativeness of the views of those they have managed to recruit is, at least in the case of the AFBF, extremely doubtful. The doubts about the representativeness of the leadership of the pressure groups are particularly acute in what should be the agricultural groups' area of greatest expertise—farm policy. It follows, therefore, that not only are American politicians not frightened by any muted threats of throwing members' votes against them, but regard interest groups as unreliable reporters of constituents' attitudes. Politicians in the United States, unlike those in Britain, do not rely on interest groups when they wish to consult an interest.

Untrusted by politicians as representative of their constituents, locked into ideological coalitions and with no sanctions available to use on politicians, what is the influence of the agricultural interests group in the United States? Their true importance is as custodians of principles. Interest groups are given institutionalized opportunities—notably at committee hearings—to air their views. By so doing they may give a cue to sympathetic Congressmen, for, as Miller notes,[75] Congressmen are always alert for cues from friends to guide them on how to vote on an issue. If the AFBF can portray a Bill as an attack on liberty or the NFU portray it as a vital step for social justice, this will have a major effect on the reception a Bill has. The interest groups have a golden opportunity to set the terms of debate on other people's proposals.

They have also great opportunities to put forward proposals of their own. The American agricultural interest group does not (for it is not equipped to) make the detailed proposals or comments on policy that come from the British NFU. But they do put forward the other sort of policy proposal that non-government bodies (such as British political parties) can make—the broad declaration of the principles that policy should follow. The AFBF has always argued strongly the principle of returning agriculture to a free market; it has always been very vague, despite prompting by politicians, on how this could be implemented. The NFU was similarly determined in its advocacy of supply management but never really faced up to the problems that supply management would cause for commodities such as cotton, where restricting American output would merely increase opportunities for America's competitors.

The fascination of the agricultural interest groups in the United States, with the broad principles rather than the practical details of farm policy, helps explain why they are so uninterested in 'consensus building' or 'interest articulation' so central to the work of the British NFU. The American agricultural interest groups have put little effort into formulating an agreed programme to present to politicians. More interesting is the willingness of the leadership of the AFBF to live with the fact that many of its constituent counties and states dislike national policy and are quietly working against it. The leadership of the AFBF is so concerned to maintain the purity of its principles that it shows little interest in achieving the prime objective of pressure group leaders in Britain—the unity of the organization.

The commitment to principle, rather than unity, which has characterized agricultural interest groups in the United States, gives a clue to the kind of influence they have tried to exert on policymaking. It is not persuading the uncommitted, for they will be repelled by the inflexibility of the organization's stand. It is not forcing politicians into line: the wide-ranging political commitments of the interest groups and their leaders' preference for consistency in principle to leading either a united organization or a united farm movement alert politicians to the vacuousness of any threats of electoral retribution the interest groups utter. The true role of the agricultural interest groups has been to act as the intellectual conscience of their ideological friends, being more consistent than politicians in their advocacy of a free market or supply management, even if by so doing they follow policies which would reduce the prosperity of their members. When friends of an agricultural interest group (the Republicans for the AFBF, the Democrats for the NFU or NFO) are out of office, the interest group will languish, unconsulted by the Executive, in the political wilderness; when its friends are in power, it will be taken for granted. The role of the interest group in American agricultural politics is to keep raising basic questions of principle about policy. However, by so doing, they are sure not to play much part in producing the detailed answers.

If American interest groups are not sufficiently powerful to intimidate or even persuade American politicians, it might be argued that these politicians do not need to be so treated. For, it may be argued, so pervasive are 'special interests' in the United States that they control section of government itself. What need of a powerful interest group does a special interest have if agencies, departments, and congressional committees dedicate themselves to its cause? Clearly, if farmers do enjoy these sort of advantages, their position is strong indeed. But is it true that either the Executive or Congress are so susceptible to their control? Let us look first at the Executive and then Congress.

Notes

1. R. Bauer, I. Pool, and L. Dexter, *American Business and Public Policy*, Prentice Hall, International, London and New York, 1961 p. 398.
2. Seymour Martin Lipset, *Political Man*, Heineman Educational Books, London, 1969, p. 195. See, also, for general agreement that the lower income groups do not join, V. O. Key, *Public Opinion and American Democracy*, Alfred Knopf, New York, 1961, esp. 502, and E. E. Schattschneider, *The Semi Sovereign People*, Holt, Reinhart, Winston, New York, 1963, esp. p. 33, where Schattschneider cities evidence agreeing with mine.
3. A. J. Crampton, *The National Farmers' Union, Ideology of a Pressure Group*, University of Nebraska Press, Lincoln, 1965, p. 59.
4. Robert A. Rohwer, 'Organized farmers in Oklahoma', *Rural Sociology*, March, 1952.
5. *Des Moines Register*, 24 January, 1972.
6. 'Deprivation, discontent and social movement participation; evidence on a contemporary farmers' movement, the NFO', *Rural Sociology*, 1971; *Farm Journal*, 18 February, 1972.
7. Crampton, op. cit.
8. American Farm Bureau Federation, *Annual Report of Roger Flemming, Secretary-Treasurer*, 1971, p. 25.
9. Wesley McCune, *Who's Behind Our Farm Policy?*, Praeger, New York, 1956, p. 15.
10. Christina McFadyen Campbell, *The Farm Bureau and the New Deal*, University of Illinois Press, Urbana, 1962.
11. O. M. Kile, *The Farm Bureau Through Three Decades*, Waverley Press, Baltimore, 1948, p. 60 ff.
12. Ibid., p. 62.
13. Ibid., p. 62 ff.
14. Charles Hardin, *The Politics of Agriculture*, The Free Press, Glencoe, 1952.
15. Campbell, op. cit.
16. Ibid., p. 89.
17. Ibid., p. 92.
18. Ibid., p. 95.
19. From American Farm Bureau Federation, *Annual Reports of Roger Flemming, Secretary-Treasurer*, 1965, 1967, 1971.
20. For an account of the conflict, see Samuel R. Berger, *Dollar Harvest*, Heath Lexington Books, Lexington, Mass., 1971, Preface; see also *Washington Post*, 19 July, 1967, and 27 September, 1967.
21. Berger, op. cit.
22. Ibid., p. 3.
23. Mancur Olson, *The Logic of Collective Action*, Shocken Books, New York, 1969. See p. 169 for his analysis of farm groups.
24. American Farm Bureau Federation, *Membership Memorandum of Agreement*, para. 6.
25. American Farm Bureau Federation, *Farm Bureau Policies for 1972* (pamphlet).
26. Ibid., p. 1.
27. Ibid.
28. *Congressional Record*, Vol. 108, part 8, 19 June, 1962.
29. US Congress, House of Representatives, Eighty-sixth Congress, First Session, Hearings, *General Farm Legislation*, 1959, p. 145.
30. House of Representatives, Committee on Agriculture, Hearings, *General Farm and Food Stamp Program*, Serial Q, 1969, p. 69.
31. House of Representatives, Ninety-first Congress, First Session, House Agriculture Committee, Hearings before sub-committee on Livestock and Grains (feed grain and wheat), 1968 *General Farm and Food Stamp Program*, p. 1121.

32. Interviews with Forest Rees and Henry Cusso, Counsels to the Senate Agriculture Committee, Washington, 12 July, 1973.
33. *Congressional Record*, Vol. 116, part 20, 4 August, 1970.
34. *Wallace's Farmer*, 6 July, 1960.
35. US Congress, House of Representatives, Eighty-sixth Congress, Second Session, Committee on Agriculture, Hearings, *General Farm Legislation*, 1960, p. 254
36. US Congress, House of Representatives, Eighty-sixth Congress, First Session, Committee on Agriculture, Hearings, *General Farm Legislation*, 1959, p. 151.
37. US Congress, House of Represenatives, Eighty-fifth Congress, Second Session, Committee on Agriculture, Hearings, *General Farm Legilsation*, 1958, pp. 265, 266.
38. House of Representatives, Ninety-first Congress, First Session, Committee on Agriculture, Subcommittee on Cotton, *General Farm and Food Stamp Program*, Serial Q, part 3, 1973, p. 1029.
39. D. E. Morrison and W. Keith Warner, 'Correlates of farmers' attitudes towards public and private aspects of agricultural organisation', *Rural Sociology*, 1971.
40. *Wallace's Farmer*, 4 May, 1957.
41. *Farm Journal*, 18 February, 1971.
42. US Department of Agriculture, Agricultural Stabilisation and Conservation Service, Background Information BI No. 10 (June, 1971).
43. American Farm Bureau Federation, *Annual Report of Roger Fleming, Secretary-Treasurer*, 1964.
44. *New York Times* 15 October, 1967.
45. M. J. C. Vile, *Politics, in the USA*, Penguin, Harmondsworth, 1970, p. 137.
46. V. O. Key, *Public Opinion and American Democracy*, Alfred Knopf, New York, 1961, p. 522.
47. United States Senate, Ninety Second Congress, First Session, Statement of H. Carl Anderson, in *Nomination of Earl Lauer Butz as Secretary of Agriculture, Hearings*.
48. Milton D. Hakel, *Farmers Union, Seventy Years of Service to Farmers*, NFU, 1972.
49. *1972 Policy of the National Farmers Union*, NFU, 1972, p. 2.
50. US Congress, House of Representatives, Eighty-sixth Congress, First Session, Committee on Agriculture, Hearings, *General Farm Legislation*, 1959, p. 97.
51. Agriculture Act of 1961. US Congress, House of Representatives Eighty-seventh Congress, First Session, Committee on Agriculture, *Hearings on HR 6400*, Serial E, part 1.
52. Senate, Eighty-seventh Congress, Second Session, Committee on Agriculture and Forestry, *Hearings on S 2786*, 22 February, 1962, p. 49 ff.
53. US Congress, House of Representatives, Ninetieth Congress, Second Session, Committee on Agriculture, Hearings, *Extend the Food and Agriculture Act of 1965*, Serial SS, 1968, pp. 33, 253.
54. Ross B. Talbot, 'The North Dakota Farmers' Union, and North Dakota politics', *Western Political Quarterly*, **10** (1957).
55. J. David Greenstone, *Labor in American Politics*, Vintage Books, New York, 1970, esp. on Detroit and Los Angeles.
56. NFU newsletter, cited above. NFU ratings of Congressmen are reprinted in Michael Barone, Grant Ujifusa, and Douglas Matthews, *The Almanac of American Politics*, Macmillan, London and New York, 1972.
57. *New York Times*, 5 March, 1961.
58. Crampton, op. cit.
59. Ibid. (quoted), p. 3.
60. Ibid. (quoted), p. 3.
61. Ibid., p. 20.
62. Ibid., p. 23 ff.
63. Lipset, op. cit. In *Political Man*, Lipset seems curiously to retreat from the point he argues so well in his earlier *Agrarian Socialism: The Cooperative Commonwealth*

Federation in Saskatchewan, A Study In Political Sociology (University of California Press, 1950) that there can be similarities in the class position of workers and farmers. 'Workers and farmers alike are forced to accept the rules laid down by the possessors of economic power' (p. 69). In this early work, Lipset notes that rural life, because of the need for cooperation, can foster socialist as well as individualist attitudes.

64. E. Shils, *The Torment of Secrecy*, The Free Press, Glencoe, 1956, p. 99. Other examples of this fear of the masses are to be found in 'Mass Society' theorists, particularly Kornhauser.

65. Michael Paul Rogan, *The Intellectuals and McCarthy, The Radical Spectre*, MIT, 1967.

66. James L. Sundquist, *Dynamics of the Party System, Alignment and Realignment of Political Parties in the United States*, Brookings Institution, Washington DC, 1973, esp. pp. 218–229.

67. Interview with Kenneth Motz, Treasurer of the National Farmers' Union, Denver, Colorado.

68. Interview with Wheldon Barton, cited above.

69. *Washington Post*, 17 March, 1966.

70. Grant McConnell, *The Decline of Agrarian Democracy*, University of California Press, Berkeley, 1953, p. 40.

71. *Washington Post*, 23 November, 1970.

72. United States Congress, House of Representatives, Ninety-first Congress, Second Session, Committee on Agriculture, Hearings, *General Farm Program and Food Stamp Program*, Serial Q, 1969, p. 60.

73. The National Grange, *Legislative Policies*, 1970 (pamphlet).

74. *Maryland and Virgina Milk Producers Association Inc. versus United States* (362 U.S. 458).

75. Clem Miller, in John W. Baker (Ed.), *Member of the House*, Charles Scribner's Sons, New York, 1962.

Chapter 7

The Executive and Agriculture

The conventional wisdom is that the Executive in the United States is fragmented. Departments and agencies have needs and interests of their own, needs and interests which may well conflict with those of the President. Much of the blame, or even credit, for this fragmentation is given to Congress. Agencies have to look to legislative and appropriations committees for Bills or funds they need, and these committees consist of members who remain in these positions of power long after a transitory mere President has retired and left town. Fenno tells us that 'the President's influence over a Cabinet member becomes splintered and eroded as the member responds to political forces not presidential in origin and direction'.[1] Truman agrees:

> The continuing unanswered question of where the responsibility for administrative action shall lie, and the expediences that consequently must guide the president's cabinet appointments turn department heads in varying degrees into political opponents. The institutionalised relationships between an established agency and its attendant interest groups and legislators may make even a personal supporter act as the president's 'natural enemy' when he heads a major department.[2]

Nor does fragmentation cease at the departmental level; the Secretary may face agencies supposedly under his control but which insist, invariably with congressional support, on freedom of action. The Army Corps of Engineers is a notorious example of agency autonomy, an agency so strong politically that Secretaries of Defence have been forced to defend its freedom to ignore them.[3]

The truth is, it is agreed, that even Presidents are ambiguous about what they want from department chiefs. Though Presidents often complain about unresponsiveness or even obstruction from departmental Secretaries, they want also a Secretary to at least speak for their department, its needs, and its opinions.

Hilsman[4] notes that the Secretary of State is the interpreter between the President and the State Department: in spite of compaints about the responsiveness of state, Presidents are not served by a Secretary who suppresses its advice. The Secretary of Agriculture is therefore expected to act within government as the spokesman for US Department of Agriculture. Some extend this role, however, to speaking for farmers, not just the Department. As one Executive Office official remarked: 'If I were President, I wouldn't want a Secretary (of Agriculture) who didn't speak for farmers.'[5]

By and large American political scientists have welcomed this apparent chaos and ambiguous accountability. Fenno, for example, comments that 'The greatest problems for Cabinet and President like the greatest problems in American politics are those which center around the persistent dilemmas of unit and diversity'.[6] It is only fitting that such a pluralist society should have a pluralist Executive. Seidman condemns the quest by those such as the Hoover Commission for orderly and efficient lines of authority as hopeless and dangerous utopianism, dangerous because the attempts to achieve it will have profound political consequences.[7]

On the Right, Aaron Wildavsky's attacks on the PPBS (Planned Program Budgeting System)[8] display a similar suspicion of organizational neatness. Even 'coordination' is seen as tantamount to 'oppression'. On the Left, writers such as Grant McConnell have criticized not the tendency of agencies to be captured by privileged groups but the weakening of agencies *representing* the less privileged, such as the Farm Security Administration.[9] For the liberal, it is so certain that government agencies will be dominated by outside interests that it is pointless to fight the trend; rather he should work to create agencies such as the Office of Economic Opportunity which will be a voice for the powerless.

Even the pluralists can see the danger implicit in a Department of Agriculture not subject to Presidential control. The Department can easily be pictured as a bureaucracy devoted to the interests of the farmer and not the consumer, staffed by sons of farmers, under the control of rural Congressmen indifferent to the national interest, and headed by a Secretary worried more about agricultural interest groups than the programme of the President. Only the President could tame such a monster. Only the President can be expected to leaven these sectional interests with the national interest. If, therefore, the Department is beyond Presidential control, then it is not surprising that subsidy programmes have been so costly and inefficient. And, as Congress delegates extensively to its rural-dominated Agriculture Committees, if reform does not come from the Executive it is unlikely to come from anyone.

There are two ways in which the question of the susceptibility of the Department of Agriculture to domination by rural interests may be considered. The first is whether the machinery of American government provides sufficient coordination and central control to offset the centrifugal tendencies of the American political system. The second is to see whether there has in fact been a real problem in keeping the US Department of Agriculture out of the hands of farmers and their congressional friends. Let us look at each in turn.

Central control: Office of Management and the Budget (OMB)

Neustadt has traced how the Office has developed from a part of the Treasury Department to a major part of the institutionalized Presidency. As the only part of the White House machinery with teeth-control over both the appropriations and legislation which departments and agencies may request from Congress, the Office had the power as well as the expertise to exercise general surveillance over the legislative requests of departments and to pronounce whether their policies were 'in accordance with the programme of the President'.[10]

In theory the Office exercises overright over all departmental proposals involving legislation as well as the appropriations. Circular A19 (11) sets out the following requirements. All agencies are required to prepare annually legislative programmes for the forthcoming session of Congress. The information supplied by agencies is issued in the preparation of the President's legislative programme, annual and special messages to Congress. The proposed programme must include all items of legislation the agency will propose or support, and should be prepared in the light of the President's known policies. The list is expected to include legislation in preparation and any laws expiring, saying whether or not extension is proposed. Attachment A orders agencies to divide their list into two parts—those items of sufficient importance to be included in the President's legislative programme and given special endorsement by him and all other measures in a list of priority. Each item is supposed to contain a statement of methods, relationship to existing programmes, appropriations required over the next five years, and any savings. Any written statement of views or report must be submitted to the office one month before submission to Congress for clearance. An agency must 'not transmit to Congress any proposal which it has been advised is in conflict with the program of the President'.

The Office regards one of its main functions as ensuring that all agencies with an interest have been consulted and have a chance to state their views before a proposal is recommended to Congress. In the case of Bills enrolled by members of Congress not on behalf of the Executive, the Office sends copies to all relevant departments and agencies demanding replies within forty-eight hours. Replies should analyse the main features of a bill, compare it with Administration proposals, identify good and bad features, estimate the effects on costs, and recommend what line the President should take.

All this seems a reasonable outline of Presidential control. Yet there are serious weaknesses. First, the Office may succeed in controlling written messages to Congress, but it does not control the attitudes of agencies. A declaration by the Office that a policy is not in accord with the President's programme is prohibition of written support, but as Circular A19 notes: 'In the case of reports on pending legislation, receipt of advice (from the BOB) contrary to the views expressed by an agency does not require the agency to modify its views.' In short, an agency has no obligation to adopt the views of the President, and therefore any Congressman worth his salt can soon persuade an agency official to reveal that his agency has been thwarted by the OMB and disagrees with Presidential policy. So long as the agency does not explicitly endorse a proposal, it can also prepare draft Bills for any Member of Congress without obtaining clearance. A suggestive telephone call from an agency to a congressional ally will prompt him to ask the agency to produce the bill it wanted anyway without the need to go through clearance by the OMB.

Not only did the Bureau make limited claims in A19—fairly easily circumvented—to control agencies on behalf of the President, it has also been probably reluctant to use the powers it claimed to the full, at any rate in the short term. For though the Office speaks for the President in theory, in practice it rarely speaks with his explicit approval. This was brought out in the hearings on the OMB by the House Agriculture Committee:

Mr Poage: My point is that it is perfectly obvious that the President, a person, Lyndon Johnson, can't possibly have any knowledge about each of the particular projects.
Mr Hughes (O.M.B.): On the routine I'm sure that is true. In special cases and in those rare instances where we are in fundamental disagreement with one of the agencies—*at least in many situations*—those would be brought to his attention (emphasis added).[11]

It is striking that the OMB has not *always* referred even 'fundamental disagreements' to the President for arbitration. Indeed, the pressure of work would have made that impossible.

The Office, therefore, has had to husband its resources for two reasons. First, the Office is expected to have some regard for the President's political interests even though it was the job of the White House staff, not them, to be the most sensitive to political issues: 'We are expected to know the mine fields, not to be experts,' one official explained.[12] The Office has to estimate the political forces behind the proposal it disapproved and to realize that the President was not served by bringing him into a fierce political fight on every issue. Not only does the Office safeguard the President's position by not pressing too hard on every issue but it safeguards its own influence by using its powers with caution. For the influence on the OMB has rested above all on the belief of departments and agencies that it spoke for the President. If decisions by the Office had been regularly appealed to the President, and particularly if the decision had gone against the Office, its prestige would have suffered. The Office, therefore, has followed a policy of setting most issues by negotiations with the departments rather than by facing reference to President. If the control of the OMB has been weak over new proposals, then its influence over continuing programmes has been even slighter. The attitude of one former Director of the OMB was clear: there is no point in attacking farm programmes *in toto* when you know you are going to lose; influence and time are far better expended on programmes where one might have some influence. The key skill for a Budget Director is knowing when to pick a fight. There is no point running to the President every week with a series of suggestions, every one of which is a major political liability.[13]

The OMB may have faced particular difficulties in safeguarding its influence in the 1960s. Gilmour argues that there was a marked decline in the influence of the OMB during the 1960s, when the Office's veritable monopoly over Executive branch legislation, built up in the Eisenhower Administration, seems to have been eroded seriously.[14] Since the Kennedy Administration, the role of the White House in legislative clearance has been multiplied several times and the White House deals directly with departments. Gilmour quotes one official:

There has to be a way of going over the O.M.B. on a regular basis without going directly to the President. There is. That's the White House staff. Ted Sorensen and Joe Califano in the Kennedy and Johnson Administration respectively were constantly available to mediate and arbitrate between the Secretary of a Department and the Director of the Budget. (p. 156).

Since then the White House bureaucracy under Ehrlichman and Haldeman has grown to even greater proportions and is probably even more obtrusive. Gilmour attributes the breakdown of clearance to the pressure of legislation, particularly during the great society period. The pressure of work also allowed departments to adopt another strategy—delay. The dynamics of the President's programme imposed deadlines, and departments (apparently including Agriculture) could minimize central control by delaying submitting their proposals to the eleventh hour: 'In the face of a firm White House deadline, the initiating Department's proposals would earn the official blessing of the President as a reward for tardiness.' (p. 197).

The Office has obviously felt that its problems are particularly great with agricultural issues. Evaluation of legislative proposals has been routed not, as is usual, through the regular legislative liaison office but through the agriculture budget examiners. Though the Office has a policy of shifting its staff from one department to another regularity (every four to five years), those covering agriculture have not been so frequently rotated. In an eloquent tribute to the complexity of the subject, the chief of the natural resources division has been within his section for sixteen years. The OMB has also encouraged what might seem to be organizational rivals in the Cost of Living Council and the Council of Economic Advisers, as these are rightly seen as allies in the struggle with the Department of Agriculture. Finally, the peculiar nature of agriculture legislation has posed special problems for the OMB. As Wildavsky has noted, budgetary politics in the United States is incremental:

An agency budget is almost never actively reviewed as a whole every year in the sense of reconsidering the value of all existing programmes as compared to all possible alternatives. Instead it is based on last year's budget with special attention given to a narrow range of increases or decreases.[15]

This approach has not been suitable for agricultural subsidies as the agriculture acts create a recurring fixed obligation on the Government to pay farmers reducing output by a certain amount per dollars per acre. Agriculture Acts create legal obligations upon government for commodity programmes and annual adjustment through the budgetary process is not possible. Legislation is required for reforms. Only with the relatively minor soil improvements or conversation schemes does the annual budget provide much opportunity for review and, as we shall see, attempts to reduce these schemes have usually foundered on widespread congressional support.

The Office has had a clear conception of its objective—to serve the wider national purpose which Congressmen with their localism are constantly endangering. It has worked, therefore, steadily to reduce the level of agricultural subsidies and guaranteed prices to the point where chance overproduction or heavy crops would not destroy the rural economy (by causing market prices to collapse). Significantly, its triumphs have been achieved by complex maneouvering. Thus its moves in 1964–65 to force the true cost of agricultural subsidies into the open by basing them on direct Treasury payments was based on recognition that only with the aid of urban Congressmen shocked by the cost of subsidies could the OMB gather enough weight to force a reassessment of agricultural subsidies. To obtain this extra help, the OMB went against President Johnson's fetish of those years—holding the budget under 100 billion dollars—by substituting conspicuous government payments for the veiled subsidies resulting from market mainpulation. But even within the Executive branch, the Office's views did not carry. Johnson was committed to the idea of financing farm subsidies by a special tax on food processors and when Congress, at the urging of the processors and the AFL–CIO (which was very influential in that Congress), refused to accept these 'bread taxes' Johnson was not pleased. He delayed signing the Act to the last possible moment before delay became a 'pocket veto'.[16] Yet it was his own Bureau of the Budget which had steered the Congress towards financing subsidies out of the Treasury.

Other central advisory agencies: the Council of Economic Advisers

A whole host of advisory councils has something to say on agricultural issues (the Cost of Living Council, the Environmental/Conservation Council committees on pesticides, etc.) but the only one of influence has been the Council of Economic Advisers (CEA). Even here, the picture is of weak influence rather than real power. Flash, the author of the most authoritative study of the Council, concluded in 1965: 'The Council's powers, however, compared to those of other Presidential advisers, have been so transitory, peripheral and intangible that as a result its competitive position has been consistently weak.' Flash also notes that the Council is weakest when it is specific, and notes 'the relative acceptance for the general as distinct from specific advice'.[17] Significantly, Sorensen singles out the agricultural subsidy issues as one in which professional economists are apt to forget the political needs of the President: 'The professional economist in urging lower farm prices supports may think more in terms of his academic colleagues than of the next presidential election.'[18]

On such reeds did the OMB lean. It was with a feeling of great triumph that Heller, Chairman of the CEA under Kennedy, secured a standing order that all agricultural issues would be referred to the CEA as well as the OMB before reaching the President. This more formal arrangement than is common with the

CEA was designed to ensure that at least two critical viewpoints reached the President. The CEA joined the OMB in taking a hostile attitude to the subsidy programmes. The lesser emphasis on 'free market' allocation of resources by Heller and President Kennedy's CEA did not blunt their concern over the mis-allocation of resources, and they were sensitive to the regressive income distribution features of the programmes. It is difficult to show that the CEA had much influence on agricultural policy, but at least it may claim that, thanks to its criticisms, the case against subsidies did not go by default; the CEA joined with the OMB to warn, advise, and discourage.

Inter-departmental dealings

Issues involving more than one department arise in the United States as in Britain. However, there is greater concern among students of administration about how they are resolved. In the absence of the structures and norms of Cabinet government, attempts at formal inter-departmental coordination rarely have been effective. In the case of national security,[19] many commentators have argued that the effect of formalized inter-departmental committees has been to submerge issues rather than to structure them for decision in a way that brings out the main issues. Departments not only fight for their clients but suppress information and conceal information from each other. A recent study has claimed that the US Department of Agriculture has been particularly wilful in disregarding the wishes and interests of other departments. For example, the Department of Agriculture, which controls the use of pesticides, has ignored successfully 185 warnings from the Department of Health, Education, and Welfare (HEW) on the effects of pesticides commonly in use. HEW also complains that the Department of Agriculture has shown little interest in focusing the food distribution programmes it controls on nutritional needs rather than the removal of surpluses. The same conflict between needs and surpluses arises with the State Department. The Interior Department has continued to increase productive acreage (the Bureau of Land Reclamation provides water to 10 million otherwise infertile acres) while the US Department of Agriculture works to take 60 million acres out of production. The author of a recent study concludes that: 'Agriculture until recently has been free to disregard recommendations from Interior and HEW and has overridden their objections regularly.'[20]

The Department itself

The US Department of Agriculture is a big spender. In the fiscal year 1970 Congress provided the Department with $9,920,166,150, and the Department collected by law 30 per cent of US Customs receipts—$657,297,000. In addition, Food for Peace is funded separately and the Commodity Credit Corporations is empowered to borrow 14·5 billion dollars to finance its price support activities. It is also a vast bureaucracy. The Department employs 101,056 full-time workers (June, 1969) plus 23,978 part-time workers. Excluding Defence, Agriculture is the fourth largest department measured by employment. The study of the US Department of Agriculture already cited argues that the myriad agencies within the Department enjoy considerable autonomy. A strong Secretary reduces but does not end this autonomy. Orville Freeman, a strong Secretary it is said, made a marginal difference so that officials of the Forest Service, nominally under his control, switched from talking of 'going over to the Department' when they went to see him talking of 'going across the street'.[21] Hardin agrees that the agencies have great autonomy. He claims that the Forest Service is the most autonomous, if only because it has its appropriations discussed separately, but the Farmers' Credit Administration, the Rural Electrification Administration (REA), and Farmers' Home Administration provide reasonable competition.[22] All these agencies carry benefits out into local districts. All are able to encourage congressional support through the fact that they have direct and friendly contacts within the Congressman's constituents. All, too, operate programmes with sufficient discretion (e.g. whether or not an area is made a soil conservation district with consequent eligibility for grants and benefits) to be able to offer help to a Congressman who wants to impress constituents by obtaining federal funds.

Lowi has drawn attention to the 'system of subgovernments' linking local groups, bureaucracies, and congressional committees in agriculture.[23] He gives as examples the Soil Conservation Service, subcommittees of the Appropriations Subcommittee, and the National Association of Soil Conservation Districts. A well-documented relationship is the one between the REA and the National Council of Rural Electric Co-operative Associations (NCRECA). The REA's duty is to create rural cooperatives to bring power to rural areas; the NCRECA is the national association which such cooperatives join. As a pressure group the NCRECA is, of course, free to campaign for increased appropriations for the REA; in 1968 the NCRECA was able to give $82,392,63 to ninety-one congressional campaigns.[24]

But of greater importance to general policy is the Agricultural Stabilisation and Conservation Service (ASCS). This is the agency that implements on behalf of the CCC the agricultural subsidy programmes, and it does so through an extensive network of farmer-elected committees. These committees operate at the state, county, and community level, and about 65,000 farmers throughout the United States[25] are members of such committees. One of their main duties is to distribute acreage allotments[26] for wheat, feed grains, cotton, etc., and there is much evidence to suggest that the cost of participatory administration has been unjust administration. Thus in 1965, the US Civil Rights Commission found evidence of widespread discrimination against blacks in the South in the Administration of US Department of Agriculture programmes. This discrimination, it found, was mainly the fault of locally-elected farmer committees: 'Starting with a view that Negroes cannot improve as farmers, many programmes have not trained Negroes in the new technology nor encouraged them to acquire larger acreage or to make their smaller acreage more productive.' The Extension Service was found to be separate and unequal (in quality) for blacks, too, in the South.[27] The first black was not elected to an ASCS committee in the South until 1968; now there are two out of 4,150, though blacks comprise 13 per cent of the Southern farm operators.[28]

Not surprisingly, the committees tend to attract farmers who believe in the farm programmes they administer. The ASCS has therefore provided a pressure group within the US Department of Agriculture for their continuation of subsidy programmes, and it has been a constant temptation to Democratic Administrations to turn this weapon on recalcitrant rural Congressmen. Though barred by federal law from political campaigning, the ASCS has been encouraged to make its presence felt. Thus in 1962 President Kennedy, working for his Agriculture Act, told the ASCS committeemen holding a government-sponsored conference in Washington that, while he did not want them to lobby, he hoped they would not let the opportunity pass to 'acquaint' Congressmen with their views.[29] Hadwiger and Talbot note[30] the major role given the ASCS in rallying 'yes' votes in the 1963 wheat referendum after the Grange, NFU, and allied groups reported the US Department of Agriculture that they themselves lacked the resources to act effectively and quickly. The ASCS was subsequently criticized by the AFBF and Republicans for being extensively involved in politics, whereas the ASCS claimed it was merely educating farmers on the issues.

The ASCS therefore fulfills the dual roles of propagandizing for the US Department of Agriculture and exerting pressure within it. That the ASCS exists with its extensive network of farmer-elected committees means that there is an alternative to the pressure groups as a source of advice and contact with farmers. Indeed, one further reason for the weakness of interest groups as organizations in the United States is the obsession with administration through elected committees representing the group administered. What need is there to listen to the AFBF when the US Department of Agriculture has, through its administrative structure, an equally democratic consultative machinery of its own? And, if, as is almost certain, the AFBF and ASCS disagree, it is not the ASCS which has the greater and more trusted access to policy-makers? The ASCS is a further example of the well-worn point that distinguishing between pressure groups and agencies in the United States is not always easy. The ASCS, nominally the administrative agent of US Department of Agriculture policy functions too as a pressure upon it.

The picture, therefore, of agency autonomy within the US Department of Agriculture is well founded. The agencies commonly have their own clienteles and interests. These can be safeguarded by links with Congress that are independent of general US Department of Agriculture congressional liaison. But we shall now see that imposed on the Department network of conflicting and semi-independent empires have been Secretaries who are very much the President's men.

The Secretaries

About 100 jobs in the Department in policy-making areas are political appointments. Eight are Presidential appointments with the advice and consent of the Senate, the chief of which is the Secretaryship. How far does Senate confirmation of the Secretary constrain the choice that the President makes? The answer would seem to confirm Harris's[31] general finding that a President has considerable freedom of choice.

The hearings on the nominations of Freeman and Benson were largely formalities. Freeman had an extraordinarily easy ride—Senator Young (Republican, North Dakota) expressed confidence in him; the candidate assured Senator Talmadge that he saw his first responsibility as being to farmers; and the Chairman noted that no objections had been received and promised to forward the nomination to the Senate as soon as the President could get around to formally presenting it.[32] Benson had a slightly harder time but was never in any danger. He was pressed by a Senator Young to endorse Eisenhower's campaign pledge to continue farm price supports at 90 per cent of parity. Benson did so, but prevented any long-term commitment on, for example, supporting a Bill from Senators Young and Russell for an additional three years (beyond 1954) by saying that he needed more time to study the issues before commenting. This need to study the issues was the shield behind which Benson sheltered from any attempts to commit him. Senator Aiken, chairing the committee again, noted that there were no requests from anyone to comment on the nomination, and it was forwarded to the Senate when formally presented.[33]

It was, therefore, somewhat unsual that the nomination of Earl Butz led to serious hearings and a strong challenge to his confirmation. The links between Butz and agribusiness and his close association with Benson in the 1950s prompted the NFU and the NFO to oppose the nomination. The Senate Agriculture Committee, according to its Chairman, Senator Talmadge, received (probably at the prompting of these groups) 'many' protests at the nomination. But it was clear that Butz, though disliked by most farm groups and members of the Committee, was going to be confirmed because it was accepted as the right of the President to pick his advisers. Thus the Grange opposed most of the policies Butz advocated, but felt unable to oppose his nomination:

We are supporting the President' nomination on the basic concept and precept that the President of the United States should have the right to choose a person for his Cabinet who he would like to have serve with him.[34]

The confirmation was duly confirmed in the Senate by 51 votes to 44 (Republicans 37:4, Democrats 14:40, with Northern Democrats 5:31 and Southern Democrats 9:9).

The role of the Secretary

The Secretary is likely to encounter expectations of the role he should play. This role is essentially that of being the spokesman for farmers. A Secretary of Agriculture must show no signs of putting the interests of taxpayers or consumers above those of farmers. Thus not only Freeman eased his confirmation by stating this but Butz, too, was eager to state that 'the President has told me that he wants me to be a spokesman for agriculture at the White House level'.[35] Any departure from this role is punished by hostility from farm groups and from congressional agriculture committees. Benson was condemned because he seemed to be trying to stir up consumers against the farmer in an effort to have Congress adopt his plan for lower price supports. The ranking Republican on the House Appropriations Subcommittee complained bitterly, 'I cannot accept your failure to stand up before America and defend our farm people.'[36] When Freeman, reacting to concern about the level of prices in the shops, welcomed a fall in the market prices for hogs, he was assailed by Democratic Senators Burdick (North Dakota), McGovern (South Dakota), Mondale (Minnesota), Gaylord Nelson (Wisconsin), Paul Douglas (Illinois), Magnuson (Washington), and Harris (Oklahoma). Freeman compounded his sins by selling government stocks to reduce prices; Evans and Novak warned, 'He had better speak up for the farmers' point of view or face demands for his resignation.'[37] Freeman moved quickly to placate his critics. He announced that he would ask the Department of Defence to continue buying pork, though this support buying was designed originally to prop up prices during gluts. The sudden wave of criticism did, therefore, cause Freeman to change some minor policies. Freeman responded to the demand of *Wallace's Farmer* that he put the farmer and not the consumer first.[38] This aberration apart, Freeman was regarded as making the pro-farmer statements a Secretary should, and was duly rewarded. 'I have been pleased with the statements as you have made,' Whitten told a grateful Freeman. 'As I listen to you I do not see how you could work harder at trying to do things for the majority of farmers.'[39] '(My criticisms) were of the Budget, not of the Secretary. We are very fond of the Secretary.'[40]

Every Secretary wishes to be thought well of, not only to satisfy his personal vanity but to ease his relations with Congressmen whose attitudes will have a real impact on the appropriations or legislation that his Department requests. But approval in this role of 'speaking for farmers' is easy to obtain *and has no substantive major policy implications*. Above all, the fact that Benson opposed farm subsidies did not mean that he was automatically disliked. The count against him was a failure in public relations for agriculture, not a failure of policy. Thus Earl Butz who was as opposed as Benson to farm programmes was considerably more popular, largely because he vigorously denied that farmers were responsible for the rise in food prices. Senator Curtis commented:

We are living at a time when inflation is quite a problem in every household, ... there are many propagandists out there who are exploiting the consumers' fears, ... farmers ... out there feel that they have a voice that speaks for them, meaning you, Mr. Secretary.[41]

Indeed, the farming community rated Butz as one of the best Secretaries even though he worked steadily to abolish the farm programmes. Secretary Freeman was often pressured to oppose Administration plans to help farm workers from unions. This prompted discussion of where his loyalty lay:

Mr. Horan (R.): We expect the Department of Agriculture to defend the proper rights of the American farmer. Don't you?
Sec. Freeman: Yes sir.[42]

The gap between what Freeman and Horan considered 'proper rights' was never bridged, and the Kennedy–Johnson Administrations did much to help farm workers, particularly migrants. In Edelman's language,[43] a Secretary of Agriculture can satisfy his audience not only by the policy positions he takes but by the impression he creates and by the symbolic benefits he offers his policy audience. Thus Butz could attack farm programmes partly because he makes sufficient speeches about the glories of the American farmer. Only by understanding this can we see how Secretaries with such diverse policies as Freeman and Butz can be equally popular.

The need to offer symbolic gestures to farmers, making them feel that you are on their side, avoiding any reference to 'cheap food policies', is one which Secretaries do not find irksome. That this need is not a major constraint is further demonstrated by the fact that far from being trimmers and compromisers, Secretaries of Agriculture in the postwar period have been men whose views were clearly known before their appointments and who, indeed, are regarded as somewhat extreme.

We have noted earlier the moralistic fervour with which Ezra Taft Benson pursued his policies aimed at increasing the influence of the market on prices. Benson's views were well known before appointment, which presumably was made partly on the basis of his known views and partly on the obduracy with which the Elder of the Mormon church could be expected to pursue them. Freeman was firmly committed to his policy of supply management by physical controls before his appointment; we have seen that he testified in favour of a supply management programme designed by Midwestern Governors before his appointment. Freeman was also a major figure in the Democratic party, and apparently had been seriously considered both in 1960 and 1964 as a Vice-Presidential candidate.[44] He was not therefore really a bipartisan figure. Butz was so controversial that his nomination was challenged, and Hardin, the only mild Secretary with claims to non-partisanship, was asked to resign, at least in part for being too conciliatory. His compromising strategy on the 1970 Act (described in Chapter 5) was criticized and his lack of principle was exemplified to many Republicans by his failure to appoint more Republicans to the Department of Agriculture.[45]

It is difficult to appreciate in Britain just how clear the division on farm policy was in the United States and how far down the policy community that split went. The split certain includes economists, and typically certain schools of thought massively dominate particular universities. Thus Purdue University has functioned as 'shadow USDA' for the Republicans in opposition. Hardin was a graduate student and member of staff there; Butz taught; and Don Paarlberg, Director of Agricultural Economics, served as economic adviser to Benson and when dsimissed by Democrats returned to Purdue as Professor of Agricultural Economics. Thus Presidents-elect come to office with clearly differentiated groups of policy-makers available. It is not merely that Eisenhower knew that Benson had extreme *laissez-faire* beliefs or that Kennedy knew that Freeman had already testified in favour of production controls before they were appointed. Benson and Freeman were a part of two intellectual traditions in the United States in agricultural economics. Not only their prescriptions on future farm policy but their analysis of what constituted the farm problem were fundamentally opposed. The Republicans believed in the beneficence of the market-place; the Democrats did not. The Republicans believed that the price system would automatically balance demand and supply; the Democrats, following J. K. Galbraith,[46] not only believed that the market system was unacceptably brutal in its social costs but denied that the market system was properly self-adjusting. Without government intervention, the technological revolution in agriculture would drive farming into deeper and deeper recession. Low factor mobility would prevent this being self-adjusting.

Not only are Secretaries of Agriculture, on the whole, men of known and pronounced views. Once in office they find that the pressures from Congress[47] for conformity are more than matched by the need to have extensive help from the President. In the case of Benson, the Secretary was, as we have seen, under severe pressure from Congress (especially from Midwestern Republicans) to resign. Only Eisenhower's commitment to him as a 'pious man' (he led the prayers at Cabinet meetings) following sound policy kept him in a job. For most of his Secretaryship Benson was, in terms of relations with Congress, a liability and not an advantage to the President. Freeman was never under comparable pressure from Congress, but Goldman still tells us that Freeman was one of the most eager and successful at convincing President Johnson that his loyalty could be transferred from Kennedy.[48] Before Kennedy was assassinated, Freeman was placed in a tenuous position by the rejection of the 1963 wheat referendum, and many observers expected his resignation. For Secretaries of both parties, failure has been too probable to make independent political strength likely. Moreover, as we have seen, no Agriculture Act has an easy ride in Congress. The Secretary has been dependent on the White House for help, for, as one US Department of Agriculture congressional liaison official explained, 'The Administration has more lobbying punch in a day than a lobbying organization has in a week.'[49] No alliance the Secretary can make which does not include the Administration can hope to succeed, for only the Administration can turn the heat on such a variety of Congressmen. Thus during the 1962 campaign for the Kennedy Farm Bill, the New York Democrat, Otis Pike, complained of heavy Administration pressure.

The Republican leader, Hallek, quoted during the debate a letter Pike had sent to his constituents:

I did receive both phone calls and a visit from a friendly representative of the Post Office Department. He didn't want to talk about eight new applications for post offices which are pending in the district; he wanted to talk about the farm bill. Now isn't it odd that the man who came to talk about the farm bill should come from the Post Office Department and not the Department of Agriculture? Do you suppose that it had anything to do with those pending post offices? The arm aches this week but the voice is still loud and clear.[50]

Significantly Pike was not shifted from his opposition, but in reply to Hallek he noted that the Administration had carried existing practices to excess rather than done anything totally new. 'The gentlemen on the opposite side of the aisle are no strangers to the gentle art of persuasion.' The sort of benefits that an Administration can offer Congressmen are well known. Hadwiger and Talbot detail four sorts of benefit offered during the campaign for the 1962 Act. Jobs may be offered with federal government to friends of Congressmen or even Congressmen themselves. Thus Carl Anderson, who voted consistently with the Administration when he was serving out his time in Congress after being defeated in a Republican Primary, was afterwards given a job in the US Department of Agriculture. As in the case of Otis Pike, the federal government may give or take away projected federal installations such as highways or post offices from the districts of Congressmen who fail to support the Administration; amendments may be put forward to the Bill in question to provide special exemptions to favour wavering Congressmen's districts, or help may even be given them in some unrelated bill; and the US Department of Agriculture could be particularly helpful to the districts and Congressmen who supported its proposals.

Perhaps the most important Executive weapon available to Secretaries has been the Presidential veto. Every Republican Secretary of Agriculture has made extensive use of threats to veto any Bill which he disliked sufficiently. This negative power has been used to shape legislation on several occasions. In 1973 Butz forced Congress to lower its proposed support prices by frequently threatening to veto legislation embodying higher support prices than he wanted. In 1958 Benson was able to force a widening of the party range on the agriculture committees—notably in the Senate—because he threatened to veto a major Bill favoured by Southern Democrats. Without the Bill, an automatic formula embodied in legislation dating from the New Deal would have reduced drastically cotton acreage allotments. There were frequent pleas to Eisenhower not to follow Benson's advice to veto certain high support prices Bills, but Eisenhower invariably supported his Secretary, vetoing one Bill in an election year (1956) and two others in a midterm election year (1958). A veto is always difficult to override; in the case of agriculture Bills which always cause such sharp divisions, they are never overridden. A close relationship with a President so that this weapon is available is as important to a Secretary as the goodwill of Congress, where he can please only some of the people some of the time.

If it is true, as I have argued, that the congressional constraints on how a Secretary should act are relatively minor and the dependence on the President great, how have Presidents used that influence? The traditional argument is that the President is the custodian of general interests. Elected by all the people, he is held to ransom by none. In particular, it would be argued that farmers, though now a small proportion of the population (5 per cent), can maintain their influence with Congress because of the unequal distribution of power within Congress typified by the committee system. Consumers and taxpayers who are, of course, more numerous find their interests better protected by the President. No matter how plausible such an argument, it is incorrect. Presidents have shown an eagerness to court the farm vote which fully matches and probably exceeds competition for the farm vote in Britain.

Much of the evidence of competition for the farm vote appeared in Chapter 5.[51]

We have seen how Truman's surprise victory in 1948 was attributed to his popularity with farmers; Eisenhower, mindful of Dewey's mistakes, tried to bury the issue in 1952 with a masterpiece of purposeful political equivocation. Eisenhower's position seemed clear:

And here and now and without any 'ifs' or 'buts' I say to you that I stand behind—and the Republican Party stands behind—the price support laws now on the books. This includes the amendment to the basic Farm Act passed by the votes of both parties in Congress to continue through 1954 the price supports on commodities of parity.[52]

Eisenhower's genius was in not stating (and, indeed, implying the opposite) that in 1954 he would move to abolish subsidies at 90 per cent of parity. We have also seen that great attention was paid to agriculture in the 1960 campaign and that concern about Goldwater capturing the farm vote helped persuade Johnson to support the 1964 Wheat/Cotton Bill. Finally, we noted the role that the quest for the farm vote played in the 1968 Primaries as well as the General Election. Unlike the situation in Britain, it is highly rational for Presidential candidates in the United States to compete for the farm vote.

Campbell *et al.* in *The American Voter* [53] point to several characteristics of the farm voters which make competition worthwhile. The farm vote is unusually unstable; both turnout and party allegiance vary unusually. The 'American farmer ... showed himself to be sporadic in his voting and inconstant in his partisan attachments' (p. 213). Outside the South, party identification is unusually weak (p. 214). However, the farm vote is hard to play for, because farmers show abnormally little interest in elections unless times are bad (p. 215), are ill educated, and isolated from all forms of political activity (p. 217). The farm vote is unusually responsive to the pressures a farmer feels as an individual, and because of his low identification with party, is likely to 'kick the rascals out' even if he put them there himself. Conversely, history shows that once relief has been obtained 'from the most immediate economic grievances' farm discontent dies down, 'as rapidly and as unexpectedly as it coalesced' (p. 227). Perhaps one of Campbell *et al.*'s most striking comments is that farmers in the United States are unusually likely to vote on the basis of one issue—the farm vote. They cite the response of a small Mississippi farmer in an interview:

There is the familiar profession of great ignorance about politics with virtually no other content. However Stevenson's name elicited the remark, 'Now wait a minute—ain't he the one gonna give money to the farmers? My boys and me needs that.'[54]

The authors comment, 'their criteria for political decision are totally wrapped up in the tangible benefits that may flow to the farmer.' Though Campbell *et al.* would recognize great differences between farmers, especially by size of holding, they would agree that the farm vote is open to competition to a degree that is not true in England.

It is, of course, reasonable to point out that the sharp decline in the number of farmers suggests that the farm vote has declined in importance to Presidents.

Even in 1972, however, President Nixon claimed to have granted an increase in dairy prices partly to avoid the Congressional Democrats taking the credit and partly because John Connally (Secretary of the Treasury) warned that 'their (dairy farmers) votes would be important in several Midwestern States'. If Congress did pass a price increase, the President 'could not veto it without alienating the farmers—an essential part of his political constituency'. It is only fair to note in the light of a heavy contribution to Nixon's campaign fund that Democrats had a cruder explanation—bribery.[55] There are two less obvious reasons why the prosperity of American agriculture is of significance to the Presidential aspirant.

First, though the number employed in agriculture has diminished, the importance of agriculture to the economies of several states is clear. A striking feature of Table 7[56] is that not only is agriculture a significant source of income in many states (with twelve states showing 5 per cent or more of personal income coming from farming) but those states in which agriculture is a significant source of income are not those in which are the largest agricultural producers. Thus Illinois, Texas, and California with over 2·5 million dollars in the case of the first two and over 4 million dollars in the case of California in personal income coming from agriculture are not dependent on it as a source of income. Agriculture supplies a low percentage of personal income. But in South Dakota (seventeenth in cash receipts) farm income is 19 per cent of the total and in Idaho (thirtieth in cash receipts) 10·1 per cent. In short, states differ in the degree to which they industrialized, and this gives agriculture a great significance in some. The twelve states where agriculture does provide a significant (5 per cent or more) proportion of personal income command a not-insignificant 64 electoral votes (about the same as New York and Illinois together). A recession in agriculture in these states could lead to a more general recession, hurting any incumbent or candidate from his party.

Second, though the autonomy and even antipathy of the congressional from the Presidential party is a cliché of American politics, the Presidential candidate does have a vested interest in the success of congressional candidates of his own party. In spite of well-publicized exceptions, party is the best predictor of voting in Congress: a President usually gets more help from his own party. Severe losses among Congressmen of one's own party are a serious matter, if only because they make passing legislation more difficult. That an unpopular farm policy can cost a party strength in the House seems established in the case of Ezra Taft Benson and the 1958 Midterm Elections. Contemporaries certainly attributed Democratic inroads in the Midwest to Benson's unpopularity. A *Congressional Quarterly* enquiry, 'Does Benson hurt GOP in midwest', concluded that he did.[57] The article reached three conclusions. First, the Republican ticket which had scored big gains in the Midwest farm areas in 1952 performed less well in 1952. Eisenhower received a smaller share of the vote in 33 of 60 studied districts. Not surprisingly, Eisenhower's losses were greatest where the Republican Representative (probably knowing that feeling in their districts) opposed his farm policy. Republican Representatives lost strength in 49 out of 60 districts with more than 5 per cent in

Table 7   Farming in the states' economies. (Reproduced by permission of *National Journal*, 1 March, 1970)

State	Cash receipts from commodity sales in 1968 ($ thousands)	Farm income as percentage of personal income
Alabama	659,687	3·5
Alaska	4,087	0·1
Arizona	587,187	4·7
Arkansas	986,405	10·0
California	4,274,054	2·4
Colorado	903,595	3·5
Connecticut	161,880	0·5
Delaware	125,518	1·9
Florida	1,232,543	3·4
Georgia	1,038,731	3·3
Hawaii	204,505	3·8
Idaho	546,148	10·1
Illinois	2,591,362	1·6
Indiana	1,352,473	2·7
Iowa	3,461,510	11·0
Kansas	1,535,914	6·8
Kentucky	824,811	5·1
Louisana	628,743	3·5
Maine	209,807	2·5
Maryland	346,514	0·8
Massachusetts	161,026	0·3
Michigan	849,500	1·1
Minnesota	1,864,931	4·5
Mississippi	646,868	9·7
Missouri	1,402,215	3·9
Montana	509,505	10·4
Nebraska	1,757,556	9·9
Nevada	57,240	1·0
New Hampshire	56,403	0·6
New Jersey	248,016	0·3
New Mexico	322,353	5.2
New York	1,041,992	0·5
North Carolina	1,238,620	4·5
North Dakota	720,314	17·0
Ohio	1,223,580	1·2
Oklahoma	845,983	4·1
Oregon	512,801	2·4
Pennsylvania	932,848	0·8
Rhode Island	20,278	0·2
South Carolina	374,180	2·5
South Dakota	958,035	19·0
Tennessee	623,450	2·8
Texas	2,669,031	3·9
Utah	197,521	2·1
Vermont	141,243	3·4
Virginia	520,419	1·5
Washington	813,298	3·0
West Virginia	100,265	0·6
Wisconsin	1,458,743	4·1
Wyoming	242,047	7·2

agriculture and in all but one of 23 districts covered employing more than 25 per cent in agriculture. It remains uncertain whether or not a Representative could safeguard his seat by opposing the Administration. Where there were less than 25 per cent but more than 5 per cent of the workforce directly employed in agriculture, the anti-Benson Representatives fared less well than the pro-Benson Representatives; with more than 25 per cent employed in agriculture, anti-Administration Republican Representatives did better. This might suggest that Benson's rural appeal was more to small towns than to farmers—a finding supported by odd opinion polls. However, the study also found significant variations between states: in Illinois and Kansas anti-Administration and pro-Administration Republican Representatives fared equally well (or badly); in Wisconsin, Minnesota, and Nebraska anti-Administration Representatives did better. (This again seems to show the significant differences between the meaning of Republicanism within the Midwest to which I have alluded.)

Gilpatrick shows a common scepticism about the knowledge which voters have about the details of candidates' policies. He finds[58] that:

... there was virtually no discernible difference in the way farmers on adjacent farms and engaged in the same type of farming but on opposite sides of a congressional district line voted for congressmen from the same party when these men had gone on public record on opposite sides of the prices support issue. . . . High as well as flexible support Republicans suffered losses at the polls in fine disregard of their policy stands.

Gilpatrick did find that Republicans lost about 12 per cent of the farm vote, however, attributing this, after Lubell, to the idea that *voters* instinctively turn to Democrats during Depressions or, he would argue, periods of falling prices. Gilpatrick's findings could well be modified to support the general argument that Benson cost the Republicans votes. His survey does seem to show that rural voters were not able to distinguish pro-subsidy Republicans from Benson, and instead punished all Republicans for the policies of a Republican Administration—a case of the electorate acting as if there was the responsible party system as so many commentators have wanted. The evidence then seems to suggest the idea that an unpopular Secretary cost the Republicans congressional strength, though experts are. uncertain whether these Congressmen could escape their fate by opposing Benson. Any President as leader of his party must be concerned by such losses.

Given these concerns about the farm vote (to win Presidential elections and to preserve the strength of the congressional party), it is not surprising that Presidents, far from defending the general will fearlessly, have tried to restrain their Secretaries. The clearest example of Presidential restraint was Eisenhower and Benson. Benson in his memoirs and Eric Goldman provide at least two instances. In 1954, Benson acting under the discretionary powers of the Secretary, cut dairy price supports from 90 to 75 per cent of parity. There was a storm of protest, and Eisenhower sent for Benson and explained to him as an old soldier that there were other, and often better, strategies than frontal assault. In 1956, Eisenhower accepted Benson's recommendation that a high support Agriculture

Bill which passed Congress that election year should be vetoed, but insisted on more than compensating for this by extending high support for a year to farmers who did not even offer to restrict production. Jamie Whitten, Chairman of the House Agricultural Appropriations Subcommittee, for one was impressed by the political artistry displayed:

If any of you read the President's veto message, he vetoed a Democratic farm bill on the grounds that it fixed high level price supports and on that statement he got commendation of almost 100 per cent of the press of this country.

In the second paragraph or rather the second part of that message he told the Secretary of Agriculture to fix high level price supports and then the press eulogised him the next day for helping the farmer.[59]

Eisenhower's gesture of supporting commodities with production restrictions was always seen by the Democrats as one of the major causes of the surpluses in the late 1950s. We also saw in Chapter 5 how Kennedy damaged the chances of the wheat referendum by not endorsing Freeman's claim that rejection of the Administration's wheat programme would mean no programme at all. When the programme was rejected, Hadwiger and Talbot tell us,[60] the inclination of Orville Freeman and the US Department of Agriculture was that wheat farmers should be left without a programme; the resulting slump in prices would teach them a much-needed lesson. However, as Chapter 5 also noted, Lyndon Johnson refused to take any chances with the farm vote and ordered Freeman to find a programme that could be passed, which meant a return to higher subsidies for wheat. Johnson himself put in a major personal lobbying campaign for the 1964 Act. Johnson's instructions to Freeman to emphasize continuity in agricultural programmes and not to look for 'dramatic new programmes' in effect meant an end to the quest for less costly farm programmes.[61] When the cards have been down, it has been Presidents, not their Secretaries, who have lost confidence and backed off in the shadow of the agricultural vote.

The influence of the Executive

The danger that a President might lose control over his Secretary of Agriculture is, then, not as great as is feared. If an Administration changes policy on agriculture, it is more likely to be because the President is worried about re-election than because the Secretary has been 'captured' by agricultural interests. Yet another obvious problem remains—Congress. Little can be changed in agricultural policy without fresh legislation.

Even though there may have been a general reduction in Congress's power, it has certainly not shown in agricultural policy. Both in committee and on the floor, Congress has remained very willing to amend or reject the proposals of the Administration and substitute its own. Even Secretaries of Agriculture have been forced to promise that their Department will make every effort to help Congress draft Bills entirely inconsistent with their policies.[62] An Administration is not powerless; Presidential vetoes can prevent the enactment of legislation which commands a simple majority in Congress. Neither can an Administration force Congress to accept its proposals *in toto*. Indeed, one reason commonly advanced for the failure of Kennedy's 1962 Farm Bill was that his Administration had antagonized Congressmen by attempting to coerce them into approving his proposals. As one Congressman complained, 'The President has done the one thing he should not have done—twisted our arms.'[63] Secretary Freeman's polite requests for support and attempts at persuasion were much better received.[64] Congressmen cannot be forced to support a Secretary of Agriculture, even from their own party. As one Republican somewhat cynically argued in debate:

Maybe you are going to feel that you are going to have to support your Secretary of Agriculture. I faced that situation for eight long years. At times, the viewpoint of the Secretary of Agriculture differed from that of my constituents. . . . These constituents live in my district, and the Secretary of Agriculture did not. Had he lived in my district, he would have had only one vote.[65]

Though Secretaries of Agriculture of both parties have been unable to coerce Congress into accepting their plans *in toto*, the consequences have been somewhat different for Republicans and Democrats. Congress, which has been under Democratic control since 1954, has found itself in deadlock with *laissez-faire* Republicans such as Benson and Butz. Harold Cooley, Chairman of the House Agriculture Committee, found the situation during Benson's tenure of office particularly galling. Benson's insistence on principles not shared by the Democrats made any progress hard to achieve:

(if) Instead of coming back and saying to this committee 'We will not take 85%' [of parity as a target price] you would say 'We don't like 85% but we will take $82\frac{1}{2}$%', (and) show some willingness to compromise, we might make some progress. . . . Just to oppose everything we send to the White House is not my idea of making progress at all.[66]

Democratic Secretaries such as Freeman face a different problem. They share the same broad approach as their majority in Congress, but find that Democratic Congressmen and Senators are always ready to argue that farmers in their district are a special case. A typical example is that a Democratic Secretary and Congress will agree on production controls only for controls to be undermined by detailed exemptions. The result can be that controls cease to be effective. Ezra Taft Benson astutely outlined the process at work:

We might as well be frank about this whole thing. There is always a tendency for us to vote legislation with guaranteed high prices and what we can consider to be effective controls.
Then when the formula starts to work we pass another piece of legislation in which we set a minimum acreage of 55 million acres so the formula cannot work. And then in order to satisfy the hundreds of farmers who don't grow very much wheat . . . why we give them a 15 acre exemption without any penalty.[67]

Faced with such pressures, Republican and Democratic Secretaries have but two choices. Either they can see their proposals go down in defeat (as Chapter 5 showed many have) or they can make concessions. Republican Secretaries cannot, because theirs is a minority party in Congress, win any vote without Democratic help. Democratic Secretaries, faced with the steady opposition of the Republicans in Congress, have been unable to afford a significant number of defections from the ranks of their party. The wise Secretary has been willing to settle for legislation far short of this general objectives.

The lot of Secretaries of Agriculture has not been altogether happy. They have been men selected because they are known to take a clear stand on farm policy, but they have been constrained by Presidents who have been more sensitive than they to the farm vote. The Secretaries have tried to present Congress with a coherent approach, but have been forced to accept either defeat or compromise. It is not surprising that no Secretary of Agriculture succeeded from this impossible situation in reducing the cost of farm subsidies. (That reduction was to be achieved only by capricious changes in climate and the world market.) Yet it would be unfair to blame Secretaries of Agriculture and their Department for failing to reform the subsidy system.

In different ways, both Republican and Democratic Secretaries tried to reduce the burden. Both lacked the necessary political support from the President and Congress. We have explored the nature of the Secretaries' problems in the Executive; it is time now to turn to the congressional politics of agriculture.

Notes

1. Richard Fenno, Jr., *The President's Cabinet*, Harvard University Press, Cambridge, 1959, p. 249.
2. David B. Truman, *The Governmental Process*, Alfred Knopf, New York, 1951, p. 406.
3. See A. Maas, 'Congress and water resources', *APSR*, **44** (1950).
4. Roger Hilsman, *The Politics of Policy Making in Defence and Foreign Affairs*, Harper's American Political Behaviour Series, 1971, pp. 1–39.
5. Confidential interview.
6. Fenno, op. cit.
7. Harold Seidman, *Politics, Position and Power, The Dynamics of Federal Organization*, Oxford University Press, Oxford and New York, 1970, p. 14.
8. A. Wildavsky, 'The political economy of efficiency', *Public Administration Review*, **30** 1970.
9. Grant McConnell, *The Decline of Agrarian Democracy*, University of California Press, 1953.
10. Richard Neustadt, 'The growth of central clearance', *APSR*, **48** (1954).
11. US Congress, House of Representatives, Eighty-ninth Congress, Second Session, Committee on Agriculture, *Legislative Policy of the Bureau of the Budget*, Serial MM.
12. Confidential interview.
13. Confidential interview.
14. R. S. Gilmour, 'Central clearance, a revisited perspective', *Public Administration Review*, March/April, 1971.
15. A. Wildavsky, *The Politics of the Budgetary Process*, Little Brown, Boston, 1964, p. 15.
16. *Wall Street Journal*, 3 November, 1965.

17. Edward S. Flash, *Economic Advice and Presidential Leadership: The Council of Economic Advisers*, Columbia University Press, 1965, pp. 318–319.
18. Theodore Sorensen, *Decision Making in the White House*, Columbia Paperback, New York, 1963, p. 66.
19. In the late 1950s attempts by Eisenhower to run the NSC on almost British Cabinet lines prompted a great deal of comment, mostly critical. Hearings were held by a Subcommittee of the Senate Government Operations Committee under Senator Jackson; there are many associated newspaper articles. For a short bibliography, see Hilsman, op. cit., pp. 156, 157(n), and 'The National Security Council under Truman, Eisenhower and Kennedy', *Political Science Quarterly*, 1964.
20. Prentice Bowsher, 'CPR Department Study/The Agriculture Department', *National Journal*, 3 January, 1970.
21. Agriculture is housed in buildings separated by Independence Avenue on Fourteenth Street. Forestry is not in the same building as the Secretary.
22. National Advisory Committee on Food and Fiber, *Food and Fiber in the Nation's Politics*, Vol. III of the technical papers by Charles M. Hardin.
23. Theodore Lowi, 'Agriculture's Subgovernments', *Reporter*, 21 May, 1964.
24. Andrea F. Schoenfeld, 'Washington Pressures/The National Rural Electric Co-operative Association', April, *National Journal*, April, 1970.
25. US Department of Agriculture, ASCS, *Background Information*, BI No 6, July, 1972.
26. The number of acres a farmer is allowed to plant without losing eligibility for subsidies.
27. As reported, *New York Times*, 1 March, 1965.
28. Bowsher, op. cit.
29. *New York Times*, 5 April, 1962.
30. Hadwiger and Talbot, op. cit., pp. 287, 288.
31. Joseph P. Harris, *With the Advice and Consent of the Senate*, University of California Press, Berkeley, 1953.
32. US Senate, Eighty-seventh Congress, First Session 1961, Committee on Agriculture and Forestry, Hearings, *Confirmation of Orville Freeman as Secretary of Agriculture*.
33. US Senate, Eighty-third Congress, First Session 1953, Committee on Agriculture and Forestry, Hearings, *Anticipated Nomination of Ezra Taft Benson to serve as Secretary of Agriculture*.
34. US Senate, Ninety-second Congress, First Session, Hearings before the Committee on Agriculture and Forestry, 1971, *Nomination of Earl Lauer Butz*.
35. Ibid., p. 28.
36. US Congress, House of Representatives, Eighty-sixth Congress, First Session, Hearings before a Subcommittee of the Committee on Appropriations, *Department of Agriculture Appropriations for 1960*, p. 2502.
37. *Des Moines Register*, 5 May, 1966; *Washington Post*, 12 May, 1966.
38. *Wallace's Farmer*, 23 April, 1966.
39. US Congress, House of Representatives, Eighty-seventh Congress, Second Session, Hearings before a Subcommittee of the Committee on Appropriations, *Department of Agriculture Appropriations for 1963*, p. 2.
40. Appropriations, Hearings 1966 (for 1967), p. 99.
41. US Senate, Ninety-third Congress, First Session 1973, Committee on Agriculture and Forestry, *Extension of Farm and Related Programmes*, pp. 651–652.
42. Congress, House of Representatives, Eighty-eighth Congress, 1st Session, *Department of Agriculture Appropriations, 1963*, Hearings before a Subcommittee of the Committee on Appropriations, 1962, p. 173.
43. Murray Edelman, *The Symbolic Uses of Politics*, University of Illinois Press, Urbana, 1964.

44. Arthur Schlesinger, *A Thousand Days*, Houghton Mifflin and Co., New York, 1965, p. 14. Eric Goldman, *The Tragedy of LBJ*, Vintage Books, New York, 1968, p. 199.
45. *Des Moines Register*, 22 January, 1971 (esp. interview with Paul Findley).
46. J. K. Galbraith, 'Economic preconceptions and the farm policy', *American Economic Review*, March, 1954.
47. For a discussion of the influence of the Appropriations Committees, see Chapter 8.
48. Goldman, op. cit., p. 80.
49. Leo Schaffer (interview), Congressional Liaison Officer, Department of Agriculture, 2 July, 1973.
50. *Congressional Record*, Vol. 108, part 8, col. 11342, 21 June, 1962.
51. Chapter 5, 'Policy in America; Charge without Reform'.
52. The speech and commitment are reproduced in the Benson confirmation hearings cited above.
53. Angus Campbell, Philip Converse, Warren Miller, and Donald Stokes, *The American Voter*, John Wiley and Co., New York, 1964.
54. Ibid., p. 229.
55. White House statement on Milt and ITT Decisions, quoted in *International Herald Tribune*, 1 October, 1974.
56. From CPR Research Services, *National Journal*, 1 March, 1970.
57. *Congressional Quarterly Weekly Report*, 14 March, 1958.
58. Thomas Gilpatrick, 'Price support policies and the Midwest farm vote', *Midwest Journal of Political Science*, November, 1959. But for a slightly sceptical view of how far the 1948 Truman campaign succeeded because of changes in the farm vote, see Charles Hardin, *Journal of Farm Economics*, November, 1955, which argues that in general Truman held the Midwestern states not by improving on the Democratic share of the farm vote (though he did) but because he was so successful with urban voters in the region.
59. US Congress, House of Representatives, Eighty-fifth Congress, First Session, Hearings before a Subcommittee of the Committee on Appropriations, *Department of Agriculture, Appropriations for 1958*, p. 1673.
60. Hadwiger and Talbot, op. cit., p. 316.
61. For an account of these events see Chapter 5.
62. Vide Benson's promise, US Congress, House of Representatives, Eighty-sixth Congress, First Session, 1959, Senate Committee on Agriculture and Forestry, *President's Farm Message and Hearings*, p. 3.
63. *National Observer*, 23 July, 1962.
64. See, for example, *New York Times*, 13 and 21 June, 1962; *Washington Post*, 19 June, 1962.
65. *Congressional Record*, Vol. 108, part 15, Republican Belcher, col. 20117, 20 September, 1962.
66. US Congress, House of Representatives 1959, Eighty-sixth Congress, First Session, Committee on Agriculture, Hearings, *General Farm Policy*, p. 332.
67. US Congress, House of Representatives, Eighty-sixth Congress, Second Session, Hearings, *General Farm Legislation*, 1960, p. 170.

Chapter 8

Congress and Agriculture

Practical politics consists in ignoring the facts

(*Henry Adams*).

A simple pattern emerged from the description of the evolution of the United States's agricultural policies in Chapter 5. It was a pattern, familiar to students of American government, in which the Executive launched a series of proposals for comprehensive reform, only to see them founder on the rock of Congress. Brannan, Benson, and Freeman all had their competing and conflicting ideas on how to solve the farm problem. Yet none could get his proposals through Congress, and the conspicuous abuses of the subsidy laws—their expense, waste, social injustices, and inefficiences—continued.

Many will find this pattern unsurprising. Congress, it is often argued, is at best parochial in its outlook; at worst, it is the Washington home of special interests. Congressional votes are, therefore, heavily influenced by constituency interests. Representatives or Senators of differing party allegiance but from the same area will work together on its behalf, the classic example, of course, being the farm bloc of the 1920s which was prepared to bring the work of the Senate to a halt in order to obtain justice for the farmer. Congress's committees, too, are thought to be under the control of the interests on which they legislate, because they are composed of Representatives or Senators who represent areas where that interest is strong. Thus all but one of the House Agriculture Committee's members are from rural areas.[1] Because the committees of Congress control the content of legislation on their subject, it is further argued, agricultural legislation has been in the hands of agriculture's representatives; only the naïve, therefore, can be surprised by the failure of Congress to de-rail the gravy train of farm subsidies.

This chapter seeks to explain why Congress has been the graveyard of so many attempts to change the agricultural subsidy laws. It argues that the classic interpretation of agricultural politics outlined above (which is based on the politics of immediate, material constituency interest) is unhelpful, and then proposes an alternative explanation for Congress's failings in agricultural policy. We turn first to the nature of agriculture committees and their impact on policy; we shall then examine the pattern of voting on Agriculture Bills.

The agriculture committees

From the earliest works of political scientists on Congress, tremendous importance has been attached to the committee system. Woodrow Wilson noted, and deplored, the shift of power and debate:

... from the Floor of Congress to the privacy of the committee rooms. ... Whatever is done must be done through or by the committee. ... Congress, or at any rate the House of Representatives, delegates not only its legislative but its deliberative function to its Standing Committees.[2]

Though more recent writers have sometimes liked and sometimes loathed the effects of the committee system, writers continue to stress its importance.[3] Committees, it is argued, are the graveyard of most Bills introduced into Congress; there is no effective way to get a Bill to the floor if it is opposed by the relevant committee.[4] Moreover, because committees carry out the detailed work on Bills, they determine their content. Not only do committees set the agenda of Congress, but their decisions are likely to become the decisions of Congress. It is a widely held congressional ethic that members of a committee are the experts on a Bill and that their views ought to be respected.

We might expect, therefore, to find that Congress's major impact on agricultural legislation comes through its committees on agriculture. As we shall see that these committees are composed of legislators from rural areas, we might suspect that Congress's poor record on farm policy reflects the power of the agriculture committees. On the other hand, recent scholarship[5] has emphasized that congressional committees differ in their power and authority. How much, then, of Congress's refusal to reduce farm subsidies does the committee system explain?

The House Agriculture Committee

Determinants of membership

As Masters demonstrates,[6] the seniority system leaves important discretion to those who select House committees (until members of Ways and Means for the Democrats and the Committee on Committees for the Republicans). They use this discretion partly to match the Representative to the committee (e.g. in terms of partisanship), partly to insulate certain committees from constituency pressure (by appointing Representatives with safe seats), partly to maintain a geographical balance, and partly to put a Representative where he can help his constituents and thus help himself get reelected. Jones[7] shows how the last two considerations shape the House Agriculture Committee. All but one member (Anfuso, Democrat, New York) had major agricultural interests in his constituency. (The urban Democrat appointed was usually one who, trained in the traditions of machine politics, could be relied upon not to make too much fuss.) A limited geographical balance was preserved too because every subcommittee was staffed with Representatives from districts which produced that commodity on which it deliberated. The Committee as a whole however has had until recently a distinctly Southern flavour; in 1961, fourteen of the eighteen Democrats were from the Southern or Border states. Seniority, the tradition of appointing Representatives of rural areas to the Committee, and the fact that the South was, until the late 1950s, the Democrats' only loyal rural region area have also placed Southerners in the chair of the Committee since 1954. In 1961, for example, the Chairman and the nine top-ranking Democrats were from Southern or Border states.

The Committee has, come therefore to be known as one which is highly unrepresentative of the House as a whole. Goodwin argues that the members of the House Agriculture Committee are more conservative than the members of any other, including UnAmerican Activities.[8] Members who have links to the liberal wing of the Democratic party are prized anomalies. Even before Thomas Foley became Chairman of the Agriculture Committee he played a crucial role in its work because he was the only man with power on the Committee (as Chairman of the Subcommittee on Livestock and Grains) with a liberal voting record. Foley, whose ADA rating is 88 per cent and COPE rating 83 per cent, could round up Democratic votes for Committee proposals in a way which its Chairman could not because Foley was not identified as a Southern reactionary unlikely to follow the party line on other issues.

The most influential congressional committees are committees which maintain a high degree of unity and cohesion.[9] Ways and Means and Appropriations are frequently cited examples. The House Agriculture Committee faces formidable difficulties in maintaining unity, however.

The first of these difficulties is the nature of the industry on which it legislates. The Ranking Republican on the Committee, Page Belcher, noted that even when the Committee tried to be fair to everyone, divisions between commodities made life difficult. Describing the 1970 Act, uniquely a compromise measure, he said:

Regardless of what kind of general farm bill you try to write, you have got all kinds of different interests. . . . On this Bill, I would go down and get the Administration to agree to a little benefit for wheat, and the cotton people would say, 'Now listen, if you are going to do that for wheat, then you have to do it for us.' And then we would get everyone satisfied, and then in a little bit we would have the cotton people getting a few extra acres and the gentleman sitting right here would say, 'Well now, listen. If you are going to do that for cotton, why not do it for feed grains?' So that is what you are up against every time you try and write a farm bill. And in this particular farm bill, everyone has had their feet stepped on just enough times that we got a sort of balance now. If we upset that balance now, if we accept just one amendment that helps feed grains tomorrow, the cotton people will vote against that bill.[10]

If all this was not bad enough, the problems of striking a balance between commodities are compounded by problems of striking a balance within them. Belcher again made the point effectively:

I remember at one time when I started up one of those hearings that we had across the country, that cattle were very cheap, and so many of the people in Oklahoma were raising Cain about the fact that cattle were so low. And then I was up in Nebraska, and I was telling the people up there, 'You know, it beats the dickens how low cattle are.' 'Well,' they said, 'Why, what do you mean, low? Why, you doggons Oklahomans are getting twice what cattle are worth. And how do you think we can pay that price in Oklahoma and feed them corn in Nebraska and sell them on the market in Chicago?' So I found out.[11]

Even more important, however, than the difficulties of pleasing all of the farmers all of the time has been the sharp partisan divide which has plagued the Committee. The Committee has divided on clear party lines on every major Agriculture Act in the 1960s. Indeed, the Committee split on party lines throughout the 1960s: all bar one of the Republicans voted against reporting the Kennedy Farm Bills to the House; every Republican on the Committee opposed the 1964 Wheat/Cotton and 1965 Agriculture Bills. Behind such figures lies a mood of bitterness and enmity between Republicans and Democrats on the Committee which prompted Congressman Bolling to describe it in 1962 as 'perhaps the most bitterly divided in a partisan sense'.[12]

A standard explanation for this partisan division is that some commodities are produced in predominantly Republican areas and others in predominantly Democratic territory. Thus an anonymous writer in the *Yale Law Journal* in 1962 argued that:

... farm policy is one of the few issues in American politics on which the Republicans and Democratic parties clearly differ. If, however, the make-up of the parties is examined, this behaviour (partisan Congressional voting) can be easily explained on the theory that crop interests are the dominant forces.[13]

Some crops are 'represented' by Democrats, others by Republicans. The article also contained the following table.

Table 8 Twenty largest producing farm districts (major crops). (Reprinted by permission of The Yale Law Journal Company and Fred B. Rothman & Company from *The Yale Law Journal*, **71**, 963)

Crop	No. of districts held by Democrats	No. held by Republicans
Rice	20	0
Peanuts	20	0
Cotton	20	1
Tobacco	17	3
Wheat	7	14
Dairy	4	16
Corn	2	18

It is commonly argued that not only do commodities divide on party lines but that they do so because they conflict. This is partly an argument that, as we saw in Chapter 5, some commodities are very much more subsidized than others. Those that do well are invariably 'Democratic' and often Southern. This, it is argued, reflects the balance of power in Congress. Republicans have long been aware of this fact. In 1962, Representative Jensen complained that:

... every member who has spoken today in support of this conference report represents the cotton–tobacco–rice and peanut producing districts and every member who has spoken against ... represents a feed grain producing district ... which is not a new situation but one as old as the time since the South has controlled the Committees on Agriculture both in the House and the Senate. The facts are that after the South got what they wanted for their farmers, they cared little and have done less about the problems of our corn hog farmers.[14]

In the course of a 1958 debate, Michel (Republican, Illinois) was more scathing:

Those of us from the corn and soya bean producing areas have been concerned over the extraordinarily benevolent attitude Congress has taken with regard to such crops as cotton, tobacco, rice and peanuts. I just cannot help but have a feeling that we are still being asked to pay reparations to the South for the Civil War.[15]

The South, it is argued, benefits from the wheat and feed grain programmes because it is allowed to grow feed grains, wheat, and soya beans—Midwestern products—on acreage farmers are paid not to use to produce cotton, tobacco, and other traditional Southern commodities. Feed grain and wheat programmes have usually contained a clause allowing small producers to maintain without reduction the acreage they use for these crops, at times as much as 40 acres, and it is this loophole the South has exploited. Southern agriculture, which needed to diversify anyway, has been helped to move into producing feed grains, wheat, and soya beans as the government already is paying to keep the land used out of production of traditional Southern crops. Thus the Midwestern farmer faced the galling spectacle of Southern farmers moving into the production of 'his' crops while the government required him to cut output. Ninety per cent of Southern feed grains producers but virtually no Midwestern would have been exempted from controls in the 1962 Agriculture Bill. Belcher voiced the anger of the specialist producer in 1960:

... I fought it (the wheat programme) all the way ... my farmers have constantly seen their acreage requirements reduced year after year until in my district about 42% of the acreage is idle. ... I would not consent to further reduction in these allotments to these traditional wheat raisers when the same acreage was being picked up by 15 acre farmers who never in the history of America had raised a bushel of wheat until the price support system made it profitable for them to raise wheat without penalty and sell it in the open market.[16]

It is also true, of course, that some farm subsidy policies can have an immediate, sharp effect on other producers. Thus if a successful 'supply management' programme raises the price of feed grains, those who feel the pinch immediately are livestock farmers. As livestock producers who rely on feed grains (e.g. corn–hog producers) are Republicans, this provides some short-term rationale for their hostility to farm subsidies.

The explanation of partisan conflict within the Committee in terms of the political allegiance of commodities and of conflicting constituency interests has, then, a certain plausibility. It is also a convenient argument for Republican Representatives to make when they have to explain to their farming constituents why they have voted against a Farm Subsidy Bill. It is, nevertheless, an inadequate explanation.

The Democrats would have benefited greatly by placating the Republicans on the Committee. As we shall see, farm subsidy legislation has been carried on the floor of the House by very narrow margins. The main reason for this has been the steady opposition of Republicans. This opposition has been made more probable and more effective because the Republicans on the House Committee, instead of supporting the Bill drafted by their Democratic colleagues, have led the opposition to the Committee's proposals. As members of the Committee, they have alerted and guided opposition to the Bill. Had the Democrats on the Agriculture Committee secured the cooperation of their Republican colleagues, it would have been much easier to steer Agriculture Bills through the House.

If the conflict between Republicans and Democrats on the Committee had been caused merely by conflicts of interest between commodities, then it could have been solved easily by the traditional congressional expedient of logrolling. There are numerous precedents for this; as we shall see, the standard procedure in the Senate Agriculture and Forestry Committee is for legislation to be drafted by the Senator whose state is the leading producer of the commodity in question, irrespective of party. Indeed, Jones[17] argued that the House Committee itself functioned in the same way; legislation on wheat was entrusted to a subcommittee of Representatives from cotton states, and the results were combined in an omnibus Farm Bill. In fact, Jones, whose article was based on the unusual situation in 1958 when the Democrats were trying to obtain Republican votes in order to override an anticipated Presidential veto, presents a misleading picture of the usual way the Committee worked. The Committee was characterized by partisan conflict, not inter-commodity logrolling. But the plausibility of his description is a useful reminder of how easily mere differences between commodities can be solved—by giving something to them all. The easy solution to the political problem caused by the fact that government subsidies for feed grains raised the costs of pig and cattle producers was to subsidize pigs and cattle too. Yet the standard Republican response to the inequity of the farm laws has been not to demand fair shares for 'their' commodities but to work for the abolition of the laws.

The truth of the matter is that agricultural policy in the United States involved, if it was to be workable, making difficult choices. Congress could choose between high farm prices, which would bolster farm incomes but require tough controls of production, or low farm prices, the abolition of subsidies, and the freeing of the farmer from government controls. Any failure to make this choice (by giving high subsidies without production controls) would lead, because production was stimulated by the subsidies, to impossibly costly surpluses. Yet this choice, simple to formulate, caused great difficulties for the House Agriculture Committee because it was the practical expression of a central ideological divide in the United States between Democrats on the one hand (including most Southerners) and Republicans on the other.

The ideological divide

It is a standard finding of studies of voting in Congress that Democrats, particularly from the North, Midwest, and West are more willing to accept a high degree of government involvement in the economy than are Republicans.[18] Yet the anti-union attitudes of the South, coupled with its conservatism on race, foreign policy, and social issues, too often still lead to an identification of its traditions with those of the conservative Midwest. The South, in fact, has a populist and therefore interventionist tradition which the Republican heartlands of, for example, Illinois, never fully experienced. (Those Midwestern areas which were once both Republican and interventionist, e.g. the Dakotas, have steadily gravitated towards the Democrats since 1952.) As C. Van Woodward has shown, Southern populists like Tom Watson were, if shaky on race, steady in their belief that business ought to be regulated.[19] Cash, too, illustrates how the South, anxious to catch up with the North even after the Civil War, retained, nevertheless, a certain scepticism about the entrepreneur and nostalgia for a mythical but cultural benevolent, planter aristocracy.[20] *Laissez-faire* was always faintly Yanky.

It was against this background that the Depression made a profound impression on the South, hitting it harder than perhaps any other region. The New Deal Agricultural programmes were but one of the Roosevelt programmes which the South felt had rescued it. The South, Cash writes of the early New Deal period:

... took Mr. Roosevelt and all his purposes to hear with a great burst of thanksgiving. ... From every platform the politicians of the established Democratic machines, enjoying such patronage as they had never before imagined, unanimously declaimed over and over again every utterance of Mr. Roosevelt's.[21]

The Tennessee Valley Authority, one of the most interventionist features of the New Deal, revitalized a region, and most Southerners appreciated such economic benefits.

Many of the influential Southern Democrats (including Poage himself) were starting their political careers in the 1930s. It is not surprising, then, that they should share the acceptance of government regulation in the New Deal programmes, and so reject *laissez-faire*. 'I am not for freedom,' Chairman Cooley told his Committee in 1960, 'if it means freedom only to go into bankruptcy.'[22] Representative Abernethy (Democrat, Mississippi) was equally clear: 'I do not shudder when anyone speaks of controls. I do not run out, get scared and frightened when they make reckless use of the word "regimenation".[23] Poage, in the same debate, argued that the choice for the farmer was between controls and rural penury as the way to control surpluses. Representative Whitten (Democrat, Mississippi) asked the House to recognize, even if reluctantly, that *laissez-faire* was no longer the guiding principle of American economic policy, and that this had to be recognized. Either everyone returns to unadulterated laws of supply and demand, or not just the farmer or the South does. 'Do those who ask farmers to be paid at world prices ask that labour be paid at world rates?'[24] Many Southern Senators have argued the same point, including the Chairman of the Senate Agriculture and Forestry Committee, Senator Talmadge:

I am a conservative man. The idea of getting government out of agriculture is basically appealing to me. But I would be a traitor to the people of my state and nation if I were a participant in such a scheme. It would be the rankest sort of discrimination to insist that the American farmer survive in a free market when other segments of our economy are not forced to do so.[25]

The attitude of the Congressional Republicans to farm subsidies needs clarification. They have not been as extreme in their hostility to price supports as Republican Secretaries of Agriculture such as Benson or Butz. But they are, nevertheless, hostile. Republican Congressmen have usually been spared the difficulty of making positive proposals because they are the apparently permanent minority party. Thus, in 1962, early Republican stragey was to do no more than oppose the Democratic proposals; after an embarrassing memo stating this became public, the Republicans were more or less forced to make a 'Declaration of Republican Principles'.[26] Though the declaration did propose ways of boosting farm income (by a programme of voluntary land retirement that probably would not work and would benefit mainly richer farmers), the statement hankered after the free market. Farm subsidy programmes should be changed so that they 'encourage' a 'shift in resources'; the emphasis was on saving American agriculture by improving marketing and distribution. The sting of the statement was in its tail; price supports should be 'adjusted' to permit the development and growth of markets and to remove the incentive for overproduction. This is a polite way of saying that prices should be lower. Thus the quest for the free market was present, though disguised. Republicans recognize that the cost of subsidies is control, and prefer not to pay it. We shall return to the importance of party ideology when we turn to voting on the floor of the House.

Unity would have been difficult for the House Agriculture Committee to achieve. Yet the example of the Ways and Means Committee, which deals with such contentious issues as Medicare, shows that greater unity and so greater influence might have been achieved by the Committee. Two reasons account for the Committee's failure to surmount the ideological divide between the parties. The first is that a very high proportion of the Committee's time has been spent discussing legislation requested by Republican and Democratic Secretaries of Agriculture who, as we have seen in Chapter 5, have dramatized the differences between the parties on this issue. The second reason is the personality of the

Democrats who have led the Committee. The former Chairman of the Agriculture Committee, Bob Poage, is far from a winning man; it was a tribute both to his politics and personality when he became one of the first committee chairmen to be voted out of office when the Democratic caucus breached the seniority principle in 1975. His predecessor, Harold Cooley, was scarcely more popular.

Indeed, the *Washington Post* attributed the defeat of the first 1962 Agriculture Bill to Cooley's rudeness to fellow Democrats. He affronted Virginia Democrats by pointedly allocating the powerful Representative Howard Smith (Democrat, Virginia) only $1\frac{1}{2}$ minutes to speak on an amendment.[27] The votes of five Virginia Democrats against the Bill were enough to turn victory into defeat. Republicans, of course, were treated with even shorter shrift than fellow Democrats, and were not encouraged to believe that they had a real opportunity to shape the content of agricultural legislation through the Committee's work.

The characteristics of the Committee's chairmen have had another effect. Both Cooley and Poage represented districts which were almost a parody of the South. Poage, for example, represents a district of Texas, the Eleventh, which produces cotton and some livestock; a one-party district, Poage has not had a Republican opponent in Congressional elections since 1936, when he secured 81 per cent of the vote. Neither has the character or appearance to appeal easily to Northern, liberal Congressmen. Poage has recognized the need to try to win the confidence of the House as a whole. For example, he introduced a symbolic limitation on the size of payments that any one farmer could receive, a move unpopular with the large-scale cotton producers of his own district, because 'though if I bring out a bill with a payment limitation, my folks back home will never forgive me', if he did not, 'some members up here (on the Hill) never will'.[28] Yet Poage continued to make the sort of blunder associated with Cooley. Relying on organized labour's help in securing votes from urban Democrats for the 1973 Agriculture Act, Poage allowed his Committee to report out a Bill with a clause denying food stamps to the families of strikers, which the unions fiercely resented.

The Committee's floor record

Political scientists versed in the literature on congressional committees would predict, from the evidence above, that the House Committee would not have a great influence on legislation. They would notice that the Committee is disunited, that most Republicans oppose most of its recommendations, and that the Committee does not foster confidence among the House as a whole. Indeed, the partisan spirit of the Committee, created by differences not so much in commodity by in ideology between the parties, guarantees the opposition of Republicans on the floor. Simultaneously, the unrepresentativeness of the Committee's Democrats (predominantly Southern and conservative on non-agricultural issues) makes it more difficult for them to enlist the support of members of their own party. Anyone who predicted that the Committee would have little authority within the House as a whole would be absolutely right. Though a Committee may maintain its influence by anticipating the wishes of the House, and may therefore not be truly 'powerful' because it does not impose its preferences on the House, a minimal condition for saying that a Committee is influential is that its proposals should usually be adopted.

The House Agriculture Committee regularly failed to carry major Farm Bills. In 1958 it failed twice to secure passage of its proposals. In 1962 the Committee saw its first Bill defeated; a modified version from Conference Committee was carried very narrowly (202 votes to 197) after intense pressure from the Administration. In 1964 the crucial vote on the Wheat/Cotton Bill was carried by only eight votes after extensive bargaining. The Committee is too weak to defend farm subsidies.

The House Appropriations Subcommittee

The Appropriations Committee, Fenno tells us,[29] likes to save money; budget-cutting is the norm. It is interesting, therefore, to ask why it did so little to save money wastefully spent on agricultural subsidies. We shall see that though the Committee follows the Appropriations norms of saving money by criticizing the Administration of the subsidy programmes, it has also emphasized defending existing programmes rather than working to improve them.

Certain points of comparison between the subcommittee and the legislative Agriculture Committee may be noted. First of all, it is small—eight members with a majority of three from the Democrats at present. Until recently when members from Colorado and Illinois were added, the Southern Democrats dominated the majority. Whitten, the Subcommittee Chairman since 1946, like Poage, is a parody of a Southern Democrat. He represents a district of the Mississippi Delta (the Second). There is a large black community—34 per cent of the population—but it has been effectively excluded from political life, which is dominated by mighty plantation owners. One might expect, therefore, that Whitten would have the same problems in securing the respect of the House that Poage and Cooley have had. That would be incorrect, and Whitten's performance shows how good generalship can compensate for a poor strategic situation.

Fenno notes that agricultural appropriations are rarely decreased by the Subcommittee or the House. Agriculture was one of two departments (the other was HEW) which accounted for the 'great bulk' (sixteen out of seventeen cases) where Appropriations gave agencies more funds than they requested. The House has supported the Subcommittee's willingness to supply funds. Fenno concludes that: 'Agriculture's friends clearly dominated on the floor as they did inside the Committee.'[30] The success of the US Department of Agriculture in obtaining funds from the Subcommittee has been the despair of the Bureau of the Budget, for whenever the Bureau has tried to reduce expenditure on agriculture the agencies affected have passed the word to the Subcommittee that they have lost out, and the Subcommittee has restored the cut. This is known as an agency making an 'end run'.

A glorious example occurred in 1958, and the Subcommittee's report to the

House during the Agriculture Appropriations's debate makes clear exactly what happened:

> The budget sent down to the sub-committee by the Bureau of the Budget provided 150 million dollars (for the Rural Electric Administration). ... In testimony before the committee the Department witnesses including the head of the R.E.A. ... testified that the original 120m. dollars was sent down to cover a half year and requests for a full year were some 350 million dollars as I recall. The committee provided 300 million dollars with 25 million dollars contingency.[31]

The Budget Bureau was steadily defeated until the late 1960s in its attempt to pare away the agricultural conservation programme which, by funding farm improvements, expanded farm production as other farm programmes paid farmers to reduce it. Congressmen found its projects, which could be scattered around the districts to grateful constituents, irresistible. As early as 1958, the Subcommittee Chairman could boast to the House that for the third time since the war the Budget Bureau had tried to cut AOP funds, and for the third time the Subcommittee had restored them.[32]

Fenno attributes the funding success of agriculture to a combination of bipartisanships and 'exceptionally widespread support for their program'.[33] Yet we have seen that support for the agricultural programmes is far from unanimous. Why then has the Appropriations Subcommittee been more successful than the legislative? The answer is partly that Congressmen want to maintain House influence over budgeting and therefore support their Subcommittee. In 1965, Langen (Republican, Minnesota) expressed his pleasure 'to see a bill before us that does not bear the stamp "Written in the White House". ... The bill under consideration today represents a substantial change from the budget recommendations submitted by the administration.'[34] It is partly, too, due to a feeling that the House, once programmes are passed, should fund them adequately.[35]

More important has been the House tradition of trying to keep party politics out of appropriations subcommittees. Republicans have been appointed who are either naturally mild consensus builders or who actively favour the agricultural programmes. H. Carl Anderson (Republican, Minnesota), for many years ranking minority members of the Subcommittee, was non-partisan that he sounded like a Democrat. Few Democrats have launched attacks as ferocious as his on the Republican Secretary of Agriculture, Benson, in 1959:

> I know of no Cabinet officer with whom I have more completely disagreed. ... Our farm economy has been in a downward trend ever since you took office. ... I cannot accept your failure to stand up for the farm people of America.[36]

Whitten noted that his views and Anderson's coincided.[37] Yet more important has been the Subcommittee's willingness to adapt to opinion in the House.

Kotz has argued that Whitten has systematically obstructed welfare programmes such as food stamps by refusing funds.[38] On the contrary, what is striking is the willingness of the Subcommittee and its Chairman in particular to make concessions to clear majorities in the House. This has sometimes involved making strategic retreats on the floor. In 1969, the Subcommittee eliminated appropriations for the school milk programme on the grounds that a more selective and hence efficient substitute had been adopted. Led by the Chairman of the legislative Committee, Poage, liberals and rural Representatives moved to restore the funds. It became obvious that there was widespread support for the amendment; Whitten quickly conferred with other members of the Subcommittee and announced, 'we have no objection to the amendment.'[39]

Indeed, far from suppressing welfare programmes, the Subcommittee has funded them more and more readily in order to pick up support. Mrs. Sullivan (Democrat, Missouri) and creator of the food stamp programme has paid tribute to Whitten:

The subcommittee on Agricultural Appropriations has generally given full support to the food stamp program, and has recommended almost every cent for the program. It has always been like pulling teeth getting anything out of the Committee on Agriculture in the way of improvements in the law; it has generally not been difficult getting the full amount from the subcommittee on Agricultural Appropriations.[40]

There is no reason to suppose that there is a liberal in Whitten struggling to get out. Indeed, he was brutally honest about the reasons why he is prepared to carry welfare programmes on the Agriculture Budget. In 1968, Whitten was asked by Latta whether programmes such as food stamps should not be carried by the Department of Health, Education, and Welfare's (HEW) Budget rather than the US Department of Agriculture's. Whitten replied:

... from a consideration of the law angle, I would agree with the gentleman that there are many things that are possibly carried in this bill that should not be charged to agriculture. But at the same time, we have had the burden of trying to get this bill through the Congress, and each year it becomes more difficult. At present we have 47 out of 435 districts that contain as much as 20% farmers. There is considerable doubt in my mind whether if we did not have some of these programs in the Department of Agriculture that affect the whole country, we could not get a shirt-tail's worth of support to pass this program. . . . Possibly these programs are of some help to some of our friends in realising the necessity of this bill. For that reason alone I believe it necessary to keep these items in the bill.[41]

While urban Representatives are kept in line by throwing in welfare programmes, rural Representatives should be kept together by linking the legislative fate of all commodities:

While a commodity by commodity approach may be sound, I trust that you will realise that we need to have all the commodities in one bill legislatively. We must all pull together. If you let the sugar people out, they have no interest in the common problem thereafter. If you let the diary people out, they have no interest. We have seen this kind of thing happen. . . . In other words, we must support one bill . . . otherwise we haven't any chance to pass anything.[42]

The solidarity of the Subcommittee, its reputation for winning any contested votes on the floor, and the well-founded impression of expertise fostered by unity have given the Subcommittee great influence over the general direction of thought on agricultural policy, particularly within the US Department of Agriculture. Chairman Whitten has, by his extraordinary knowledge of agricultural legislation, developed by hard work over thirty years and by the trust among the subcommittees which he has fostered, secured the right to exercise this right personally on behalf of the Subcommittee. It was not surprising that Whitten, though at least as conservative as Poage, survived the purge of committee chairmen in 1975.

Kotz has provided us with several examples of the way in which officials of the US Department of Agriculture hold Whitten in awe. Secretary Freeman used to tell his staff, 'I've got to get along with two people in Washington—the President and Jamie Whitten. How can you help me with Whitten?'[43] Surveys by the US Department of Agriculture which could have embarrassed Whitten, e.g. on the extent of malnutrition in Mississippi, were deliberately suppressed. When Secretary Benson failed to use legal powers at his disposal as Whitten wished; the Chairman called him before the Agriculture Appropriations Subcommittee and abused him soundly. One instance came when Secretary Benson, conscious of the general trade policy of the Administration, refused to dump surpluses of cotton on world markets. Dissatisfied with the explanation, Whitten attacked Benson for failing to obey congressional instructions. 'I was formerly a district attorney,' Whitten told the Secretary, 'and I have seen a lot of people who broke the law, and I have never seen one that didn't have an excuse.'[44] A year earlier, in 1958, Whitten used the annual appropriations procedure as a general seminar on farm policy, at which he brought great pressure to bear on the Secretary to change the whole direction of his policy. Though Benson did not change his approach, the episode was a graphic demonstration of the influence that the 'Opposition' can exert on policy through the prerogatives of Congress.[45]

Representative Whitten has a clear, though simple, conception of his Subcommittee's purpose: 'to attempt to get funds and results for the Nation's agriculture'.[46] Whitten is convinced that the farm subsidy laws are merely fair compensation for the distortions in the economy caused by labour bargaining and the ability of industry to fix prices.[47] Above all, farm subsidies are nothing to do with welfare or redistributive politics. Indeed, Whitten argues it is not the small farmer but the large-scale producer with a lot of capital invested (men not unlike the plantation owners in his own district) who need help the most. Because Whitten sees his role as that of defender of the inefficient and socially regressive farm subsidy laws, he has rendered those laws a signal service. An Appropriations Subcommittee can be a valuable forum for those who dislike a programme over whose funds it presides. Enjoying the real power to vary a budget and armed with the expertise obtained through pouring over the detailed accounts of the relevant agency each year, a Subcommittee concerned to attack the waste of America's farm laws could have achieved much. By defining its role as that of defender of the subsidy laws, not critic, the Subcommittee has staved off a possibly serious threat to their existence.

It is important to emphasize, however, that Whitten and his supporters on the

Subcommittee have exercised influence, not control. The whole trend towards direct subsidy payments, traced in Chapter 5, is one which Whitten finds most unwelcome. Whitten has also had to live with schemes such as cropland retirement, which he dislikes. But most clearly of all, Whitten's *bête noire*, a limitation on the total of subsidy payments which any one farmer could receive, has been passed into law. Indeed, amendments providing for payment limitations had been added to Appropriation Bills by the House since 1967, but the Senate had rejected them; in conference with the Senate, Whitten and his chosen conferees concurred in the Senate version. Payment limitation, though pioneered in House Agriculture Appropriations debates, had to wait until the 1970 Agriculture Act, but it is significant that long before this the Subcommittee had been steadily defeated on the issue in the House. Counter to Kotz's view that Whitten has some sort of veto, the truth is that if a majority of the House know what they want, they can achieve it in spite of subcommittee—or committee—opposition. Whitten's influence is usually based on making concessions (e.g. on food stamps) which he has to make to keep the trust of the House on other issues. When an issue such as agricultural conservation payments is arcane when members of the House know nothing about it and suspect they care less, Whitten's influence is strong. As soon as an issue attracts attention, Whitten either has to accommodate to the majority or face defeat. The genius of Jamie Whitten is that by yielding sufficiently quickly and gracefully to the House when faced with defeat, much of his Subcommittee's work does not attract the attention of the House. If Whitten was more obstinate he would be more often defeated, his Subcommittee less trusted, and its freedom of action considerably reduced. Whitten's power is based on willingness to withdraw. Had the House as a whole turned against farm subsidies, Whitten could have done little.

The Senate Agriculture Committee

One might expect that the Senate Agriculture and Forestry Committee would be rather like the House Committee, if only because it deals with the same legislation. In fact, there is a remarkable contrast in style between them.

Fenno offers a succinct summary of the differences between the House and Senate Committees: 'Senate Committees are less important as a source of Chamber influence, less preoccupied with success on the chamber floor, less personally expert, less strongly led, and more individualistic in decision making than are House Committees.'[48] Most of these points are applicable to the Senate Agriculture Committee. In addition, the Senate's Committee is much less partisan and much less divided by commodity interests than is the House's. Unlike Congressmen, Senators practise classic logrolling tactics on agricultural legislation, whereby all commodities can have something as long as the responsible Senators support the package. Unlike the House Committee, the Senate's is characterized by unity—by shared assumptions and objectives, mutual tolerance, and willingness to accommodate Senators' constituency interests.

Internal organization of the Committee

The Committee is characterized by no formal but high informal decentralization. That is, there are only six subcommittees and all deal with uncontroversial topics. On the other hand, it is traditional to defer to the views of Senators representing states in which a commodity is concentrated. Thus when in 1973 the Agriculture and Forestry Committee, in the absence of Administration programmes, drafted the new Agriculture Act, *ad hoc* subcommittees of the Committee were formed on the basis of commodity, and irrespective of party. The wheat section was drafted, for example, by Republican Senators Dole and Milton Young.[48] This emphasis on commodity, not party, was nothing new. Ripley reported the comment on an anonymous Senator: 'I never think who is on the Agriculture Committee, I think of it in crops, and I think right where they sit at the table. We start with rice, cotton, sugar, tobacco, peanuts, broilers and then you have a little wheat in there.'[50] Today wheat has progressed higher up the table with McGovern's increasing seniority. Hubert Humphrey complained bitterly when, for once, in 1958, the tradition of leaving commodities to their Senators was not followed:

In the Senate Committee on Agriculture and Forestry I said to my colleagues: 'If you want to mess around with cotton and rice because they are produced in areas you represent *that is your privilege. But do not tell the farmers of my state that they are not entitled to a better shake* than the one this bill provides' (emphasis added).[51]

The failure of the Committee to follow the principle of allowing Senators to write programmes for their commodities caused considerable criticism on the floor. Senators felt that failure to follow the usual practice had caused non-Southern commodities to be sacrificed to getting Southern programmes passed by Benson and Eisenhower. An angy Democratic Senator Douglas called the Bill 'a monstrosity' and demanded a more equitable share-out:

I am not here to logroll but whenever everybody else is under the mistletoe and is being accepted but corn and soya beans [important in his state] are left out, then in self defiance I must protect the commodities grown in my state and the farmers who grow them.[52]

Southern Senators who supported the Bill did so because, without it, production allotments for commodities produced in their states would have been sharply reduced by the Republican Administration to the detriment of their constituents. They were deeply apologetic about forcing an unacceptable Bill on their colleagues.

Leadership

Not surprisingly, this tradition of logrolling and devolution has been accompanied by a tradition of mild chairmanship. Though the Senate Chairman has the same prerogatives as the House Chairman, he is not expected to use them as harshly. Thus it is clear that Senator Ellender profoundly disapproved of the shift towards direct subsidy payments in the 1964 Wheat/Cotton Act. But it is equally clear that he made no effort to impede progress on the Bill, let alone prevent it reaching the floor. His opponents paid generous tributes. McGovern, introducing the wheat section on the floor, said:

I should like to take this opportunity to thank the chairman ... despite his personal views in opposition to some portions of the Bill, the Senator from Louisiana conducted extended hearings and committee sessions and worked more diligently than any other member of the committee.[53]

In 1965, the situation was repeated. Again Ellender's views did not prevail; again he yielded gracefully; and Senators Talmadge, Carlson, Bass, and Miller paid handsome tributes. Miller thanked the Chairman for his fairness: 'each member of the committee has been given complete discretion as to the amount of time devoted to questions ... each member was given ample time to set forth his views.'[54] Replying, Ellender conceded that he did not like the Bill, but said that he had been unable to persuade the Committee. It is uncommon for a House Committee to be run in so relaxed a way.

This is not to argue that the Chairman has no influence. The rapid progress of proposals for deficiency payments (paying farmers a supplement to the market price per unit sold) when Talmadge replaced Ellender is probably significant. Talmadge, in alliance with Hubert Humphrey, had pushed deficiency payments in the 1950s, but they were given little serious consideration until 1972–73. Both chairmen were, of course, Southerners. Allen J. Ellender (Democrat, Louisiana) had been Huey Long's lieutenant; he therefore did not need persuading that strong government was legitimate. Talmadge, too, has represented a Southern state, Georgia, touched by the populist tradition for it was Tom Watson's home. Elected with a reputation as a conservative, Talmadge's natural base is in the rural rather than the urban part of the state. Talmadge's rural base inclines him to support farm programmes; he reconciles any conflict with conservative views, as we have seen, by viewing subsidies merely as compensation for such measures as the minimum wage.

The atmosphere of the Senate Agriculture and Forestry Committee is completely free from the partisan feeling and tension that has split its House counterpart. This is noticeable even among its staff, whereas the Republican Counsel and Democratic Counsel to the House Committee rarely speak to each other and are clearly not on good terms, the two Senate Committee Counsels invariably draft Bills together and wonder why feelings should run high in the House.[55] The answer is that though the Senate divides on the *methods* of agricultural support, the ideological conflict so obvious in the House over the proper role of government is clearly absent. Dissenting from the 1965 Committee report, Senator Miller (Republican, Iowa) argued: 'I have said many times that there are few Members ... who advocate doing away with farm programs. ... Those who speak of the danger of Congress doing away with farm programs are merely throwing up a straw-man to frighten farmers.'[56] No member of the House could so argue. The split over the methods of support does not follow neat party lines; Democrat Senators Spessard Holland (Florida) and Clinton Anderson (New

Mexico) were as severe critics of high prices and mandatory controls as Benson. Similarly, Republicans were vehemently opposed to Benson's plans for a free market; in 1958 Republican Senator Aiken (Vermont) and ranking minority member joined with Democratic Senators in criticizing Benson so fiercely that he could hardly complete his presentation.[57]

In short, the Senate Committee does conform to the pattern which we expected to find fitted the House Committee but did not. That is, Senators representing different agricultural commodity areas work together to provide subsidy programmes for each others' constituents. In general, Senators defer to each others' judgement on what is best for their states, and the fact that six of the eight Democratic majority are from Southern states has no doubt meant that the Southern commodities have done particularly well.

We shall attempt to explain this striking difference between the bitterly divided House Committee and logrolling Senate later.

The Committee's floor record

Fenno's findings that Senate Committees are less influential than their House counterparts is difficult to apply to the case of agriculture, if only because of the meagre success of the House Committee.[58] Yet even if the Senate Committee does not suffer from the distrust and even antipathy which attends its House counterpart, it has no more control over events. Because farming of one sort or another is a significant source of employment in almost every state, every Senator is either interested personally or has a member of his staff keeping a watching brief. Senators, in brief, are convinced that farm laws are too important to be left to the Agriculture Committee.

The Senate has shown itself, therefore, very ready to make very significant changes in Bills its Committee has reported. In 1962, for example, the Senate took the advice of the Administration and the Committee's Chairman in restoring to the first Agriculture Bill of that year the controversial plan for strict controls of feed grain production. With no sense of the alleged enormity of amending Committee proposals, the Senate went on to make another twelve changes in the Committee proposals. Not content with this, the Senate made ten changes of some consequence in the second version of the Bill the Committee reported after the demise in the House of the early Bill. In 1965, the Senate made a smaller number of changes in the Committee's version of the Agriculture Act of that year,[59] but they were of considerable importance as they completely changed the cotton and wheat sections. The Senate continued to demonstrate its willingness to amend in 1970, and thereby demonstrated the weakness of the Committee.

One sort of amendment which the Senate has no wish to adopt is that which would phase out agricultural subsidies. When Senator Buckley offered an amendment to the 1973 Agriculture Bill to phase out agricultural subsidies by 1977, he could attract the support of a motley bag of only thirteen colleages, in spite of the fact that his amendment embodied the official policy of the Administration. Significantly, though Buckley attracted the support of some Eastern Democrats

(Ribicoff and Pell), he failed to mobilize the conservative wing of the Republican party effectively, which would have constituted the basis of his following in the House.

The conclusion is obvious. The strength of agriculture in the Senate is not the farmers' grip on the Agriculture and Forestry Committee, for that Committee's authority is limited. It is to be found on the floor of the Senate. It is true that the Committee would impede any attempt to repeal the agricultural subsidy, laws, but in so doing it would be acting with the whole-hearted consent of the Senate. If the Committee were out of line with the Senate, the Senate would reject its proposals.

The Senate Agriculture Appropriations Committee

There is little to be said about this Subcommittee which is not implicit in our account so far. We have noted already the tendency of Senate appropriations sub-committees to restore cuts made by the House. Fenno[60] points to the fact that whereas the Senate usually increases cuts made by the House, in the case of agriculture, appropriations are increased by the House and further increased by the Senate. Fenno notes that to increase an appropriation not cut by the House is quite unusual and the mark of a programme having considerable political support. The Subcommittee works more closely with its legislative counterpart and the Chairman, ranking majority and ranking minority members of the legislative committee, are *ex officio* on the Subcommittee. It is interesting to note that the Sub-committee not only has a more equal geographic representation of status than the others dealing with agriculture, but that the balance is achieved across party lines. That is, the interests of the wheat-producing states are entrusted to two Republicans (Young and Mundt) and no Democrat from the major wheat states is on the Subcommittee. This reflects a low level of partisan feeling, and this is clear, too, in the Subcommittee's hearing. The Senators delight in complimenting each other on the bipartisan way in which they rally round on the subsidies, as the following exchange makes clear:

Senator Holland (Chairman): ... the sections of this committee have always been bipar-tisan. We have stuck together before the full (Appropriations) Committee and on the floor. Senator Young (Ranking Republican): I don't know of a time we have divided on party lines. You get so used to working in a bipartisan way that sometimes people in your own state wonder what has happened to you.[61]

Senator Hruska (Nebraska), too, was a conservative Republican, but when he succeeded Mundt he made no attempt to disturb the cosy consensus, but rather worked to supplement it:

'Affluent Society' is a mockery for farmers. ... Sometimes I hear it said that if all the so-called farm subsidies were cut, it would make the job of budget balancing easier. If we should liquidate the farm programs and liquidate the farmer also, would we not thereby be liquidating and destroying our food supply also? The farmer is losing ground fast enough.[62]

The impact of the committee system

In his vignette, 'How the farmers get what they want', Theodore Lowi attaches a crucial role to the agriculture committees. Because they are all composed of Representatives of the farm interest, Lowi argues, the agricultural legislation before Congress is effectively decided by Representatives of those who will benefit from it.[63] Agricultural policy is formulated by a farmer-orientated coalition of interest groups, the Department of Agriculture, and Representatives and Senators on the agriculture committees representing rural areas.

The evidence here suggests that any explanation of how the farmers get what they want which rests on the power of agriculture committees in Congress is radically wrong. For a variety of reasons, the legislative agriculture committees were not in control of events. The weakness of the House Committee is related to its disunity (caused ultimately by ideological differences) and its unrepresentativeness of the House as a whole. Its Recommendations were regularly discarded. So, too, were the recommendations of the Senate Agriculture and Forestry Committee, though this was due more to the generally weak authority of Senate committees than to any flaws in the Committee itself. Only in the case of the appropriations committees did we find examples of committees which seemed to have the sort of influence that the classical account of the strength of congressional committees suggests. Even the appropriations committees had limited influence, however. The most powerful of the congressional committees on agriculture which we encountered, the House Agriculture Appropriations Sub-committee, retained its authority only by taking care to act in a way which was acceptable to a majority of the House.

It seems, therefore, that Congress's role as the rock on which attempts to reform the subsidy system have foundered is not explained by the autonomous power of its Agriculture Committee but by the political power of farmers in the House and Senate as a whole. We shall dig deeper therefore by examining the way in which farm subsidy legislation attracts the support of a majority of the entire House and Senate.

Floor votes on subsidies

There were, according to the 1970 Census, only fourteen congressional districts in which 'acutal farm population' accounted for more than 20 per cent of the residents. Even if we use the low, and necessarily arbitrary, cut-off point which commentators such as *Congressional Quarterly* employ to decide whether or not a district is rural (5 per cent or more of the population living and working on farms), there are still only 134. Only twelve members of the Senate and thirty-four of the House of Representatives are themselves farmers.[64]

Not only has Congress not repealed the agricultural subsidy laws but it has passed improvements to them with regularity. In 1958, 1961, 1964, 1965, 1970, and 1973, Congress adopted new farm laws, demonstrating that the political power of agriculture in Congress extends beyond the agriculture committees.

How, when the primary effect of all these acts has been to transfer money from the majority of America's population to the farming minority, has it been possible to find a majority for these Acts in either the House or Senate?

We shall look for the answer first in the House and then in the Senate.

The House

Three plausible explanations can be outlined. The first is that Representatives from rural areas act as a bipartisan block, voting for policies which benefit urban America in return for farm subsidy laws. The historical example which demonstrates the plausibility of this strategy is the farm bloc in the Senate in the 1920s, which was prepared to bring the Senate's work to a standstill until subsidy laws were obtained.

The second plausible explanation is that outlined by Mayhew, in his stimulating study of roll-call voting in the House of Representatives:

It is important to ask why the farm laws were kept on the books at all. If the actions of Congressmen were governed by a crude reading of constituency interest, the farmer would have been abandoned by the federal government some time ago. The answer, at least in these sixteen postwar years, is that party pressures intervened to magnify the power of the congressional farm minority. In this period of declining farm population, the commodity programmes were sustained in the House by the propensity of Democrats from urban and industrial districts to support them by deferring to their rural colleagues.[65]

Mayhew argues that Congressmen can be expected consistently to support laws which bring their own districts material benefits. However, the Democratic party, as the party which has held a majority in the House for all but four of the postwar years, has developed a skill or instinct which goes beyond this. Representatives from districts which have differing interests have learnt to support each others' pet interests. There is, in short, recurring logrolling within the Democratic party. Urban Democrats, therefore, vote for farm subsidies and rural Democrats hopefully reciprocate by voting for laws which will help the cities. (Mayhew shows that in fact the rural Democrats have not kept this bargain very well, which is not surprising because most of them are Southerners.)

The final plausible explanation we shall consider for the ability of farm subsidy laws to command a majority in a House more and more dominated since the reapportionment cases[66] by Representatives from the cities and suburbs is party competition. It is possible that urban Representatives of both parties have backed farm subsidy laws so that their party could expand its strength in the countryside. Thus, just as British political parties have been mesmerized by the supposed strategic importance of a handful of rural marginals, Republican attempts to break into the South and Democratic assaults on the Midwest have induced urban Representatives to vote for farm subsidies to prove that their party is the true friend of the farmer.

We can, in fact, discard nearly all of these explanations by looking at the recorded attitudes of Congressmen to farm legislation. In the section which follows, we shall look at the potential support for farm laws as revealed mainly by roll-call votes, but supplemented by such declarations of support or opposition as being paired for or against a Bill. In all cases which are mentioned, the criterion used for deciding whether or not a district is rural or non-rural (urban or suburban) are those of the *Congressional Quarterly Almanac*, outlined in the volumes for 1957 and 1963. All the material used in this section is reproduced in tables in the Appendix.

The primary lesson of the tables is that the farm subsidy laws have split Congress more along party lines than on any other. In the first vote on the Agriculture Bills of 1958, for example, of the 222 Congressmen who favoured the proposals to continue subsidies at a high level, 191 were Democrats (Table 11). Of those voting against (196), 169 were Republicans. A similar pattern emerged in the same year when the House voted against high subsidies by refusing a rule for a Bill reported by the House Agriculture Committee. Of the 201 Congressmen who favoured the Bill, 179 were Democrats, and of the 232 who opposed the bill, 173 were Republicans (Table 12). In 1962, the Kennedy Farm Bill which provided for high subsidies cleared Congress when the Act narrowly cleared the House of Representatives. Of the 225 Congressmen who favoured accepting the report, 220 were Democrats; all but five Republicans opposed it (Table 14). This repeated, with marginal adjustments, the pattern of the earlier vote of that year when the House voted against high subsidies (Table 13). The year 1964 witnessed another narrow vote on farm subsidies, when the innovative Wheat/Cotton Bill was squeezed past the House by 14 votes. Of those in favour of the Bill (including pairings), 212 were Democrats, and of the 210 opposed, 167 were Republicans (Table 15). Ninety-four per cent of the votes for subsidies came from Democrats. Finally, in 1970, when the Democratic leadership of the House Agriculture Committee and the Republican Administration negotiated a compromise, which continued subsidies at a high level, an attempt was made to kill the Bill by referring it back to Committee. The move foundered on the opposition of 228 Representatives of whom 151 were Democrats; of the 198 Congressmen opposing this Administration-backed Bill, 112 were Republican (Table 16).

Constituency influence

It is important to compare the impact of party with that of constituency influence. Our task here is aided considerably by the work which the influential *Congressional Quarterly* has done to identify those Congressmen whose districts contain a significant proportion of farmers. Until 1964, the *Congressional Quarterly* contented itself with identifying those districts in which 5 per cent or more of the population were engaged in agriculture; after 1963, the redistribution of seats which followed the usual census and the effects of rural depopulation caused the *Congressional Quarterly* to adopt a more restrictive definition. As the trends are clear in both the pre- and post-1963 techniques, the results have been subsumed into one table and, for the sake of simplicity, the adjective 'rural' is used

Table 9   Positions of rural Republicans on Bills to continue farm subsidies

	1958 (ii)	1962 (i)	1962 (ii)	1964	1970
For	22	1	5	4	8
Against	99	111	105	20	13

to refer to all Congressmen representing districts in which, by either measure, the *Congressional Quarterly* detected a significant farm interest.

In every vote except 1970, Republicans with substantial farming interests in their districts voted by sizeable margins against agricultural subsidies.

Equally startling is the tendency for urban Democrats to favour farm subsidy laws which operate against the immediate material interest of their constituents. Clearly, though urban Democrats have varied in the unanimity with which they have supported farm subsidies, they have been more stalwart than rural Republicans in supporting farm subsidy laws.

Table 10   Positions of urban Democrats on Bills to continue farm subsidies

	1958 (ii)	1962 (i)	1962 (ii)	1964	1970
For	49	108	112	185	137
Against	57	19	9	42	80

What sort of politics does this represent? Clearly, it represents none of the plausible explanations for the success in the House of farm subsidy laws that were outlined above. It cannot represent the politics of a bipartisan farm block, for the major feature of voting on Farm Bills was the steady opposition of the Republicans. Nor, for the same reason, can the success of Farm Bills be explained by party competition; the Republicans did not compete. Even Mayhew's explanation for the success of Farm Bills support by a coalition of rural Republicans and Democrats backed by the urban wing of the Democratic party founders on the simple objection that most rural Republicans have consistently opposed proposals for high subsidies.

The basic feature of voting on Farm Bills in the House which requires explanation is why Democrats from both town and country rallied to support the Bills and Republicans as consistently opposed them. We may imagine two explanations for this phenomenon. The first would be that the farm laws are the result of bargaining between rural and urban Democrats. Rural Democrats, who are predominantly from the Southern wing of the party, exchange their votes on policies of benefit to the cities in exchange for urban votes for farm subsidies. Farm laws are, therefore, the result of bargaining, but it is *intra*-party, not *inter*-party, bargaining. The proponents of this explanation could point, too, to the fact that 'Democratic' commodities seem better served than 'Republican', suggesting that rural Democrats have been anxious merely to look after their constituents, and not farming in general. Another explanation, however, would be that the reason why nearly all Republicans, irrespective of their constituency interest, have opposed the farm subsidy laws which most Democrats have supported is that the issue touches on an issue of principle or even, to use the much overworked word, ideology, which divides the parties. This explanation is slightly heretical because it implies that ideas are important in American politics, something writers on the subject, particularly if they are American, are keen to deny. Nevertheless, we shall see that, as is so often the case in the social sciences, there is some evidence to support each theory.

Evidence of bargaining between urban and rural Democrats is easy to find. We have, indeed, come across one important example already—the use by Jamie Whitten and the Agriculture Appropriations Sub-committee of food stamps, which entitle the poor to food at reduced prices, to ease the passage of appropriations for farm subsidies by putting both programmes into the same Appropriations Bill. The votes of urban Democrats, who want food stamps, are thus secured for farm subsidies, while the rural Southern Democrats, who want farm subsidies, are forced to vote simultaneously for food stamps. It was, indeed, this strategy which secured the adoption of food stamps in the first place. In a case study of the deal, Randall Ripley rightly notes the informality with which it was made:

Gradually, during March, it became clear that the trade would involve the food stamp bill and the wheat/cotton bill (of 1964). No formal announcement was made of such a trade. Indeed, no formal meeting was held at which leaders of urban and rural blocs agreed on it. Instead, and this is typical of the operations of the House, it was a matter of favourable psychological advantage. The more the individual members and the press talked about a specific trade of rural votes on food stamps for urban votes on wheat/cotton, the more firmly the exchange became rooted in the minds of the members. It was in short based on shared perceptions of the legislative situation in the House. This was bolstered by individual lobbying efforts relying on it as a persuasive point. Thus, Birkhead (Congressional Liaison Officer of the U.S.D.A.) and (Secretary) Freeman . . . lobbyists for the various parts of the cotton industry and Democratic Senator James O. Eastland of Mississippi all made extensive contacts and used this argument.[67]

One reason why this bargaining in 1964 needed so little formal arranging was that it takes place so regularly. The *Congressional Record* contains many appeals to Democrats from their colleagues to honour implicit bargains. Thus McCormack (Democrat, Massachusetts) made a strong appeal for rural–urban trades when he was Majority Leader:

I think the record should show that throughout the years, members from non-agricultural districts, members from the city districts, have always appreciated the importance of farmers and agriculture to the way of life of our country, and we have supported farm legislation. On many occasions, the city vote has not only supported farm legislation, but on a number of occasions has actually saved farm legislation. In the next few days when legislation comes up that is of great concern to the cities, we know, at least we hope, that our friends from agricultural areas will reciprocate and look on that legislation with an understanding mind.[68]

McCormack's plea echoed the call of Representative Anfuso (Democrat, New York) in 1958:

I have always supported farm legislation and I do not have a single farm in my district. . . . At the same time, I must caution you that we as representatives from the cities do not want this to be a one way street. If we support you (rural Democrats) in legislation, we expect some kind of consideration.[69]

In 1970 Representative Obey (Democrat, Wisconsin) reversed the plea:

I have not been here very long, but in the time I have been here, I have many times seen urban members of this House ask for support from rural congressmen (on issues) which are not at all understood in rural America. Today I am asking my colleagues to turn the coin around.[70]

There are certain facts, however, which explanations of the adoption of farm laws through bargaining do not successfully account for. One is why rural Republicans have not been in on the trade. The other is why both rural and urban Republicans have opposed the farm laws with such vehemence.

The trouble with roll-call analysis is that it presents votes under headings which are all too simplistic. Thus our analysis so far presents us with almost incomprehensible facts, such as rural Republicans voting against Farm Subsidy Bills. We must return to the point which arose during our discussion of the House Committee; Farm Bills raised major issues of principle for Republicans. In particular, there were two aspects of farm subsidy laws which worried Republicans. The first is that farm subsidy laws seemed an almost perfect example of inefficient 'big spending, big government' which Republicans love to attack. If there is one cause to which Republicans steadily dedicate themselves, it is opposing the growth of government activity. The traditional cry of the Republican, at least since the secession of the Progressives in 1912, has been that a problem is best left to the beneficent workings of a free-enterprise system. If government action is truly unavoidable, then it is better handled by state rather than federal authorities. Farm subsidy laws, which, as Republicans could rightly argue, lead to inefficiency and do almost nothing to help the poor farmer, seemed a perfect example of the evils of federal government out of control.

The second aspect of farm subsidy laws which offended Republicans was that their inevitable concomitant was close government control of production. If the market system was not allowed to avoid surpluses by reducing the price, and hence profitability, of agricultural commodities, it was certain that the government would try to avoid surpluses by strict physical controls. Shonfield noted[71] the paradox that the United States, supposedly the land of *laissez-faire*, had, in its farm laws, draconian controls of how much its farmers could produce, under what conditions, and of how much they could market. These restrictions were the inevitable consequence of the attempt to keep farm prices above the market level. Without controls, the United States would have been flooded with surpluses and the cost of farm policies would have been astronomical. But the inevitability of controls did not alter the fact that Republicans, with their commitment to minimal government activity, found these controls deeply (almost morally) objectionable. So objectionable in fact did even rural Republicans find these controls that they felt that it would be better for their constituents to have low incomes and freedom than tutelage and prosperity.

The congressional debates on farm subsidies are dotted, therefore, with highly principled speeches from Republicans objecting to the degree of government involvement in the industry. Representative Quie (Republican, Minnesota) voted against the 1962 Kennedy Farm Bill because he saw this issue as being whether or not agriculture would take the path of 'regimentation and control'.[72] Representative Paul Findley (Republican, Illinois) was more emphatic in his warnings about the sinister purposes of Farm Bills: 'This bill (the Kennedy Bill) is but a skirmish, it is skirmish in a long range assault on the private enterprise system.'[73] Even in 1958, when Benson's *laissez-faire* policies were not exactly popular, Representative Miller (Republican, Nebraska) argued:

I think all of us would recognise that the only true solution to the farm problem will be when we get the farmer back on the old law of supply and demand, the day when he will be free of Government subsidies, Government handouts, and Government interference.[74]

If the Republicans have seen in the farm laws serious issues of principle, or 'ideology', which caused them to attack the farm subsidy laws, the Democrats have seen in them principles to defend. The basic principle which both urban, liberal and Southern 'conservative' Democrats have defended in their advocacy of the farm laws is that the government has a duty to mitigate the effects on the farmer of the effects of a market economy. Both the Southern and non-Southern sections of the Democratic party are much more favourably disposed to government intervention in the economy than are Republicans. It is true that the South may be less enthusiastic about expanding the role of federal government than Northern Democrats, but particularly when it has been the beneficiary of government intervention in the economy (as with the Tennessee Valley Authority) it has found any scruples easy to swallow. In particular, farm laws can easily be portrayed as simple justice, giving the farmer the collective power to regulate this output and prices which business and labour already enjoy through collusive price fixing and trade unions. Chairman Cooley voiced both Southern doubts about a free market economy and this quest for justice when he spoke in the debate on the Kennedy Farm Bill:

Everywhere there is an effort to balance supply and demand. Labour has learned the same thing. All other segments of our economy do this. Why should not the farmer have the same right to do it? Do you want to go back to the days of 1931? I was farming then, and that is what finally convinced me that I had better sit under the electric fan in town because it is so much more comfortable than farming in that free economy.[75]

Northern Democrats, with their history of being the dominant force behind the expansion of the role of government in American society, find appeals from Southerners to the superiority a regulated, rather than the free, market economy almost irresistible. Urban Democrats can be won over by farm subsidy laws by an argument which would be expressed in student politics by the clain that 'their struggle is our struggle'. (The claim should always be disbelieved.) Spokesmen for farmers can always couple the farm subsidy laws with the liberal reforms of the New Fair Deals, dear to the hearts of urban liberal Democrats, as joint examples of the need for government to step in to redress the balance of the market-place. The enemies of farm subsidies are the enemies of every other humanitarian policy which involves government intervention in the economy. It was Senator Proxmire who made this claim most explicitly:

The economic interests and the philosphy that are behind today's attack on the principle of parity for farmers were not less opposed to other fundamental reformers initiated a quarter of a century ago (i.e. the New Deal). They have not dared attack these programmes (social security, minimum wage) head on. But their enmity for programs to help America's ordinary citizens is as unrepentant and unregenerate today as it was when they fought with all their strength against the early farm legislation, social security, and all the rest.[76]

Democrats do not have the Republicans' faith in the self-correcting qualities of the market economy. They accept, therefore, that even if their district does not suffer immediately from a farm recession, that recession will not be limited to rural America, but will snowball. The saying that 'Every Depression has been farm bred and farm led' is often quoted in Democratic circles. Urban Democrats who want to avoid a recession, therefore, should start by voting for farm subsidy laws, and any recession which does occur just shows how inadequate farm subsidies are.

Victor Anfuso, the Democrat from the heart of New York, argued this in 1958: 'This depression did not just start. It started four years ago with the farmers and now it is hitting the towns and the cities because the purcashing power of the farmers, our best consumers, has been destroyed.'[77] Representative O'Hara (Democrat, Chicago) added his voice:

Mine is not an agricultural district. All of the second district of Illinois is in the city of Chicago, but the city and the farm are closely related, and we in the city never forget that if things go wrong on the farm, the harm will sooner or later come to the city and vice versa.[78]

Santangelo, the solitary urban member of the Agriculture Appropriations Sub-committee, rushed to agree: 'The welfare of the farmer is intimately connected with the welfare and dignity of the labourer in the city and the industrialist who makes the tools. Our activities are intertwined.'[79]

We can, in short, explain the politics of agricultural subsidies in the House as successfully in terms of a clash between *laissez-faire* Republicans and interventionist Democrats as we can in terms of bargaining within the Democratic party.[80] Do we have to choose, however, between the two explanations? We do not.

The elementary key to striking a good bargain is to get what you want at the lowest possible cost. In Congress, this means obtaining the votes of one's fellow Representatives for one's favourite measure, and, in return, promising to vote for a measure about which you are indifferent or, at worst, find only mildly objectionable. A bad bargain is one where you pay a high price, such as voting for a measure you have long opposed in return for the help of your colleagues on your favourite Bill. In short, if people behave rationally, bargains take place between people who are already close to agreement, and do not take place between people who are apart. The reason for this is that the costs of bargaining are less for people who are close to agreement than for people who are apart.

Bargaining takes place between Democrats because Democrats on both wings of the party are, on balance, more likely to agree with each other than with the Republicans. Even in contentious votes on liberal issues such as the poverty programme (7 August, 1964), rent supplements for the poor (29 March, 1966), wheat sales to the USSR (16 December, 1966), and even the Voting Rights Act (9 July, 1965), House Southern Democrats gave the liberals more help than did Republicans. The bargains within the Democratic party, such as that which maintains the farm laws, rest on the ideological basis that Democrats have more in common with each other than with Republicans.

The role of constituency interest

As the Democrats have had a majority in the House since 1954, if the alliance that is the Democratic Party had, buttressed by both ideology and bargaining, worked perfectly, then Democratic Secretaries of Agriculture and the House Committee would not have had so much trouble getting their legislation adopted. Though the analysis of votes on Farm Bills contained in the tables in Appendix A can be used to illustrate how an alliance, overwhelmingly composed of Democrats, was strong enough to pass farm legislation, they can be used also to illustrate the weaknesses of that coalition. The forces which the Democratic party could rally to enact the subsidy laws were not united behind any detailed programme. Indeed, so loosely were the Democrats allied on farm issues that there was always the possibility, or even probability, that some Democrats would defect to the Republican enemy.

The first, and most predictable, group of rebels came from among the urban Democrats. Though most urban (non-rural) Democrats went along with farm subsidies, there were groups (sometimes large groups) of Democrats from the cities who did not. In the vote on the Second Farm Bill of 1958, almost as many urban Democrats opposed the Subsidy Bill as supported it. (The split was 59 votes to 47.) In the vote for Kennedy's First Farm Bill of 1962, a crucial minority, 20, or urban Democrats joined with the Republicans, giving them the victory. Even in 1964, after all the bargaining over wheat/cotton legislation in return for food stamps, a quarter of the urban Democrats voted against the Subsidy Bill.

The temptation for urban Democrats to follow their immediate constituency interest by voting against pouring money down the throats of ungrateful farmers at the expense of the constituents was obvious. It is, of course, easy to lampoon the farm subsidy laws, too. The thought of voting for a Bill which would give rich cotton plantation owners such as Senator Eastland $1 million a year for promising not to grow anything is obviously hard for a Northern Democrat to accept. The wonder is that so many did. Nevertheless, the possibility of an urban Democratic rebellion if a Subsidy Bill was too much of a 'give away' to the farmers circumscribed the freedom of action of policy makers in one crucial respect. The option of easing production controls in order to attract rural Republican support was closed by the insistence of urban Democrats, whose votes were equally important, that the cost of farm subsidies should be kept within bounds.

The second group of rebels came, surprisingly, from among rural Democrats. The proportion of Democratic Representatives with a significant proportion of farmers among their electorate who voted against Farm Subsidy Bills was usually tiny—12 out of 115 in 1958, for example. However, in one year, 1962, 34 out of 98 and 32 out of 108 rural Democrats refused to support the Kennedy Subsidy Bill. All but five of these rebels were from Southern or Border states, prompting suggestions that their opposition was due to an ideological objection to government controls. This was not the main reason for their opposition, however.

The irony of agricultural politics in the House is that, though Southerners have more influence than anyone else over the content of Bills that Congress adopts, the Bills they have written have been particularly unsuited to many Southern commodities. Cotton is the prime example. The basic method used to subsidize cotton from the New Deal was to force up the price of cotton by restricting the quantity that American farmers grew. The trouble was that the higher price encouraged other countries to grow more, and foreign and even American textile mills to buy abroad. By 1964, American textile mills had to be subsidized to buy American cotton. The damage, however, had been done already. The artifically high price for cotton in the United States had encouraged not only production abroad but also the substitution of manmade fibre for cotton. The effect of the cotton programme, designed by Southerners to help Southern producers, had been to contract their market and help their competitors. The realization of this prompted Southern Congressmen to object to any Subsidy Bill which included more stringent controls, not so much on principle but because they found the practical effects of applying that policy harmful to their constituents.

Though the Southern example is one of the clearest to understand, it is not the only case of Democratic rural Congressmen, who are perfectly prepared in principle to see the government control agricultural production and subsidize farmers, refusing to accept the application of one particular approach to their own districts' commodity. The dairy industry, for example, has always been a 'special case'. It has never been brought within the framework of production controls, because Congressmen from dairying areas find the effects of applying controls to the industry unacceptable. Farmers who grow feed grains to feed to their own cattle have always insisted that they should not be subjected to the controls applied to the producer who sells his feed grains, even though they both effect the balance between supply and demand. Wheat producers have, through their Congressmen, prevented the minimum amount of wheat that can be planted falling below 55 million acres, even if that amount could not be sold. The clauses of Agriculture Acts are bowed down by special cases.

Few of these issues reach the floor of the House. Faced with the unremitting hostility of the Republicans to Farm Subsidy Bills and the constant possibility of defections by urban Democrats, the manager of a Farm Bill, be he an official of the US Department of Agriculture, a member of the White House staff, or Chairman of the Agriculture Committee, has so few votes to spare that he usually gives in to pressure from rural Democrats. Superimposed on the ideological politics of the farm subsidy issue in the House is, therefore, a highly detailed political struggle for exemptions for specific commodities. Taken together these exemptions may undermine the whole purpose of an Agriculture Bill.

Subsidies on the floor of the Senate

The contrast between how the farm problem has been treated on the floor of the Senate compared with its reception on the floor of the House is wholly in line with the difference in the way their committees handle the issue. Table 17, for example, shows some interesting contrasts with analysis of voting in the House which appears in the preceding six tables. Only in the first vote of 1962 do we find the sort of party solidarity among Republicans that appears so regularly among their House colleagues. By 1965 nearly 20 per cent of Senate Republicans voted with the majority of Democrats in favour of the wheat/cotton subsidies. In 1965, Senate Republicans were split almost evenly on the vote for the Agriculture Act of that year, while in 1970 Republican Senators voted overwhelmingly for the Agriculture Act. It is true that the Administration supported the 1970 Act, but Republican Senators were much more eager in its support than their House colleagues. Whereas House Republicans voted against the 1970 Act by 110 votes to 78, Senate Republicans voted for it by 24 to 6.

The inference that Senate Republicans do not see the farm issue in the ideological terms of their House colleagues is supported by certain specific events. The most important of these is the overwhelming rejection by the Senate of Senator Buckley's suggestion in 1972 that subsidies be phased out. Senator Buckley obtained, as we have seen above, the support of only thirteen colleagues. What pattern, if any, can we find in the support for Senator Buckley's amendment and in opposition to the recent (post-1964) Agriculture Acts which have been so widely accepted in the Senate?

The largest stable group of anti-Farm Bill Senators is composed of Republicans from urban dominated states. Thus of the seven votes against passage of the 1970 Act six—Boggs (Delaware), Case (New Jersey), Percy (Illinois), Schweiker (Pennsylvannia), Smith (Illinois), and John J. Williams (Delaware)—were Republicans from states containing large cities. Of the fourteen Republicans voting against the 1965 Act, Boggs, Williams, and Case were joined by Republicans Saltonstall (Massachusetts) and Javits (New York). Of the fourteen votes in 1973 in favour of Buckley's resolution to phase out subsidies, five (Weicker, Roth, Percy, Case, and Buckley) fell into this pattern of Republicans from states with strong urban influences. This may in part be an example of Republicans who can afford to do so—following their anti-subsidy feelings. However, it is likely that the Senators from Delaware, Maryland, Pennsylvania,

Massachusetts, New Jersey, and Connecticut were influenced by the importance of clothing and other textile industries in their states. They were therefore keen to reduce the cost of cotton which the subsidy programme raised. Some support for the thesis that the textile industry provided a constituency interest which overrode agriculture is provided by the fact that Democratic Senators from those and similar states also voted against farm programmes. Examples are John Kennedy (Massachusetts) prior to 1958; Ribicoff (Connecticut) in 1973 and 1970; Clark (Pennsylvania) in 1964; Brewster (Maryland) in 1964 and 1965; McIntyre (New Hampshire) in 1965; and Pastore and Pell (New Hampshire) in 1973. A state interest in textiles would thus account for over half[31] of the opponents of the 1973 Act. Certainly there is little in common ideologically between Caleb Boggs and Ribicoff. Attentiveness to the interests of the state again seem important—a theme we have noted throughout in relation to the Senate.

There is a group of fiscal conservatives in the Senate who follow their principles and therefore oppose Agricultural Subsidy Bills, but they are few in number. Three obvious candidates from 1973 stand out—Republican Senators Goldwater (Arizona), Dominick (Colorado), and Buckley (New York). They were joined by several Democrats—Robertson (Virginia) and Byrd (West Virginia) in 1964, and Lausche (Ohio) in 1965 are examples. Clinton Anderson (Democrat, New Mexico) felt honour-bound to oppose Subsidy Bills favoured by other Democrats because his policy as Truman's Secretary of Agriculture had been to lower support price levels and work towards a free market. Just how individual a stand this was can be seen from the fact that his successor, Joseph Montoya, has worked equally consistently for higher subsidies. Senator Ellender felt obliged to oppose drift towards reliance on government payments in the 1964 and 1965 Acts. But the key point about the fiscal conservatives has been their erratic behaviour. Thus neither Dominick nor Goldwater opposed the 1970 Act, though they did the 1973, and they had also failed to vote against the 1965 Act. The picture of opposition to subsidies in the Senate is one of consistent individualistic opposition (like Anderson) or of inconsistent principled opposition (like Goldwater) added to the opposition of an ideologically ramshackle collection of Senators from states with important textile industries which want cheaper cotton.

All of this might be clearer if compared to the House. Unlike the House, farm programmes are often passed or opposed by coalitions frequently crossing party lines. Unlike the House, the Senate has seen few attacks on the principle of agricultural subsidies, though there are many detailed amendments to Committee suggestions. Whereas in the House opposition to subsidies has often seemed a matter of principle, of an ideological commitment to *laissez-faire*, in the Senate the most stable opposition group has been Senators with a constituency interest—textiles—in lower farm (particularly cotton) prices. In short, support for subsidies has been so strong in the Senate that the question of whether they should be paid has scarcely arisen; instead, Senators divide on how to hand out the money. Though the Senators, like Congressmen, have fewer and fewer farm constituents, majorities for subsidies in the Senate have steadily risen since 1968, while in the House passing a Subsidy Bill has seemed more and more difficult.

Two patterns of congressional politics

This chapter set out to explain why Congress had given such steady support to agricultural subsidies. In describing the political process in Congress, two quite different patterns emerged. In the Senate, we found that Senators differed on the best method to subsidize agriculture. The Senate Committee often had its proposals extensively amended on the floor and party differences did emerge, particularly when the choice was clearly posed between subsidies and high farm income, on the one hand (as in 1962), and stringent control, on the other. With the trend in the 1960s towards government buying the cooperation of farmers in production controls which it had previously sought to impose, the Senators steadily rallied round the programmes, voting final passage by greater and greater margins. In the House, however, no such accommodation was reached. With the sole exception of 1970, when House Democrats struck a bargain with a Republican Administration, the subsidy programmes passed the House on Democratic votes. In the 1960s over 90 per cent of support for major Farm Bills in the House came from Democrats (Table 14). Not only did the urban Republicans fail (as Mayhew notes) to support the programmes but rural Republicans (with the exception of 1970) also opposed the subsidy programmes by a margin of usually four to one. By 1973, the contrast had become even clearer, for, far from the cooperation of 1970 being repeated in the House, a fierce party battle took place around an Agriculture Bill drafted in a bipartisan spirit by the Senate Committee.

Why did this contrast exist? There are reasons related to the inner workings of the Senate. The greater autonomy of individual Senators, the corresponding weakness of leadership (compared with the House), and the ability each Senator has to exact revenge in many policy fields if his state's interests are threatened, all encourage giving Senators representing a commodity their heads in legislating on it.

Why, however, should individual Senators be keener on agricultural subsidies than individual Representatives? It might be useful to start by noting that electoral pressures bear more heavily on Senators than on Representatives. As Price has noted: 'What needs to be emphasised here is both the increasing number of statewide electorates which are becoming susceptible to party changes and the small—and dwindling—number of competitive House districts.'[82] The Republican Senator has, on average, more to worry about, therefore, if he alienates the farm vote than even House Republicans who represent rural districts. It was customary to portray the Representative as the slave to the parochial, clearly defined interests of his district and its special interests. More recent scholarship by political scientists such as Bauer, Poole, and Dexter has stressed the autonomy that Representatives enjoy in interpreting what constitutes the best interest of their district.[83] Representatives hear from their district messages which are in line with what they wish to do themselves. We find, therefore, that not only at the national but at the regional level the crucial determinant of whether a Representative was in favour or opposed to the Agricultural Subsidy Bills which came before Congress was not his district but his party. This is demonstrably the case in 1962, 1964, and 1965, when so few Republicans voted with the Democrats as to make further analysis worthless, as all Democratic dissidents were from a region, the South, where there were almost no Republicans. It is interesting to note in Table 18 that, even in 1958, the national difference between the parties on Farm Subsidy Bills was reproduced in almost every region, the West North Central being the one significant exception. This exception is easily explained by the special character of Republicans in that area, which dates back to the Populists and Non-Partisan League.

In short, Senators, who face more competitive elections than Representatives, are more united on farm policy. Nearly all Senators agree that farm subsidies are necessary, and though disagreements do arise over the details of subsidy policy, even these are minimized by a tradition of allowing Senators from states associated with one particular commodity to write the section of the subsidy law which will apply to that commodity. In the House, however, Representatives from the two parties have offered farmers radically different options according to the ideological predictions of the Representatives. Republicans have offered freedom, but low subsidies; Democrats have offered high subsidies and tighter controls. Party rivalry, carried on in elections, has produced cross-party voting and large majorities in favour of subsidies in the Senate. But party rivalry in the House has produced not consensus but the clear articulation of contradictory positions.

Yet in spite of the differences in the way in which agricultural subsidy politics was handled in the House and Senate, differences related basically to the greater salience of party in the House, there is one important similarity. In neither the House nor the Senate was there anyone who had the power to impose a coherent approach in an area, agricultural policy, where coherence was desperately needed. There was no united farm block to dictate an agreed agricultural charter; there were no strong agriculture committees which could agree on legislation and have it carried through Congress; and though the Democratic party could provide a majority for farm legislation, it was a majority constantly threatened by defections if details were unacceptable to any 'Democratic' commodity.

Congress's impact on agricultural policy

The assumption at the start of this chapter was that Congress was the barrier to reform of the agricultural subsidy system because agricultural legislation was controlled by farmers' Representatives. It was expected that Representatives and Senators of both parties who depended on the votes of farmers for reelection worked together on the floor and in Committee to maximize the subsidies their constituents obtained. The weakness of the congressional policy process for agriculture which, in the light of Lowi's article, it was anticipated would be found was that it placed the task of making agricultural policy in the hands of agricultural interests. This Congress has not done. The weakness of the agricultural committees and the fierce partisan war in the House between rural

Republicans and Democrats has ensured that the choices in agricultural policy have been presented to the House and the Senate as a whole.

Farm subsidies have enjoyed extensive support in Congress thanks to the Democratic party. It is inconceivable that any Congress with a Democratic majority would have ended farm subsidies during a period of low prices. Yet Congress's effect on policy has not been limited to ensuring that some form of farm subsidies continues; it has also had a marked effect on the form that subsidy policy has taken. Much of this influence has been negative, frustrating the attempts to rationalize the system described in Chapter 5. Our analysis in this chapter helps us understand why Congress has been unable to accept clear leadership on farm subsidies. Consistency and efficiency has been sacrificed in the Senate to the norm of deferring to the expertise of Senators whose states are particularly affected by a policy. The House has had to abandon consistency and efficiency because, faced with unrelating Republican opposition, a majority can be obtained only by placating any Democrat who wants to make his constituents a 'special case'. In both chambers, the weakness of the Committees on Agriculture has removed an obvious forum in which to obtain consistency. Not surprisingly, Congress has not merely sustained agricultural subsidies but it also has failed to eliminate waste. Subsidies have persisted in some form because of the Democratic party. The unnecessary waste and expense of the form they have taken result not because agricultural interests are in the saddle in Congress but because the horse is riderless.

Notes

1. C. O. Jones, 'Representation in Congress; the case of the House Agriculture Committee', *APSR*, June, 1961.
2. Woodrow Wilson, *Congressional Government*, Meridian Books, New York, 1966, pp. 70–71.
3. George Goodwin, *The Little Legislatures*, University of Massachusetts Press, 1970.
4. Laxer rules 'of relevance and procedure' make it easier to circumvent a Senate than House committee; it has, however, been traditional to stress the importance of Senate committees, too. For an example, see Donald R. Matthews, *U.S. Senators and Their World*, Vintage Books, New York, 1960, p. 147. For Fenno's downgrading of the importance of Senate committees, see below.
5. Richard Fenno, *The Power of the Purse, Appropriations Politics in Congress*, Little Brown, Boston, 1966.
6. Nicholas Masters, 'House Committee Assignments', *APSR*, 1961.
7. Jones, op. cit.
8. Goodwin, op. cit., p. 112.
9. Fenno, op cit.
10. Representative Belcher, *Congressional Record*, Vol. 116, part 20, col. 27196, 4 August, 1970.
11. *Ibid.*
12. Richard Bolling, *House Out of Order*, E. P. Dutton and Co., New York, 1965, p. 96.
13. 'The political impasse in farm support legislation', *Yale Law Journal*, 1962, p. 952.
14. *Congressional Record*, Vol. 108, part 15, col. 20123, 1962.
15. *Congressional Record*, Vol. 104, part 4, col. 4923, 1958.

160

16. US Congress, Eighty-sixth Congress, Second Session, House Committee on Agriculture, Hearings, *General Farm Legislation*, 1960, p. 167.
17. C. O. Jones, 'The Agriculture Committee and the problem of representation', *APSR*, 1961.
18. D. R. Mayhew, *Party Loyalty Among Congressmen*, The Difference between Republicans and Democrats, 1947, Harvard University Press, Cambridge, 1966 *passim;* Julius Turner, Party and Constituency, Johns Hopkins, Baltimore, 1957, p. 46
19. C. Van Woodward, *Tom Watson, Agrarian Rebel*, Glaxay (Oxford University Press), 1963, London and New York, p. 350.
20. W. J. Cash, *The Mind of the South*, Pelican, Harmondsworth, 1973, *passim.*
21. Ibid., p. 375.
22. US Congress, Eighty-sixth Congress, Second Session, House Committee on Agriculture, Hearings, *General Farm Legislation*, 1960, p. 12.
23. *Congressional Record*, Vol. 108, part 8, col. 11176, 20 June, 1962.
24. *Congressional Record*, Vol. 111, part 15, col. 20913, 18 August, 1965.
25. US Senate, Ninety-third Congress, First Session on S 517, Hearings before the Committee on Agriculture Programs, before the Committee on Agriculture and Forestry, *Extension of Farm and Related Programmes*, 1973, p. 2.
26. The text is reprinted in the *New York Times*, 8 June, 1962.
27. *Washington Post*, 27 June, 1962.
28. *Wall Street Journal*, 10 November, 1969.
29. Fenno, op. cit.
30. Fenno, op. cit., p. 458.
31. *Congressional Record*, Vol. 104, part 5, col. 6008, 1958.
32. Ibid., col. 5967.
33. Fenno, op. cit., p. 583.
34. *Congressional Record*, Vol. 112, part 7, 1966.
35. See Fenno, op. cit., *passim.*
36. US Congress, Eighty-sixth Congress, First Session, Department of Agriculture and Related Agencies, Hearings before the Subcommittee of the House Committee on Appropriations, *Appropriations for 1960*, p. 11.
37. House of Representatives, Eighty-seventh Congress, First Session, Department of Agriculture, Hearings before the Subcommittee on Appropriations, *Appropriations for 1962*.
38. N. Kotz, *Let Them Eat Promises: The Politics of Hunger in America*, Prentice Hall, 1969, p. 2.
39. *Congressional Record*, Vol. 115, part 10, col. 13756, 1969.
40. Ibid., col. 13736.
41. *Congressional Record*, Ninetieth Congress, Second Session, col. 11259, 1969.
42. House of Representatives, Eighty-seventh Congress, First Session, Department of Agriculture, Hearings before the Subcommittee of the House Appropriations Committee, *Appropriations for 1962*, p. 98.
43. Kotz, op. cit., p. 88.
44. US Congress, Eighty-sixth Congress, First Session, Department of Agriculture, Hearings before Subcommittee of the House Committee on Appropriations, *Appropriations for 1960*, 1959, p. 20.
45. US Congress, Eighty-sixth Congress, Sound Session, Department of Agriculture, Hearings before the Subcommittee of the House Committee on Appropriations, *Appropriations for 1961*, 1960.
46. Jamie Whitten, 'The Farmers' Predicament', *The Staple Cotton Review*, December, 1958.
47. See his exchange with Secretary Freeman, Department of Agriculture, Appropriations Hearings in 1965 (for 1966), p. 5 ff.

48. Richard Fenno, Congressmen in Committee, Little Brown, Boston, 1973, p. 190.
49. This and much other information was obtained from interviews with the Democratic and Republican Counsel to the Committee, Henry Cusso and Forrest Rees, on 12 July, 1973 and in November, 1972.
50. Randal Ripley, *Power in the Senate*, St Martin's Press, 1969, p. 135.
51. *Congressional Record*, Vol. 104, part 11, col. 14902, 1958.
52. Ibid., col. 14908.
53. *Congressional Record*, Vol. 110, part 3, col. 3983, 1964.
54. *Congressional Record*, Vol. 111, part 17, col. 23301, 1965.
55. When I interviewed the helpful House Minority Counsel he doubted frostily that he could put me in touch with his Democratic colleagues; the Senate Majority Counsel spontaneously and without me suggesting it asked if he could bring along the Minority Counsel to the interview.
56. *Senate Report*, Calendar 673.
57. US Senate, Eighty-fifth Congress, Second Session, *Hearings before the Committee on Agriculture and Forestry*, and *Washington Post*, 17 February, 1959, p. 1 ff.
58. Fenno (1973), op. cit., p. 146.
59. Fenno (1973), op. cit., pp. 197–198.
60. Fenno (1966), op. cit., *passim*.
61. US Senate, Eighty-ninth Congress, First Session, Hearings before the Subcommittee on Agriculture of the Senate Committee on Appropriations on HR 14596, *Agricultural Appropriations for 1967*, p. 2.
62. *Congressional Record* (Senate), Vol. 114, part 12, col. 15315, 1968.
63. Theodore Lowi, 'How the farmers get what they want', in James E. Anderson (Ed.), *Politics and Economic Policy Making*, Addison-Wesley, Reading, Mass., 1970, esp. p. 297.
64. Figures from the 1970 Census kindly supplied by the US Department of Agriculture.
65. David R. Mayhew, *Party Loyalty Among Congressmen*, Harvard University Press, Cambridge, 1966, pp. 55–6.
66. The case starting this development was *Baker versus Carr*, 369, US 186, 1962.
67. Randall Ripley, 'Legislative bargaining and the Food Stamp Act', Frederick Cleveland (Ed.), *Congress and Urban Problems*, Brookings, Washington D.C., 1969, p. 300.
68. *Congressional Record*, Vol. 105, part 6, col. 8311, 1959.
69. *Congressional Record*, Eighty-fifth Congress, Second Session, Vol. 104, part 9, 26 June, 1958.
70. *Congressional Record*, Vol. 116, part 20, col. 24785, 1970.
71. Andrew Shonfield, *Modern Capitalism, The Changing Pattern of Public and Private Power*, Oxford University Press, London, 1965, p. 300.
72. *Congressional Record*, Vol. 108, part 8, col. 11179, 1962.
73. Ibid., col. 11189.
74. *Congressional Record*, Eighty-fifth Congress, Second Session, Vol. 104, part 9, col. 4910, 26 June, 1958.
75. *Congressional Record*, Vol. 108, part 8, col. 10957, 20–21 June, 1962.
76. *Congressional Record*, Vol. 104, part 11, col. 14880 ff, 1958.
77. *Congressional Record*, Eighty-fifth Congress, Second Session, Vol. 104, part 4, col. 4912.
78. *Congressional Record*, Vol. 105, part 5, col 5984, 1958.
79. Ibid., col. 5985.
80. It is interesting to note that the stress on the importance of ideology so far is fully in accord with the conclusions of that pioneer of voting analysis, Julius Turner. He argued in his *Party and Constituency* (Johns Hopkins, 1951) that:

    ... both parties woo the farmer with great intensity on election day. It is surprising, therefore that there appears to be disagreement between the two parties over agricultural policy. ... It is more surprising furthermore, that from the point of view of *largesse*, of the payment of government money to farm groups the Democrats have far out distanced the Republicans (p. 64).

Though Turner's work was based mainly on votes taken in the 1930s, one's only comment can be *plus ça change*.

81. For summaries of the economic interests of these states, see Michael Barone, Grant Ujifusa, and Douglas Matthews, *The Almanac of American Politics*, Gambit, New York, 1972 and 1974.

82. H. Douglas Price, 'The electoral arena', in D. Truman (Ed.), *The Congress and America's Future*, Prentice-Hall, Englewood Cliffs, New Jersey, 1973, p. 51.

83. See Lewis Anthony Dexter, 'The Representative and his District', in R. Peabody and N. Polsby (Eds.), *New Perspectives on the House of Representatives*, Rand McNally, Chicago, 1963.

Chapter 9

Conclusions; State Power and Minority Benefits

Political scientists managed to speculate about differences in the power and functions of special interests in Britain and the United States for many years with few comparative empirical studies to aide them. It seems unlikely that this study will settle the debate, and, as it is based on but one policy area, there may be many good arguments why it should not. However, many of the conclusions of this book should pose problems for participants in the debate.

The book set out to answer three deceptively simple problems. The first was how much help British and American governments gave their farmers, and whose farmers therefore received the most. The second was to explain why this small and ever-diminishing section of the population was able to obtain so much government help. The third was to identify the features of the political system which explained the greater success of whichever group, British or American farmers, proved the better provided for. We may dispose of the first two questions quickly.

The question of how highly subsidized British and American farmers were is obviously basic. It is, however, hard to answer definitively. The basic reason is that any complete estimate of how much help farmers received must include not only direct payments but the effects of tariffs, quotas, and government intervention on the domestic market. The problem with assessing the effects of all these is that no one can be completely sure what the levels of supply, demand, and price would be if these government policies did not exist. Yet it is important to make the attempt in any comparison between Britain and the United States because (and this is a crucial failing in Pennock's calculations)[1] the major difference between the agricultural subsidy systems of Britain and the United States has been that whereas most subsidies in Britain come direct from the government to the farmer, most subsidies in the United States are created by the government spending a smaller amount of money to change the market price considerably. Pennock's concentration on government expenditure alone ignored the main strategy of the

American policies, which was to increase farm income by government agencies bidding up market prices.

The best surveys[2] of the effects of agricultural subsidy policies suggested somewhat surprisingly that American farmers are, on average, less subsidized than their British counterparts. This was true, it emerged, even allowing for all forms of 'indirect' subsidy through quotas, artificially raised prices, and tariffs. The average, however, was not a good figure to pursue, for it disguised the fact that subsidies were even more narrowly concentrated in the United States than in the United Kingdom in terms of both crops and size of farm. While some commodities were highly subsidized in the United States (notably corn, cotton, tobacco, peanuts, and rice), other significant commodities (notably meat) were negatively protected. That is, commodities such as meat not only receive few subsidies but were penalized by the higher costs which government policies produced in commodities they used as raw materials. Indeed, the very techniques of agricultural support used in the United States (which have been mainly raising the market prices of subsidized commodities) have increased inevitably the income differentials among farmers, as they must be distributed in proportion to output, thus helping the large-scale farmers most. It seemed, therefore, that those American farmers who did receive subsidies were more generously provided for than British farmers who received subsidies, even though all American farmers were, on average, less generously aided than all British. While answering one question, whether British or American farmers were the most protected, another question and point of comparison had emerged—why subsidies in the United States were more narrowly concentrated there than in the United Kingdom.

Differences in policy outcomes are often traceable to differences in policy processes. This study has organized the contrast by examining in each country the role of pressure groups; the nature of Executive (or inter-departmental) politics; and the difference that a clearly important legislature, Congress, makes to the policy process in the United States. Though each has been examined in some detail, it emerges that none of these headings individually provides a satisfactory explanation for the persistence of agricultural subsidies. Let us recall the argument for each of these headings.

The greater disparity in the distribution of subsidies in the United States (than in Britain) reflects less unity and common purpose in agricultural politics. Nowhere was this contrast clearer than in the contrast between British and American agricultural interest groups.

British agricultural interests are characterized above all by unity. One organization, the National Farmers' Union, had succeeded in establishing a virtually total monopoly, as it represented some 86 per cent of the commercial farmers in Britain. This alone provides a striking contrast with the United States, where more competing interest groups organized fewer farmers. Even more remarkable was the way in which the British NFU managed to conceal differences of viewpoint and interest between farmers. Conflicts of interest or conflicts over priorities in dealing with the Government between small farmers and large-scale producers, between hill farmers and East Anglian 'grain barons', and between landowners and tenants *could* divide farmers, but have not. The NFU manages to convince all types of farmer that it represents *their* interests and that they have no need for a separate organization to defend their special interest. The politics of the NFU are private and restrained.

The contrast with the American agricultural interest groups is obvious. There the agricultural interest groups have been engaged in bitter conflicts over farm—and almost every other—policy. Though members of the NFU, NFO, AFBF, or Grange are not distinguishable in terms of their incomes, the commodities they produce or the size of their farms, the interest groups could easily be placed in different parts of the American political spectrum ranging from the liberalism of the NFU or NFO to the Goldwater conservatism of the AFBF. Indeed, it emerged that each of the interest groups, far from establishing its right to represent agriculture's views to all politicians, had become locked into stable political coalitions with liberals or conservatives which hampered their efforts to have their farm policies adopted. Thus the AFBF, which should have been able to attract the support of liberal urban Congressmen for its attack on farm subsidies, failed to do so at least in part because its attack on trade unions, social security, and Medicare aroused the distrust of urban Democrats. Similarly, the NFU became so committed to the Democratic party that its influence with Republicans was sharply reduced.

Indeed, whereas the aim of the British NFU seemed to be to maintain itself as the authoritative voice of agriculture, and to that end it was prepared to compromise on tactics and policy, the aim of at least the largest of the American agricultural interest groups, the AFBF, seemed to be to maintain ideological purity. Thus considerable evidence emerged that many local units of the AFBF (and, indeed, in the case of the South, a whole region) disapproved of its policy. A drastic limitation on the influence of the AFBF was that not only the leadership of the AFBF but also politicians knew this. We may recall Congressman Foley's remark: 'I do not know how we are to evaluate presentations that come before us from the AFBF when members have so many constituents who do not agree with these presentations.'[3]

In brief, we argued that the American agricultural interest groups are more explicitly ideological and less accepted as representative of farmers' wishes or interests than is the case with their British counterparts. American agricultural interest groups play an almost totally different role to British ones. They speak not as the authoritative interpreter of what farmers want from politicians but as challengers to consensus determinedly applying principle to policy.

All this must seem grist to the mill of Pennock,[4] Beer,[5] and those who argue that interest groups play a more significant role in British than in American politics. In both the chapters on the Annual Review procedure and on the NFU itself, it was willingly conceded that the relationship between the British NFU and government is close and, particularly in discussions between the NFU and MAFF, trusting. The point is obvious, fully in accord with earlier work on British pressure groups, and there is no reason to doubt it. What is, however, contentious is whether it supports any interpretation that British interest groups have greater influence.

This study argues that the close relationship between the NFU and British governments reflects pressure groups' weaknesses as well as strengths. It emerged from the chapter on the NFU that it had no wish to bargain politically. In spite of the putative importance of the 'farm vote', the NFU could not change its members' votes and its ventures into electoral politics have been uncertain and not accepted as a legitimate tactic. The NFU, far from being in a position to dictate terms to the Government has been dependent on its goodwill. The NFU has been dependent on goodwill in two senses. First, its monopoly of representation was granted by the Government, and has been preserved by a deliberate government policy to restrict participation in decision-making to the NFU and not to extend it to groups such as the Farmers' Union of Wales, the CLA, and the NUAAW. Second, there was a threat, which sometimes became reality and which the NFU was almost powerless to prevent, that the Government might decide its policy before its annual consultations with the NFU and refuse to be influenced. While the NFU is bound by the secrecy of the Review, it must behave in a way which encourages civil servants to believe it is moderate, sensible, and worth listening to. If the NFU met all these conditions, policy-makers could afford to indulge it with promises to listen carefully to its comments, secure in the knowledge that nobody can overrule the decision of the Cabinet. It is, in short, a sign of the strength of British governments *vis à vis* interest groups they can concede interest groups such opportunities to influence them.

The leadership of the NFU has been, placed therefore in a difficult position. On the one hand, it has had to satisfy its membership by showing determination and even aggression in the pursuit of higher incomes for its members. On the other hand, its officers have always had to act in a way which fostered the trust of the civil servants and government. The Union has often, therefore, been caught between the mood of its membership and the requirements that operating in Whitehall impose. This was, in particular, the experience of Sir Gwilym Williams, and significantly he chose, as President of the NFU, to alienate his members rather than Whitehall. It seemed to Williams that he and his successors had often to give the membership the impression of militancy while assuring Whitehall that they would continue to play the game. This strategy was pursued to the point where its high officials of the Union have argued that the NFU should publicly 'agree' some Reviews it privately disapproved of in order to encourage governments to maintain interest in its official comments. The officials of the NFU have known that, though part competition for the farm vote may discourage governments from pursuing a persistently 'anti-farmer' policy, there is absolutely nothing it can do in the context of any one Review except encourage, warn, and advise. The NFU had to keep the confidence of the civil servants with which it dealt.

It was well for the NFU, therefore, that its formal and informal political structure helped it fulfil the functions of moderating and reconciling not only the differences between farmers but also their occasional militancy. The NFU's leadership needed freedom of action so that it could conform to the expectations which Whitehall has of its favoured pressure groups. This requires the NFU's leadership to avoid close control by more militant members. In fact, the membership of the NFU had little control over its officers. Some of the reasons for this are common to all voluntary organizations, and here we may recall the low turnout for NFU meetings, the fact that almost all activists are more affluent farmers, and the absence of a visible group of alternative leaders whom the membership could use to displace the incumbents. These general flaws in voluntary associations were reinforced in the case of the NFU by a cumbersome constitution, by the absence of viable, competing alternative organizations for the dissatisfied to join, and by an enormous but inevitable gulf of knowledge and authority between those full-time officers who are in close and regular contact with the government, on the one hand, and the part-time elected representatives to whom they were theoretically responsible, on the other.

Like many other studies of interest group politics, this one found that interest groups are not very reliable indicators of their members' wishes.[6] Just as we argued that the leadership of the NFU has enjoyed considerable freedom of action, so the AFBF leadership too has been subject to little control from its members who join to get cheap insurance and had, it seems, very different policy preferences to their leaders. Yet it is instructive to compare how the leaders of British and American pressure groups used their freedom of action. The British NFU's leaders have used their autonomy to maintain close and friendly relations with government in general and MAFF in particular. They have behaved less politically, more moderately, and more like an extension of the Civil Service than many of their members would have wished. The leaders of American pressure groups have, on the contrary, emphasized their dogmatism and their political commitment, and have indulged their ideological propensities on a wide variety of issues. Whereas the British pressure group leader wants to be seen as the apolitical technocrat speaking authoritatively on his subject, the American pressure group leaders speak so vehemently on so many issues that they are more like the British conception of a political party than interest group leaders.

Is this the rub? Might it not be that the differences in style between the British NFU and the American NFU, for example, reflect not some peculiarities of either but the reaction of pressure groups in America to legislative rather than executive politics in a country with weak political parties? Must any effective pressure group in the United States from wide-ranging ideological alliances in which different pressure groups exchange support across a variety of issues? Does the somewhat extraordinary involvement of the AFBF in the debates on social policy, education, and foreign policy reflect merely its attempts to build a legislative majority? Such an interpretation has a certain plausibility, but neglects the cost of such a strategy for American interest groups. That cost has been to alienate potential allies on what one presumes to be the agricultural interest groups' central interest—agricultural policy. One can imagine the effect of the American NFU's leaders endorsement of *Baker versus Carr* and subsequent cases on reapportionment on the thinking of rural Republicans, or of the AFBF's work for Taft Hartley on urban Democratic Congressmen who could so easily be convinced of its arguments against the agricultural subsidy laws.

It is interesting to note, too, the unwillingness of American politicians to accord interest groups the status they are given in Britain as authoritative spokesmen for their interests. Not only has the US Department of Agriculture fostered its own interest groups as offshoots of its 'farmer administered' projects but politicians have been less willing to accept that pressure groups represent their constituents. American politicians (always more professional than British) work harder in keeping in touch with their constituents and are correspondingly less willing to accept the verdict of pressure groups on the state of public opinion.

The disunity of the pressure groups, the lack of a collective consciousness among farmers, the fact that Congressmen are making their own imperfect estimates of what their constituents want, and the weakness of any countervailing pressures to unity are all factors contributing to the confusion and disunity which exist in Congress.

One of the most obvious differences between the policy process in Britain and the United States is the enormously greater role played by Congress than by Parliament. The difference which it was expected this greater role played by Congress would make was that policy would be dictated by rural interests. Congressional committees would be controlled by Senators and Representatives from the most rural areas of the United States, who would conspire together to impose on their colleagues a 'give away' to farmers. They would be supported in floor votes by other Senators and Representatives from rural areas who would bargain or logroll with their colleagues by pressing for farm subsidy legislation in exchange for rural votes on urban issues. The impact of the legislative process would be to place policymaking in the hands of rural vested interests.[7]

This picture of how Congress would handle the agricultural subsidy is drawn (I trust not unfairly) from the picture of American politics that has long been current. Yet the evidence of this study suggests that this picture is profoundly misleading. Congressional committees did not enjoy great freedom of action or autonomy from their parent chamber. The only committee which approached the classic model, the House Appropriations Subcommittee, had achieved that independence largely through showing considerable deference to any clearly articulated sentiment in Congress. It was true that the Senate showed considerable unanimity on the need to keep farm subsidy policies, a unity which was explained partly in terms of the deference which Senators (almost always now faced with a serious two-party conflict in elections) paid to their farmers' votes. But the House of Representatives, where the smaller constituencies presumably should encourage parochialism, turned out to contradict flatly the classic pictures of agricultural politics. Representatives were divided not so much by the interests of their districts but by party. The House divided between rural Republicans who found any proposed farm legislation unworkable, non-rural Republicans who believed any government intervention in agriculture undesirable, and Democrats, almost all of whom accepted government intervention but were sometimes divided on what sort was best.

In short, congressional politics, particularly in the House, were profoundly affected by a sharp ideological divide. Agricultural policy could not avoid the issue which, according to all the studies of congressional voting,[8] best divides Republicans from Democrats, namely the extent to which government intervention in the economy is justified. It is perfectly true that bargaining between urban liberal Democrats and their rural, often Southern, more conservative colleagues has been involved. But it has been intra-party bargaining which has gone on to get the farm subsidy laws enacted, not bargaining between a bipartisan farm bloc and legislators representing urban or suburban districts.

So long as bargaining went on, what did it matter if it was intra-party bargaining? What did it matter that the farm programmes were overwhelmingly adopted by the Democratic party rather than any coalition of rural Representatives—any sort of farm block? There have been two important consequences. First, because the farm subsidy laws have been very much the creation of the rural Democrats enacted with the help of their urban colleagues, farm subsidies inevitably have tended to benefit those commodities produced in areas represented by Democrats more than the others. That is to say, that commodities such as rice, tobacco, cotton, and of late wheat, grown in states which have had the good sense to elect Democrats, are more highly subsidized than commodities such as feed grains or hogs which are represented by Republicans. Second, because the Republicans in the House voted against almost every agricultural subsidy law the Democrats have drafted, the defection of comparatively few Democrats has proved fatal to the legislation proposed. Defections have come from two sources. Southern Democrats have defected when strict production controls, which they felt would help only overseas competitors, have been proposed. Second, there has always been a minority of urban Democrats in the House who are suspicious about farm subsidies. If they feel that the legislation proposed is too much of a 'give away' to farmers, or if provoked by Southern disloyalty, this minority is expanded to significant and decisive proportions.

Thus the main effect of the importance of the legislature in the American policy process has not been to put the representatives of rural representatives in the box-seat. They fight too much among themselves to steer the stage-coach. Congressional agricultural politics are typically led by a group of rural Congressmen, Democrats, enacting subsidy legislation by small majorities in the House. They are dependent, therefore, on maintaining a coalition which, even if it includes all rural Democratic representatives, is still dependent on the goodwill of the urban Democrats. It is the instability of this coalition in the House, aided by a slightly lesser disunity in the Senate on the best methods of subsidizing agriculture, which has prevented the adoption of a coherent policy for agriculture in the United States. Congress has been unable to choose between the clear alternatives of tighter controls or a free market which Administrations have presented to it. And Congress has been unable to make the choice because neither constituency interest nor party has been sufficient to provide stable cleavages. The Democratic party, much less any bipartisan bloc of representatives of rural areas, has been unable to provide the programmatic majorities needed to make the clear choices needed in agriculture. Reform has therefore been slow and expensive. Because Congress has failed to impose clear principles on agricultural policy, the only reforms which were possible were achieved by paying out larger and larger payments from the Treasury to persuade farmers to limit production when they would not do so voluntarily.

The British do not have, of course, legislative politics like the Americans. The Commons are entitled to comment on an Annual Review once all has been decided, though ministers always assure the interviewer that its reactions are 'taken into account'. Its influence is indirect as either a forum where rural MPs can back up the pressure from the NFU or the forum for party competition for the 'farm vote'.

Just as Huntington found that in American defence policy[9] the legislative process, defined in a broader sense as the aggregation and adjudication of interests, had been displaced from Congress to the Executive (and the Joint Chiefs of Staff in particular), so it is in nearly all British policymaking. The legislative function have been displaced from Parliament in two settings. The first is the NFU, which brilliantly fulfilled the function which the House and Senate Agriculture Committees unsuccessfully attempted to carry out of settling the balance between agricultural commodities. The NFU presented the Government with a unified picture of what farmers, or 'agriculture', wanted. British governments could, of course, change the priorities that the NFU presented to it, particularly if there was an obvious reason for so doing (such as avoiding over-production of a commodity). As with the relationship between Congress and a trusted committee, however, the presumption was against doing so. If British politicians knew the difficulty which setting the balance between commodities has caused their American colleagues, they would be grateful to the NFU for saving them from a difficult problem. What of the 'legislative' task of balancing agriculture against other interests? Where is this performed in Britain? The answer is, predictably, within Whitehall and the Cabinet, where all major political decisions are taken in Britain.

There is a case, as we saw, for saying that the real work of representing and checking interests is carried out in Britain by departments and ministries which take roughly the same attitude to agricultural policy whichever party is in power. The Ministry of Agriculture has always been receptive to the needs of farmers, particularly as formulated by its working partner, the NFU. The Treasury, the Board of Trade (or DTI), and the Foreign and Commonwealth Office have been suspicious of any policy that costs more money or seems to threaten the interests of foreign suppliers. These attitudes were reflected by the relevant Cabinet Ministers; Cledwyn Hughes was a protagonist of the farmers' interests as much as Prior and Godber, his conservative counterparts.

To what extent is it plausible to attribute the success of farmers in Britain to this penetration of the bureaucracy by their good fortune in having a ministry, the MAFF, to represent them? The answer is to be found in the distinction between 'bureaucratic politics' and 'standard operating procedures' which Allison makes.[10] The MAFF is not the ruthless servant of the NFU, but its normal way of doing business helps the Union's cause. The British policymaking process in the Annual Review is surely most impressive in the degree to which the judgement of hostile as well as friendly ministries is brought to bear on any proposed change in farm subsidies. We have also seen that the MAFF has been a moderating influence as it is a less determined advocate of the farmers' cause than the NFU. The strong, cohesive traditions of the British Civil Service, the close working relations between the civil servants in MAFF and in even the more critical ministries such as the Treasury, and the absence of any of the institutional pressures (such as the need to obtain appropriations) which are said to subvert Presidential control in the United States, have all precluded the MAFF functioning as a fervent advocate of the farmers' interest.

The weakness of the British policy process which has helped maintain farm subsidies has been the absence in British government until recently of a capacity for the analysis of existing policies. Policy change in British agricultural subsidy policy has been slow. When it has taken place, it has been forced on British governments by external pressures such as the collapse in world commodity prices in the early 1960s or the application to join the EEC in the late 1960s. Agricultural policy, like every policy area, is not self-contained, but it has seemed unusually dependent on external events to force a reconsideration of existing policy. One major reason for this is that though the MAFF is inhibited in its advocacy of the farmers' interest, it still believes in the justice of the farmers' cause. It believes that it is up to the MAFF to represent the farmers' viewpoint within Whitehall. This belief is harmless or possibly beneficial when changes in policy are considered, given the 'moderated pluralism' of British executive politics. It is less helpful, though, if we are looking for the evaluation of existing policies. Ministries (even the Treasury, but particularly other spending Ministries) feel inhibited about telling another department that the policies it is administering need changing fundamentally. Yet the MAFF itself has been extremely unlikely to evaluate critically farm subsidies. The picture of British executive politics which emerges is one which fully fits the picture of the trend in British farm policy. Increases in subsidies have been moderate so that, as total government expenditure has risen, the proportion of government expenditure taken by agricultural subsidies has steadily declined. But the outpouring of considerable sums on agriculture continued, with criticism left to the academic community.

There is, of course, as yet a gap in our discussion of the British executive. It is the politicians. Surely, it may be argued, it is the job of the politicians to force reconsideration of policies on governments. Civil servants cannot be criticized for continuing to do what they have always done. But British politicians have been wary of reducing agricultural subsidies because of party competition. Somewhat surprisingly, British politicians of both major parties have paid the 'farm vote' a deference which it has not deserved. Far from questioning farm subsidies, politicians have been at pains to make it clear that they believe in them, at least as much as the next party. It is perfectly true that the evidence suggests that the Conservative party, which holds most British rural constituencies, has been a more assiduous cultivator of the farm vote than has Labour. Yet Labour's showing has been very important, even if it has never succeeded in capturing the British farmer for socialism. The fact that the Labour party made an attempt to win the 'farm vote' put pressure on the Conservatives to maintain a farm policy that was popular in the countryside which they could not ignore. This has a more general significance to which we shall return.

Ironically, American Secretaries of Agriculture, whom the classic picture of American politics would portray as the captured servants of farmers, turned out to offer much sharper and more clearly defined policy alternatives than is common in Britain. Whether a Secretary was Republican or Democrat made much more difference to his policies than being Conservative or Labour made to the policies of Ministers of Agriculture. This comparatively simple statement of fact is surprising because we are normally taught that American politics is, particularly if compared with British or European, pragmatic and non-ideological. But of course we are taught this 'fact' by Americans, and it is scarcely surprising that authors living in the midst of an ideology are not well placed to appreciate its major features. (This point helps explain why Americans write such interesting books on Britain.) The truth is that in social and economic policy issues, Americans are highly ideological. The question is not, as in Europe, whether government fulfils a function well or best; the question so often arises of whether government *ought* to fulfil the function at all. Thus, not only agricultural policy, but medical insurance (even for the elderly), regional policy, and the overall management of the economy raise the cry, buried for a generation in Europe, that though there is a problem to be solved it is not the duty of the government to solve it.

The failure of American writers to realize, or at any rate emphasize, the ideological divide between Republicans and Democrats on economic policy issues leads to another failure in analysing Executive politics. It is the failure to make a distinction between the politics of major policy questions which involve ideological issues and minor questions where the fragmentation of the American Executive does exist just as all the textbooks say. That is, Benson's attempts to return agriculture to a free market or Freeman's attempts to introduce working production controls in 1960–63 involved a very different sort of politics to those of inter-agency rivalry or of annual appropriations fights. Whereas the politics of, for example, soil conservation districts revealed the classic triangular coalition of an expansionist agency, interest groups, and congressional committees arrayed against the President and possibly even the Secretary of Agriculture, the politics of agricultural subsidy legislation were primarily party politics.

Secretaries of Agriculture have been more determined advocates of the President's programme than have Presidents themselves. We saw that Benson and Freeman were more willing to accept unpopularity in the countryside by imposing their ideologically shaped prescriptions on agriculture than were Presidents Eisenhower, Kennedy, and Johnson. The reason for this is again obvious and summarized in the phrase 'party competition'. Roland Pennock made a crucial omission when he argued that the disciplined British party system encouraged more competition for identifiable blocks of votes than the American party system; he forgot the Presidency, the most unified centralized party unit which could be created to compete for blocks of votes. Sure enough, we found that Presidential candidates did court the farm vote and, just as in Britain, there was a myth, (based on a plausible interpretation of the 1948 Election results) that the 'farm vote' was strategic. There was, however, one rather important difference between Britain and the United States in this respect. The politicians in the United States are right to believe that the 'farm vote' is up for grabs. Electoral research, we noted, shows that farmers are one of the most mercurial groups in the electorate and also one of the most responsive to single issue—in this case the state of agriculture. Apart from the importance of the 'farm vote' in Presidential elections, rural areas in the Midwest have been the setting for one of the more important changes in party control in the postwar United States, namely the erosion of the Republican hold on the prairie states and the corresponding rise of the Democrats. This party change inevitably involved a period of congressional party competition.

It might seem, therefore, that the interesting question about party competition for the 'farm vote' in the United States is not why it takes place but why it has not had more effect. We may think, for example, of Eisenhower ignoring the warnings and pleas of his party in Congress about the effects of continuing to pursue such an unpopular farm policy with such an unpopular Secretary, Benson. His obstinancy may seem merely a result of his quixotic Presidential style, but a little historical perspective should give us cause to hesitate. President Eisenhower's lack of interest in pursuing a popular farm policy is fully in accord with a tradition established by such prewar Republicans as Coolidge (who twice vetoed the McNary Haugen Bill to protect agriculture) and Hoover who watched commodity prices collapse. The simple fact is that American politicians are not simple vote maximizers but are probably better likened to firms who, under conditions of imperfect competition, aim to make sufficient profits to satisfy their shareholders but then follow other objectives such as prestige or status. American Presidents have allowed themselves to be deflected from their agricultural policy by electoral pressure, but it is implausible to suggest that vote-maximizing tactics have determined the general direction of that policy.

Farmers enjoy, of course, an almost uniquely favourable opportunity for exploiting party competition. This is largely because they have no natural enemies. Who should be an enemy, if not of farmers then of farm subsidies? If my description of the subsidies as constituting a redistribution of income from the average and lower income groups to richer farmers is true (and I know of no authority that disputes this), then the severest critics of the programmes should be found on the centre-Left. Yet criticism of farm subsidies has come, in both Britain and the United States, almost exclusively from the *laissez-faire* Right. The moderate Left has, by its votes in Congress and by competing for the farm vote in Britain, made a major contribution to preserving farm subsidies which redistribute income to the rich.

Why? There are two explanations, one connected with agriculture and one not. The 'agricultural' explanation is that politicians continued to think of farmers as the small-scale operator, almost a worker himself, a picture that might have accurately described an earlier generation of farmers in parts of Britain or the United States but which certainly no longer accurately describes the contemporary capitalist farming which predominates in both Britain and the United

States. But of course the moderate Left, like all other sections of political opinion, operates with a conceptual framework formulated in an earlier period, and not the present day. It has, therefore, been easy to identify the farmer as a victim and not master of capitalism. As the Canadian song goes:

The farmer is the man, the farmer is the man,
Lives on credit to the fall,
Then they take him by the hand,
And they lead him from the land,
And the merchant is the man who gets it all.[11]

In short, because politicians have not fully realized just how rapidly agriculture has changed, farmers have benefited from an erroneous linkage by the moderate Left of agricultural subsidies to such redistributive measures as welfare legislation. The fact that legislation for subsidies was adopted originally as part of the New Deal in the United States or by Britain's greatest reforming Administration, Attlee's, has strengthened this illusion. Farm subsidy legislation was merely part of the task of liberating the oppressed from the excesses of *laissez-faire* capitalism.

This links with the second, more general reason for the silence of the Left on agricultural subsidies. The historic role of the British Labour party and the American Democrats has been to expand the role of government in society. Their reforms, such as the British Welfare State, have commonly been accepted subsequently by their political opponents. It is even true that their opponents have occasionally in a piecemeal way contributed to the growth in the role of the State, a commonly cited example being the National Government in Britain in the 1930s. However, the periods when British or American governments have accepted novel social and economic tasks have been periods when the Democrats or Labour have been in power.

This creditable record has encouraged a belief on the moderate Left that any extension of government intervention is a progressive step. The belief has been particularly strong in the British Labour party, where both the Marxist tradition and the Fabian can unite in contempt for the free market.

Yet a disturbing large body of research contradicts the belief that each extension of government activity advances equality or the common good. Regulatory Commissions, we learn, protect the very interests they are proposed to constrain.[12] The federal housing programme and urban renewal projects have helped the middle classes establish nicer neighbourhoods by replacing Blacks' accommodation with subsidized accommodation for middle class Whites.[13] To these examples we may add agricultural subsidies, regressive in their effects on the distribution of income but sustained by progressives. It is the willingness of the urban liberal Democrat in the House of Representatives to vote for agricultural subsidies that gets them onto the statute books. It is the willingness of the British Labour party to compete for the 'farm vote' by promising to deliver subsidies better than the Tories which gave the British 'farm vote' its illusory but effective power. Progressives have been strategic in securing the continuance of agricultural policies dubious in their efficiency but certain in their regressive effects on the distribution of incomes.

The moderate Left in Britain and the United States can make two plausible answers to the critisms above. The reason why these answers are inadequate will tell us much about the problems of government intervention in an industry. The first answer is that there has been, particularly until very recently, no way in which the effects of agriculture policies could be known. The studies of the distribution of farm subsidies on which I have relied all appeared in the late 1960s, and were at least one beneficial result from the movement for greater programme analysis, OR and PPBS. The warning from this case study is that there is often a difference between the reasons given for pursuing a policy and the effects of that policy. As British governments become involved in more and more industries, the need for us to check the effects of policies and not just their justification grows. Those in Britain who pump government funds into firms may appear, in twenty years time, to be the saviour of the British capitalism or corporatism and not builders of socialism. (Contemporary attitudes to Franklin Roosevelt show how the two can be confused.)

The second response of the moderate Left to my criticisms raises more fundamental problems. Let us agree, the progressive might argue, that most subsidies do go to larger-scale farmers. However, at least some reach the smaller farmer, and the economic costs of funnelling all aid to the smaller farmer would be too great for society to bear. For example, if we limited the amount of subsidy that each farm may receive, the immediate effect is to encourage the fragmentation of large efficient holdings into small and therefore inefficient farms. The problem for the moderate reformer is that he is caught up in an industry which has its own laws of development running directly counter to his instincts. Once the reformer recognized that the contraction of the agricultural industry's needs for manpower created a major social problem, he had no choice but to press for government action. Yet every attempt to solve the problem of low agricultural incomes within the context of the industry itself had to recognize that the size of the optimally efficient producing unit was always increasing. Any policy which encouraged small-scale farming by funnelling subsidies to small-scale farmers would, therefore, have had an ever-increasing cost to society by stopping the process of combining small inefficient units into larger. Once any policy which limits subsidies to small-scale farmers had been rejected, then the inegalitarian nature of farm policy is assured, for any level of subsidies which is sufficient to guarantee the small farmer a decent living is bound to give his larger-scale colleague a fat one.

The truth is that industry, or economics, often does have laws of its own and when government is involved, therefore, it is not master of its actions. The government which accepts partnership with a free enterprise industry often is pressed into policies of which, in abstract, it disapproves. For example, the Labour Government of 1964–70 understandably wished to help the depressed region of East Lancashire, and the obvious way to do so was through reviving the flagging textile industry.[14] Yet the only practical way to revive the industry was to concentrate ownership of the small, outdated mills into one company which had the monetary and managerial resources to modernize the industry. The Government found itself, therefore, helping a larger capitalist firm, Courtaulds, create a monopoly in areas of the manmade fibre industry, a situation which it then felt compelled to ask its own Monopolies Commission to investigate. In short, the experience of the textile industry supports the general conclusion that I have drawn from the example of agriculture; governments cooperating with an industry do not fully control the situation. Governments have no more freedom of action in industrial policy than in Foreign policy. Both have constraints that government is powerless to change.

This study has tried to devalue any explanation of what has gone wrong in agricultural policy which is based on the power of special interests in any one institution—be it interest groups, congressional committees or even penetration of the Executive by friends of the farmers. The major reason why both British and American farmers may have received unjustified (or at least poorly allocated) help from the State is that they benefitted from the inertia of government. In both Britain and the United States the same pattern exists. A quite genuine crisis for agriculture, the Great Depression, caused the governments of both Britain and the United States to adopt measures unprecedented in peacetime to help agriculture. Wartime, and immediate postwar, shortages of agricultural products seemed to confirm the wisdom of government intervention. Thereafter little basic change in the agricultural policies of either the British or American governments was made.

Some of the reasons for this inactivity are common to both Britain and the United States, an obvious example being the unwillingness of either governments to invest resources in discovering just what effects its policies were having. Yet the differences between the British and American inertias are more striking than the similarities. The major reason why British agricultural policy did not change was that both the policymaking process and party competition conspired to discourage fundamental questioning of existing policy. Though British procedures for evaluating policy changes by inter-departmental and Cabinet review were a most effective check on the growth of agricultural subsidies; no one thought that it was their job to question existing policy and levels of subsidy. The absence of consensus on farm policy in the United States has, on the other hand, meant that the fundamental tenents of farm policy are always under review, attack, and debate. The question of whether government ought to be so involved in agriculture, which cannot be isolated from discussion of the effects of that involvement, continued throughout the 1950s and 1960s with, if anything, increasing vigour. But if policy was questioned with a vigour lacking in British politics, the capacity to take decisions and to resolve the debate was obviously much less. If no one has *wanted* to change British farm policy, then no one has been *able* to change American, in the direction of either tighter control or the free market, except by lavishly financing compromises by payments to farmers out of the federal Treasury. Coherent policymaking required a political power to override ideological and regional rivalries, and that power was lacking.

Inability to question policy is sometimes a less serious failing than an inability to act firmly. Though British agricultural policy has not been subjected to searching reappraisals within Whitehall, it has at least been administered with a degree of firmness. When British governments were threatened with gluts of dairy produce and eggs in the late 1950s, they had the toughness to resist pressures from the numerous producers of these commodities and *reduced* the price. At the same time the American government was spending a million dollars a day to store surplus wheat, cotton, and feed grains, while the deadlock over farm policy persisted. It is arguable that British governments should not have been subsidizing farmers as much or even at all. But at least British government had the capacity to make decisions in implementing that policy which spared Britain the more obvious absuridities of American farm policy, such as parity, surpluses, and production controls known to be ineffective.

The conclusions of this book might be read as message of comfort to the citizens of the United States and Britain. Agricultural interests do not have any dangerous grip on the political institutions of Britain or the United States. Pressure groups are less powerful than was thought, the MAFF and USDA are not the captured servants of farmers, and Congress is not in the hands of a farm block on agricultural policy. Yet this reassuring message may also suggest that more difficult problems remain. If agricultural policy has not been dictated by agricultural interests, then its obvious weaknesses, high costs, waste, and inefficient allocation of resources, suggest that there are disturbing problems which beset governments intervening in industries even if those industries lack political power. The major criticism of the politics of agricultural policy is that the policymaking process has failed to monitor and adjust to the consequences of decisions. There has been a large gap between the alleged purpose and actual effect of farm policy. This gap reflects different but basic weaknesses in the British and American political systems. These are the tendency for any policy or decision in Britain, once made, to become fossilized or an immutable part of the administrative landscape, and the difficulty of obtaining clear, consistent policy decision in the United States. Both failings are serious in industrial policy. If detailed government intervention in the economy continues to increase in both Britain and the United States, the difficulties and mistakes of agricultural policy provide an important warning, all the more striking because those failings are not the consequence of pressure group power.

Notes

1. J. Roland Pennock, 'Responsible Government, separated powers and special interests; agricultural subsidies in Britain and America', *APSR*, 56 (1962).
2. See Chapters 1 and 5.
3. US Congress, Ninety-first Congress, First Session, House of Representatives, Committee on Agriculture, Hearings before the Subcommittee on Livestock and Grains, *General Farm and Food Stamp Program*, p. 1121.
4. Pennock, op. cit.
5. Samuel Beer, 'Pressure Groups and Parties in Britain, *APSR, 50,* 1956.
6. Many of these studies relate to the trade union movement. See Seymour Martin

Lipset, *Political Man*, Heineman Educational Books, 1969, ch. XII, for a useful introduction.

7. This, after all, is the argument of Theodore Lowis's widely reproduced article, 'How the farmers get what they want', *The Reporter*, 21 May, 1964.

8. David Raymond Mayhew, *Party Loyalty Among Congressmen, The Difference Between Democrats and Republicans, 1947–62*, Harvard University Press, 1966; Julius Turner, *Party and Constituency, Pressures on Congress*, Johns Hopkins University series in historical and political science, Series 69, No. 1, 1951.

9. Samuel Huntington, *The Common Defence, Strategic Programmes in National Defence*, Columbia University Press, New York and London, 1961.

10. G. T. Allison, *The Essence of Decision, Explaining the Cuban Missile Crisis*, MIT Press, Cambridge, 1971.

11. Political Science Union, *The War of 1812 Memorial Song Book*, University of Waterloo, 1970, p. 16.

12. There is a considerable literature on Regulator Commissions; the most stimulating attack on them remains Samuel Huntington, 'The marasmus of the Interstate Commerce Commission', *The Yale Law Journal*, LXI (April, 1952).

13. Lawrence M. Friedman, *Government and Slum Housing*, MIT Press, Cambridge, 1972, p. 227.

14. See Caroline Miles, *Lancashire Textiles, A Case Study of Industrial Change*, National Institute for Economic and Social Research, Cambridge University Press, 1968; Edmund Dell, *Political Responsibility and Industry*, George Allen and Unwin, London, 1973; Arthur Knight, *Private Enterprise and Public Intervention, The Courtaulds Experience*, George Allen and Unwin, London 1974. The similarities between governments' relations with textiles and agriculture are quite striking, and the sensitivity which Miss Miles notes in her work and in interview, which not only politicians but civil servants displayed to the handful of 'textiles' constituencies, supports my arguments on the importance of the 'farm vote' in helping farm subsidies in Britain.

Appendix

The tables which follow were constructed from computer analysis carried out in accordance with my instructions by the Nuffield College Research Services Unit. The computer tape used was supplied by the historical records section of the Michigan Survey Research Center. The tape was modified in two ways. First, Congressmen were distinguished according to the criteria employed by the *Congressional Quarterly Almanac* to determine whether or not their districts are rural. In the Congresses prior to and including 1962, the *Congressional Quarterly* counted as rural all districts which had more than 5 per cent of the population employed in agriculture. The *Congressional Quarterly* took advantage of the discontinuities in the data set which were inevitable following the 1962 redistrictings to introduce a more complicated classification which distinguished urban, suburban, and rural districts. This tighter classification magnified the trend, based on demographic factors, for the number of rural districts to fall. At my request, however, the urban and suburban classifications were recombined, as my interest was in the contrast between Congressmen with a constituency interest in farm subsidies and Congressmen who had no such interest. The second major alteration made to the tape at my request was that, following the examples of David Truman in his influential study, *The Congressional Party*, Congressmen who had taken steps to support or oppose a Bill (e.g. by being paired for or against) but who had not voted were included in the analysis. The tables, which follow, therefore, are not analyses of recorded votes; they are analyses of the recorded preferences of Congressmen.

STATE

NEW ENGLAND

01. CONNECTICUT
02. MAINE
03. MASSACHUSETTS
04. NEW HAMPSHIRE
05. RHODE ISLAND
06. VERMONT

MIDDLE ATLANTIC

11. DELAWARE
12. NEW JERSEY
13. NEW YORK
14. PENNSYLVANIA

EAST NORTH CENTRAL

21. ILLINOIS
22. INDIANA
23. MICHIGAN
24. OHIO
25. WISCONSIN

WEST NORTH CENTRAL

31. IOWA
32. KANSAS
33. MINNESOTA
34. MISSOURI
35. NEBRASKA
36. NORTH DAKOTA
37. SOUTH DAKOTA

SOLID SOUTH

41. ALABAMA
42. ARKANSAS
43. FLORIDA
44. GEORGIA
45. LOUISIANA
46. MISSISSIPPI
47. NORTH CAROLINA
48. SOUTH CAROLINA
49. TEXAS
50. VIRGINIA

BORDER STATES

51. KENTUCKY
52. MARYLAND
53. OKLAHOMA
54. TENNESSEE
55. WASHINGTON, D.C.
56. WEST VIRGINIA

MOUNTAIN STATES

61. ARIZONA
62. COLORADO
63. IDAHO
64. MONTANA
65. NEVADA
66. NEW MEXICO
67. UTAH
68. WYOMING

PACIFIC STATES

71. CALIFORNIA
72. OREGON
73. WASHINGTON

NON-CONTINENTAL STATES

81. ALASKA
82. HAWAII

Table 11   First Agriculture Bill of 1958

	Yes	No
Democrats	27	191
Republicans	169	31
Totals	196	222

Table 12   Second Agriculture Bill of 1958; motion to adopt a rule so that the Bill could be debated

	Urban Democrats	Rural Democrats	Urban Republicans	Rural Republicans	Total
Yes	59	115	5	22	201
No	47	12	74	99	232

Table 13   First Agriculture Bill of 1962; motion to refer Bill back to Committee, 21 June, 1962

	Urban Democrats	Rural Democrats	Urban Republicans	Rural Republicans	Total
Yes	19	34	64	110	230
No	108	96	0	1	205

Table 14   Second Agriculture Bill of 1962; motion to accept the Report of the Conference Committee, 20 September, 1962

	Urban Democrats	Rural Democrats	Urban Republicans	Rural Republicans	Total
Yes	112	108	0	5	225
No	9	32	64	105	210

Table 15   To adopt the Wheat/Cotton Bill, 8 April, 1964

	Urban Democrats	Rural Democrats	Urban Republicans	Rural Republicans	Total
Yes	185	27	9	4	225
No	42	1	147	20	210

Table 16   Agriculture Act of 1970; motion to recommit the Bill to Committee, 5 August, 1970

	Urban Democrats	Rural Democrats	Urban Republicans	Rural Republicans	Total
Yes	80	6	104	8	198
No	137	14	64	13	228

Table 17   Percentage of vote for subsidies supplied by Democrats

Date	Percentage of vote *for* subsidies supplied by Democrats	Percentage of vote for subsidies supplied by *rural* Republicans
1958 (second vote)	86	11
1962 (i)	99	—
1962 (ii)	97	2·0
1964	94	0·02
1970	66	6·0

Table 18   Resolution to refer back to Committee the Second Agriculture Bill of 1958; preferences for region, party, and character of districts

Region	Rural Republicans (yes–no)	Rural Democrats (yes–no)
New England	2–2	1–0
Mid Atlantic	25–1	0–1
East North Central	41–3	0–6
West North Central	8–15	0–14
Solid South	3–1	4–65
Border (South)	7–1	2–18
Mountain	6–1	0–5
Pacific	3–1	1–7

Bibliography

Primary sources of British material

Analyses of the industry

One of the advantages the student of agricultural politics starts with is that governments have collated more information on agriculture than on almost any other industry. The following official analyses of the state of British agriculture are readily available.

Ministry of Agriculture, Fisheries, and Food and the Department of Agriculture and Fisheries for Scotland, *A Century of Agricultural Statistics*, HMSO, London, 1966.

Ministry of Agriculture, Fisheries, and Food, Department of Agriculture and Fisheries for Scotland, Ministry of Agriculture, Northern Ireland, *The Structure of Agriculture*, HMSO, London, 1966.

Ministry of Agriculture, Fisheries, and Food, Department of Agriculture and Fisheries for Scotland, Ministry of Agriculture, Northern Ireland, *The Changing Structure of Agriculture*, HMSO, London, 1970.

Central Statistical Office, *National Income and Expenditure* (annually), HMSO, London (contains tables on agricultural income and on government expenditure).

Department of Agriculture for Scotland, Report of the Department of Agriculture for Scotland (annually up to 1971), *Agriculture in Scotland*, HMSO, London.

However, for most scholars a satisfactory information on the industry can be obtained from the appendices to the Annual Review White Papers. These are:

Annual Review and Fixing of Prices, Cmnd. 8239, 1951.
Annual Review and Fixing of Prices, Cmnd. 8556, 1952.

Annual Review and Fixing of Prices, Cmnd. 8798, 1953.
Annual Review and Determination of Guarantees, Cmnd. 9104, 1954.
Annual Review and Determination of Guarantees, Cmnd. 9406, 1955.
Annual Review and Determination of Guarantees, Cmnd. 9721, 1956.
Annual Review and Determination of Guarantees, Cmnd. 109, 1957.
Annual Review and Determination of Guarantees, Cmnd. 390, 1958.
Annual Review and Determination of Guarantees, Cmnd. 696, 1959.
Annual Review and Determination of Guarantees, Cmnd. 970, 1960.
Annual Review and Determination of Guarantees, Cmnd. 1311, 1961.
Annual Review and Determination of Guarantees, Cmnd. 1658, 1962.
Annual Review and Determination of Guarantees, Cmnd. 1968, 1963.
Annual Review and Determination of Guarantees, Cmnd. 2315, 1964.
Annual Review and Determination of Guarantees, Cmnd. 2621, 1965.
Annual Review and Determination of Guarantees, Cmnd. 2933, 1966.
Annual Review and Determination of Guarantees, Cmnd. 3229, 1967.
Annual Review and Determination of Guarantees, Cmnd. 3558, 1968.
Annual Review and Determination of Guarantees, Cmnd. 3965, 1969.
Annual Review and Determination of Guarantees, Cmnd. 4321, 1970.
Annual Review and Determination of Guarantees, Cmnd. 4623, 1971.
Ministry of Agriculture, Fisheries, and Food, *Farm Incomes in England and Wales* (annual series), HMSO, London.

Statements of government policy

General statements are to be found in the Annual Review White Papers, cited above, and in the statements of ministers reported in Hansard, *House of Commons Debates*, on the day that the Annual Review decisions were announced. There were, in addition, regular debates on agriculture in the House.

Statements of government policy of particular importance are:
Long Term Assurances for Agriculture, Cmnd. 23, 1956
Assistance for Small Farmers, Cmnd. 553, 1958
The National Plan, Cmnd. 2764, 1965, esp. p. 135 ff
Proposed Changes in the Work of the Ministry of Agriculture, Fisheries and Food, Cmnd. 4564, 1971

Though not of direct relevance to this book, discussion of the effects of agriculture of British entry into the European Economic Community forced government to define the importance it attached to the existing system of agricultural subsidies. In particular, the following are helpful:

The United Kingdom and the E.E.C., Report by the Lord Privy Seal on the meeting with Ministers of Member States of the EEC at Brussels, 25 and 27 October, 1962, Cmnd. 1847, 1962, esp. paras. 4–7.
Membership of the European Communities, Cmnd. 3269, 1967.
The United Kingdom and the European Communities, Statement by the Secretary of State for Foreign Affairs, the Hague, 4 July, 1967, HMSO, 1967, esp. paras. 28–31.

The Common Agricultural Policy of the E.E.C., Cmnd. 3274, 1967.
The U.K. and the European Communities, Cmnd. 4715, 1971, esp. paras. 82–87 and 148–151.

The following Parliamentary debates are relevant in this context:

Hansard, *House of Commons Debates*, Vol. 645, 1961, cols. 1486–1487 and 1659. Discussion of the first application to the EEC.
Hansard, *House of Commons Debates*, Vol. 661, 1961–62, col. 596. Statement by the Minister of Agriculture on the progress of negotiations and implications for agriculture.
Hansard, *House of Commons Debates*, Vol. 664, 1961–62, col. 648. Report by R. A. Butler on the progress of negotiations.
Hansard, *House of Commons Debates*, Vol. 671, 1962–63, col. 949 ff. and 442–452. Implications of failure of negotiations for agriculture.

Other sources on policy and commentaries on it

Agricultural Economics Society: 'The economic activities of the Ministry of Agriculture, Fisheries and Food', Presidential Address, J. H. Kirk, 1964.
J. Ashton and S. J. Rogers (Eds.), *Economic Change and Agriculture*, Oliver and Boyd, London, 1967.
'Agriculture's Contribution to the Balance of Payments', *District Bank Review*, September, 1966.
H. Frankell, *Economic Change in British Agriculture, 1959–64*, University of Oxford Economic Research Institute, Oxford, 1964.
Hill Samuel Occasional Paper No. 5, *Agriculture and Import Saving*, Hill Samuel, London, 1970.
Richard W. Howarth, *Agricultural Support in Western Europe*, Institute for Economic Affairs Research Monography 25, 1971.
Gavin McCrone, *The Economics of Subsidising Agriculture*, George Allen and Unwin, London, 1962.
Organisation for European Economic Co-operation,
  Agricultural Policies in Europe and North America, Paris, 1956.
  Agricultural Policies in Europe and North America, Second Report, Paris 1957.
  Agricultural Policies in Europe and North America, Third Report, Paris 1958.
  Agricultural Policies in Europe and North America, Fourth Report, Paris 1960.
Organisation for European Economic Co-Operation and Development, *Agricultural Policies in 1966*, Paris, 1966.
Twelfth Oxford Farming Conference, *Report and Proceedings*, 1958.
Twenty-first Oxford Farming Conference, *Report and Proceedings*, 1967.
Twenty-third Oxford Farming Conference, *Report and Proceedings*, 1969.
Twenty-fifth Oxford Farming Conference, *Report and Proceedings*, 1971.

Institute for Agricultural Science, Oxford.
United Nations, Council of the Food and Agriculture Organisation, Fifty-fifth
Session, *The State of Food and Agriculture in 1970* (and annually before.)

The House of Lords, as may be expected, debates agriculture frequently and
well; their debates are recorded in Hansard, *House of Lords Debates*. Neither
should the debates of the Standing Committees on the Agriculture Bills of the
period be overlooked; the two most important are the 1957 and 1963 Acts.

The Report of the Economic Development Committee for Agriculture,
Agriculture's Import Saving Role, HMSO, London, 1968, was very influential,
though not fully accepted by the government.
It is probably true that of greater importance than any of these sources for this
book (or any other student of the subject) were three reports from Select Committees of the House of Commons.

Select Committee on the Estimates, Sixth Report, Session 1957–58, *Treasury
Control of Expenditure*, particularly the section on Annual Review procedure.
Second Report from the Estimates Committee, Session 1961–62, *Agricultural
Food Grants and Subsidies*.
Select Committee on Agriculture, Session 1966–67, *British Agriculture, Fisheries
and Food and the Common Market:*
Vol. I, *Report,*
Vol. II, *Appendices to the Report, Minutes of Evidence, Appendices and Index.*
Select Committee on Agriculture, *Report from the Select Committee on
Agriculture*, Report, Minutes of Evidence and Index, Session 1968–69.

Lynden Moore and G. H. Peters, 'Agriculture's balance of payments contribution', *Westminster Bank Review*, August, 1965.

The *Journal of Agricultural Economics* contains many fascinating pieces on all
aspects of agricultural policy, and even politics.
The Press is another obvious source: *The Times* and *Financial Times* have out-
standingly good agricultural correspondents, and the former, as it is indexed,
provides a good guide to agricultural politics. I should like to thank Alistair
Hetherington of *The Guardian* and the Press Department of the National
Farmers' Union of England and Wales for aloowing me access to their press clip-
pings library; this allowed me to consult unindexed papers such as *The Guardian,
Financial Times*, and the popular Press. There is also the specialist farming press.
The *British Farmer* is of importance because it is the official journal of the NFU,
The Farmer and Stockbreeder because it is the best, and *The Farmers' Weekly*
because it is one of the largest in circulation. *The Economist* contains many
articles on farm policy; it is also indexed.

Interest group material

The agricultural and national Press (cited above) is an obvious source. In addition, the following publications of the interest groups contain much detailed information on their policies and activities.

Country Landowners' Association (The Association's *Journal*).
National Farmers' Union of England and Wales, *Annual Report* (yearly, but
   published in the 1950s as Vol. I of its yearbook).
National Farmers' Union of England and Wales,
   British Agriculture and the Common Market, 1961.
   British Agriculture and the Common Market, 1966.
   British Agriculture and the Common Market, 1971.
National Farmers' Union of England and Wales,
   NFU News (internal newsletter).
   The N.F.U. of England and Wales (unpublished history).
   Information Service Reports, Vol 11, 1956, to Vol. 25, 1970.
   Report on the Organisation and Management of the N.F.U., London, 1971.
   *Survey and Report on the Structure and Administration of County Branches of
   the N.F.U.*, by T. J. Cowen, 1968.
   What our Union Does for Us, 1970.
National Union of Agricultural and Allied Workers, *The Landworker* (The
   official journal of the Union, formerly the National Union of Agricultural
   Workers).
National Farmers' Union of Scotland, *Annual Reports* (yearly), 1958.
Chief Registrar of Friendly Societies, *Report* (annual), HMSO, London, part 4
   (trade unions), gives membership figures for the NUAAW.

Secondary sources

George Allen, 'The N.F.U. as a pressure group', *Contemporary Review*, June,
   1959.
Alan Butt-Philip, *The Political and Sociological Significance of Welsh
   Nationalism Since 1945*, D. Phil. Thesis, Oxford, contains a useful section on
   the Farmers' Union of Wales.
Helen Ingrid Dawson, *Agricultural Interest Groups in Canada and Britain*, B.
   Litt. Thesis, Oxford, 1966.
Reg Groves, *Sharpen the Sickle!*, The History of the Farmworkers' Union, Por-
   cupine Press, London, 1948.
Richard Hyman, *The Workers' Union*, Clarendon Press, Oxford, 1971. Contains
   a history of the attempts by the Transport and General Workers' Union to
   organize farmworkers.
Robert J. Lieber, *British Politics and European Unity; Parties, Elites and
   Pressure Groups*, University of California Press, Berkeley, 1970.
S. J. Rogers, 'Farmers as a pressure group', *New Society*, 5 February, 1970.

P. L. H. Walters, *Farming Politics in Cheshire, A Study of the Cheshire County Branch of the N.F.U.*, Ph.D. Thesis, Manchester, 1970.

Sources on party policies

Conservative party

National Union of Conservative and Unionist Associations,
Seventy-sixth Annual Conference, Official Report, 1956.
Seventy-seventh Annual Conference, Official Report, 1957.
Seventy-eighth Annual Conference, Official Report, 1958.
Seventy-ninth Annual Conference, Official Report, 1960.
Eightieth Annual Conference, Official Report, 1961.
Eighty-first Annual Conference, Official Report, 1962.
Eighty-second Annual Conference, Official Report, 1963.
Eighty-third Annual Conference, Official Report, 1965.
Eighty-fourth Annual Conference, Official Report, 1966.
Eighty-fifth Annual Conference, Official Report, 1967.
Eighty-sixth Annual Conference, Official Report, 1968.
Eighty-seventh Annual Conference, Official Report, 1969.
Eighty-eighth Annual Conference, Official Report, 1970.
Conservative and Unionist Central Office,
Campaign Guide, 1964, 1966.
Notes on Current Politics, 1965, 1966, 1967, 1969, 1970.
Agriculture and the Nation, 1964.
The Next Five Years (1959 manifesto).
Putting Britain Right Ahead, 1965.
The Agricultural Charter, 1948. A statement of Conservative agricultural policy.

Labour party

The Party's 1959, 1964, 1966 and 1970 manifesto contain brief reference to agriculture. More extended discussion is in:

Prosper the Plough, 1958.
British Farms a New Security, speech by the Rt Hon George Brown at Swaffham, Norfolk, 17 July, 1963.
Report of the Sixty-second Annual Conference of the Labour Party, Scarborough, 1963, esp. Appendix 1.
Action Agriculture, 1967.
The Labour Party, Industry and Society, 1957.
Report of the Fifty-seventh Annual Conference of the Labour Party, Scarborough, 1958.

The Liberals

Publications are scantier. In addition to the party's manifesto, a useful souce is *The Guardian*.

The Guardian Report, Liberal Assembly
(There is no official conference report).
Liberal Publications Department, *Liberal Policy*, 1964, esp. p. 20.

Other primary sources—interviews

For better or for worse, this book could not have been written without the help of numerous politicians and civil servants who agreed to be interviewed.

I have been torn by the need to respect my interviewees' desire for anonymity and the need to cite my sources. I have compromised by citing interviews only when necessary and without immediate attribution.

The following gentlemen have been particularly helpful:

Mr S. W. Astrop, Confederation of British Industries
Mr Tim Boswell, Conservative Party Research Department
Mr A. Buck, MP
Mr J. H. V. Davies, Ministry of Agriculture, Fisheries, and Food
Mr James Douglas, Director, Country Landowners' Association
Sir Basil Engholm, Permanent Secretary, Ministry of Agriculture, Fisheries, and Food
Sir John Gilmour, MP
Rt Hon Joseph Godber, MP, PC
Mr Cledwyn Hughes, MP, PC, Former Minister, Agriculture, Fisheries, and Food
Mr Michael Jopling, MP
Mr John Mackie, MP
Mr J. P. Mackintosh, MP
Mr Alf Morris, MP
Mr Napolitan, Chief Statistician, Ministry of Agriculture, Fisheries, and Food
Mr Roy Pateman, an economist, NFU of England and Wales
The Rt Hon James Prior, MP, PC, Former Minister of Agriculture, Fisheries, and Food
Mr Brendon Sewill, former head of the Conservative Research Department
Sir John Winnifrith, KCB, former Permanent Secretary, Ministry of Agriculture, Fisheries, and Food
Mr Asher Winegarten, Chief Economist and Deputy Director, NFU of England and Wales (who gave me several interviews)
Mr G. W. Wilson, Head of ATI Division, the Treasury
Lord Woolley, Former President, NFU of England and Wales

190

General books of direct relevance

Samuel Beer, *Modern British Politics*, Faber and Faber, London, 1965.

Reginald Bevins, *The Greasy Pole*, Hodder and Stoughton, 1965, contains a good description (pp. 89–109) of activities a pressure group—that for commercial television.

R. G. S Brown, *The Administrative Process in Britain*, Methuen and Co., London, 1971.

Robert Blythe, *Akenfield*, Penguin Books, London, 1972.

Samuel Brittain, *Steering the Economy, The Role of the Treasury*, Pelican Books, 1970.

Lord Bridges, *The Treasury*, Geo. Allen and Unwin, London, 1964.

Richard A. Chapman and A. Dunsire (Eds.), *Style in Administration. Readings in British Public Administration*, George Allen and Unwin, London, 1971.

Edmund Dell, *Political Responsibility and Industry*, George Allen and Unwin, London, 1974.

Harry Eckstein, *Pressure Group Politics, The Case of the British Medical Association*, George Allen and Unwin, London, 1960.

S. E. Finer, *Anonymous Empire*, Pall Mall Press, London, 1962.

J. W. Grove, *Government and Industry in Britain*, Longmans, London, 1962.

R. J. Hammond, *History of the Second World War, Food*, Vol. I, HMSO and Longmans, Green and Co., 1951.

Hugh Heclo and Aaron Wildavsky, *The Private Government of Public Money*, Macmillan, London, 1974.

Arthur Knight, *Private Industry and Government Intervention, The Courtaulds Experience*, George Allen and Unwin, London, 1974.

Dick Leonard and Valentine Herman (Eds.), *The Backbencher and Parliament*, Macmillan, London, 1972.

Louis Moss and Stanley Parker, 'The Local Government Councillor', in Ministry of Housing and Local Government, *The Management of Local Govt.*, Vol. II, HMSO, London, 1967.

Keith A. H. Murray, *History of the Second World War, Agriculture*, HMSO and Longmans, Green and Co., London, 1955.

Geoffrey K. Roberts, *Political Parties and Pressure Groups in Britain*, Weidenfeld and Nicolson, London, 1970.

Richard Rose, *Politics in England*, Faber and Faber, London, 1965.

A. Roth, *The Business Background of M.P.s*, Parliamentary Profile Services, London, 1963, 1965, 1967.

Peter Self and Herbert Storing, *The State and the Farmer*, George Allen and Unwin, London, 1962.

J. D. Stewart, *British Pressure Groups, Their Role in Relation to the House of Commons*, Oxford University Press, Oxford, 1958.

Patrick Gordon Walker, *The Cabinet*, Jonathan Cape, London, 1970.

Lord Williams of Barnbrugh, *Digging for Britain*, Hutchinson, London, 1965.

Harold Wilson, *The Labour Government, 1964–70, A Personal Record*, Pelican, 1973.

H. H. Wilson, *Pressure Group, The Campaign for Commercial Television*, Secker and Warburg, London, 1961.

Graham Wootton, *The Politics of Influence, British Ex-Servicemen, Cabinet Decisions and Cultural Change, 1917–57*, Routledge and Kegan Paul, London, 1963.

Sir John Winnifrith, *The Ministry of Agriculture, Fisheries and Food*, George Allen and Unwin, London, 1962.

Kenneth Young, *Sir Alec Douglas Home*, J. M. Dent and Sons, London, 1970.

Articles, pamphlets, theses, etc.

Sir Douglas Allen, The Department of Economic Affairs, *Political Quarterly*, 1967.

V. H. Beynon and J. E. Harrison, *The Political Significance of the British Agricultural Vote*, University of Exeter, Department of Economics, Report 134, 1962.

P. J. Giddings, *Agricultural Marketing Boards as Political and Administrative Instruments*, D. Phil. Thesis, Oxford, 1971.

Richard W. Howarth, 'The political strength of British agriculture', *Political Studies*, 1969.

J. P. Mackintosh, 'The problems of agricultural politics', *Journal of Agricultural Economics*, 1969.

National Opinion Polls, *Political Bulletin*, February, 1970.

J. Roland Pennock, 'Responsible Government, separated powers and special interests: agricultural subsidies in Britain and America, *APSR*, 1962.

Sir Eric Roll, 'The machinery for economic planning; the 1966 Department of Economic Affairs', *Public Administration*, 1966.

Sir Robert Shaw, 'The machinery for economic planning; the National Economic Development Council', *Public Administration*, 1966.

American material

Primary sources

Most of the official sources, such as committee hearings or reports of congressional debates, are very confusing to follow. It is well, therefore, to start by reading the relevant reports in:

Congressional Quarterly Inc., The *Congressional Quarterly Almanac*, an annual publication. The same organization publishes indexed weekly reports, which offer even more comprehensive accounts. After this, the official sources make more sense.

United States Congress, *Congressional Record*, Vol. 104 onwards.

United States Congress, House of Representatives, Committee on Agriculture,

Eighty-fifth Congress, Second Session, Hearings on *General Farm Legislation.*

Eighty-sixth Congress, First Session, Hearings on *General Farm Legislation.*

Eighty-seventh Congress, Second Session, Hearings on *General Farm Legislation.*

Eighty-seventh Congress, First Session, *Agriculture Act of 1961,* Hearings on HR 6400, Serial E, part 1.

Eighty-seventh Congress, Second Session, *Food and Agriculture Act of 1962,* Hearings on HR 10010.

Eighty-ninth Congress, First Session, Hearings on *Food and Agriculture Act of 1965,* Serial K.

Ninetieth Congress, First Session, Hearings on *The Agricultural Situation, 1967,* Serial A.

Ninetieth Congress, Second Session, Hearings on *Extend the Food and Agriculture Act of 1965,* Serial SS.

Ninety-first Congress, First Session, Hearings on *General Farm and Food Stamp Program,* Serial Q.

United States Congress, House of Representatives, Committee on Agriculture, Subcommittee on Cotton, Ninety-first Congress, First Session, Hearings on *General Farm and Food Stamp Program,* Serial Q, part 3.

United States Congress, House of Representatives, Committee on Agriculture, Subcommittee on Livestock and Grains, *Hearings* Ninety-first Congress, First Session.

United States Congress, House of Represenatives, Committee on Agriculture, Subcommittee on Tobacco, Eighty-ninth Congress, Second Session, Hearings on *Problems in the Tobacco Program,* serial BB.

United States Congress, House of Representatives, Committee on Appropriations, Subcommittee on Agriculture,

Eighty-fifth Congress, Second Session, Hearings on *Department of Agriculture Appropriations for 1960.*

Eighty-sixth Congress, First Session, Hearings on *Department of Agriculture Appropriations for 1960.*

Eighty-seventh Congress, First Session, Hearings on *Department of Agriculture Appropriations for 1960.*

Eighty-seventh Congress, Second Session, Hearings on *Department of Agriculture Appropriations for 1960.*

Eighty-eighth Congress, First Session, Hearings on *Department of Agriculture Appropriations for 1960.*

Eighty-eighth Congress, Second Session, Hearings on *Department of Agriculture Appropriations for 1960.*

Eighty-ninth Congress, First Session, Hearings on *Department of Agriculture Appropriations for 1960.*

Eighty-ninth Congress, Second Session, Hearings on *Department of Agriculture Appropriations for 1960.*

Ninetieth Congress, First Session, Hearings on *Department of Agriculture Appropriations for 1960.*

Ninety-first Congress, Second Session, Hearings on *Department of Agriculture Appropriations for 1960.*

United States Congress, Senate Committee on Agriculture and Forestry,

Eighty-fifth Congress, Second Session, Hearings on *President's Farm Message, 1959.*

Eighty-seventh Congress, Second Session, Hearings on *Food and Agriculture Act of 1962,* S 2789.

Eighty-ninth Congress, First Session, Hearings on *Food and Agriculture Act of 1965,* S 1702.

Ninetieth Congress, Second Session, Hearings on *Agriculture Act of 1968,* S 3590.

Ninety-third Congress, First Session, *Farm Programs; Studies and Data on the Farm Program* (prepared for the Committee).

Ninety-third Congress, First Session, Hearings on *Extension on Farm and Related Programs,* S 517.

Eighty-third Congress, First Session, Hearings on *Anticipated Nomination of Ezra Taft Benson to Serve as Secretary of Agriculture.*

Eighty-seventh Congress, First Session, *Confirmation of Orville Freeman as Secretary of Agriculture.*

Ninety-second Congress, First Session, *Nomination of Earl Lauer Butz* (to serve as Secretary of Agriculture).

United States Congress, Senate Committee on Appropriations, Subcommittee on Agriculture,

Eighty-fifth Congress, First Session, Hearings on *Agricultural Appropriations for 1958,* HR 7441.

Eighty-sixth Congress, Second Session, Hearings on *Agricultural Appropriations for 1960,* HR 7175.

Eighty-seventh Congress, First Session, Hearings on *Department of Agriculture and Related Agencies, Appropriations for 1962,* HR 7444.

Eighty-seventh Congress, Second Session, Hearings on *Agricultural Appropriations for 1963,* HR 12648.

Eighty-eighth Congress, First Session, Hearings on *Agricultural Appropriations for 1964,* HR 6754.

Eighty-eighth Congress, Second Session, Hearings on *Agricultural Appropriations for 1965.*

Eighty-ninth Congress, First Session, Hearings on *Agricultural Appropriations for 1966.*

Eighty-ninth Congress, Second Session, Hearings on *Agricultural Appropriations for 1967,* HR 14596.

Ninetieth Congress, First Session, Hearings on *Department of Agriculture and Related Agencies, Appropriations for Fiscal Year 1968,* HR 10509.

Ninetieth Congress, Second Session, Hearings on *Department of Agriculture and Related Agencies, Appropriations for 1969.*

Ninety-first Congress, Second Session, Hearings on *Department of Agriculture and Related Agencies, Appropriations for Fiscal Year 1971,* HR 17923.

Primary souces: pressure group material

American Farm Bureau Federation,
  Farm Bureau Policies for 1956 (and then annually).
  Annual Address of Charles B. Shuman, President, 1960–70.
  Annual Report of Roger Flemming, Secretary-Treasurer 1963, and annually
    since.
Proceedings of AFBF Conventions are not published, but typescript copies
were made available in the Washington and Chicago offices. In addition, all
member state Federations publish newsletters and policy statements. Most
national and state policy positions are presented to Congress in the Committee
hearings outlined above.

American National Cattlemen's Association, *There is A Time and A Place, The
  History of the American National Cattlemen's Association*, by Lyle Liggett.
National Farmers' Association, *The N.F.O. Reporter*, Vols. I to XVII (1972).
National Farmers' Association, *The Biggest Farm Story of the Decade*, by
  Charles Walters (official history pamphlet).
National Farmers' Organisation, *Annual Report* (1960–72).
National Farmers' Union,
  1957 Policy of National Farmers' Union (and annually thereafter).
  A Practical Guide to Effective Lobbying.
  Washington Newsletter (weekly).
Typescripts of the Union's Conventions are kept in its Denver office.
National Grange,
  Legislative Policies, 1973 (and annually before).
  Policies and Programs (annual summary of preceding item).

Other primary sources

Presidential messages to Congress calling for, or vetoing, Bills on Agriculture are
reproduced in the *Congressional Quarterly Almanac* for the relevant year. Party
platforms can be found in the same source.

The Press

The New York Times is indexed and is widely available on microfilm in Essex.
Unlike *The Times*, it remains a journal of record.
  A great piece of good fortune, for which I must thank Dr Rasmussen of the US
Department of Agriculture, was being allowed access to the Department's press
library. This provided easy, catalogued access to not only famous American
papers such as the *Washington Post* and *Wall Street Journal* but also less famous
papers, including:

  The Des Moines Register
  The Farm Journal

Wallace's Farmer
Washington Evening Star
and all the newsletters of the major agricultural interest groups.

Books of relevance to the American section

Dean Albertson, *Roosevelt's Farmer, Claude Wickard in the New Deal*, Columbia University Press, London and New York, 1961.

James Anderson (Ed.), *Politics and Economic Policy Making, Selected Readings*, Addison-Wesley, Reading, Mass., 1970.

A. Bauer, Ithiel de Sola Pool, and Louis Anthony Dexter, *American Business and Public Policy*, Prentice Hall International, London and New York, 1964.

Samuel R. Berger, *Dollar Harvest*, Heath Lexington Books, New York, 1971 (an exposé of the Farm Bureau).

Daniel M. Berman, *In Congress Assembled, The Legislative Process in National Government*, Macmillan, New York, 1964.

Richard Bolling, *House Out of Order*, New York, 1965.

James MacGregor Burns, *The Deadlock of Democracy, Four Party Politics in America*, Prentice Hall, New York, 1963. Contains a useful discussion of rural dominance in Congress prior to *Baker versus Carr*.

Christina McFadyen Campbell, *The Farm Bureau and the New Deal*, University of Illinois Press, Urbana, 1962.

Charles L. Clapp, *The Congressman, His Work as He Sees It*, The Brookings Institute, Washington, 1963.

Les M. Christenson, *The Brannan Plan, Farm Politics and Policy*, The University of Michigan Press, Ann Arbor, 1959.

Congressional Quarterly Service, In., *Congress and the Nation*, Vol. 1, 1945–64, Vol. 2, 1964–68, Washington, DC, 1965 and 1969.

J. A. Crampton, *The National Farmers' Union, Ideology of a Pressure Group*, University of Nebraska Press, Lincoln, 1965.

Julius Duscha, *Taxpayers' Hayride*, Little Brown and Co., New York, 1964.

Leon D. Epstein, *Politics in Wisconsin*, University of Wisconsin Press, 1958.

Gilbert Fite, *George N. Peek and the Fight for Farm Parity*, University of Oklahoma Press, 1954.

Richard Fenno, Jr., *Congressmen in Committees*, Little Brown and Co., New York, 1973.

J. K. Galbraith, *American Capitalism, The Concept of Countervailing Power*, Hamish Hamilton, London, 1957.

Eric F. Goldman, *The Crucial Decade*, Vintage Books, 1960.

G. Goodwin, *The Little Legislatives*, University of Massachusetts Press, Cambridge, 1970.

Don F. Hadwiger and Ross B. Talbot, *Pressures and Protests, The Kennedy Farm Program and the Wheat Referendum of 1963*, Chandler and Co., San Francisco, 1965.

Donald R. Hall, *Co-operative Lobbying, The Power of Pressure*, University of Arizona Press, 1969.

R. J. Hildreth (Ed.), *Readings in Agricultural Policy*, University of Nebraska Press, Lincoln, 1968.

Barbara Hinckley, *The Senority System in Congress*, Indiana University Press, Urbana, 1971.

A. O. Hirschman, *Exit, Voice and Loyalty*, Harvard University Press, Cambridge, 1970.

D. Gale Johnson, *World Agriculture in Disarray*, Fontana/Collins, London, 1973.

V. O. Key, *Public Opinion and American Democracy*, Alfred Knopf, New York, 1961.

V. O. Key, *Politics, Parties and Pressure Groups*, T. J. Crowell, New York, 1964.

O. M. Kile, *The Farm Bureau Through Three Decades*, Waverley Press, Baltimore, 1948 (an official history).

John J. Lacey, *Farm Bureau in Illinois, History of Illinois Farm Bureau*, Illinois Agricultural Association, Bloomington, 1965 (official history).

Joseph LaPolambara, *Interest Groups in Italian Politics*, Princeton University Press, Princeton, 1964.

Earl Latham, *The Group Basis of Politics, A Study in Base Point Legislation*, Cornell University Press, 1952.

William E. Leuchtenburg, *Franklin D. Roosevelt and the New Deal, 1932–40*, Harper and Row, London and New York, 1963.

C. E. Lindblom, *The Policy-Making Process*, Prentice Hall, New York, 1968.

S. M. Lipset, *Agraran Socialism, The Co-operative Commonwealth Federation in Saskatchewan, A Study in Political Sociology*, University of California Press, Berkeley, 1950.

Russell Lord, *The Wallaces of Iowa*, Houghton Mifflin, New York, 1947.

Duncan MacRae, *Dimensions of Congressional Voting*, University of California Press, Berkeley, 1958.

Theodore Marmor, *The Politics of Medicare*, Library of Social Policy and Administration, Routledge and Kegan Paul, London, 1970 (contains an excellent discussion of the impact of the AMA).

Donald R. Matthews, *U.S. Senators and Their World*, Vintage Books, New York, 1960.

Allen J. Matusow, *Farm Policies and Politics in the Truman Years*, Harvard University Press, Cambridge, 1967.

David R. Mayhew, *Party Loyalty Among Congressmen, The Difference Between Republicans and Democrats, 1947–62*, Harvard University Press, Cambridge, 1966.

Grant McConnell, *The Decline of Agrarian Democracy*, University of California Press, Berkeley, 1953.

Wesley McCune, *Who's Behind Our Farm Policy*, Praeger, New York, 1956.

Stanley D. Metzer, *Lowering Non-Tariff Barriers, U.S. Law Practice and Objectives*, Brookings Institution, Washington, DC, 1974.

George McGovern (Ed.), *Agricultural Thought in the Twentieth Century*, Bobbs Merrill and Co., New York, 1967.

Raymond Moley, *The First New Deal*, Harcourt Brace and World Inc., New York, 1966.

R. Joseph Monsen and Mark W. Cannon, *The Makers of Public Policy, American Power groups and Their Ideologies*, McGraw Hill, New York, 1965.

Richard Neustadt, *Presidential Power*, John Wiley and Sons, New York, 1960.

Russell B. Nye, *Midwestern Progressive Politics*, Michigan State University Press, 1959.

Wayne D. Rasmussen and Gladys L. Baker, *The Department of Agriculture*, Praeger, New York, 1972.

Randall Ripley, *Power in the Senate*, St. Martin's Press, New York, 1969.

Michael Paul Rogin, *The Intellectuals and McCarthy*, The Radical Spectre, MIT Press, Cambridge, Mass., 1967.

E. E. Schattschneider, *The Semi Sovereign People*, Hott, Reinhart, and Winston, New York, 1960.

E. E. Schattschneider, *Politics, Pressures and the Tariff*, Archon Books, New York, 1963.

Arthur Schlesinger, *The Coming of the New Deal*, Houghton Mifflin, New York, 1959.

Harold Seidman, *Politics, Position and Power, The Dynamics of Government Organisation*, Oxford University Press, London, 1970.

Philip Selznick, *The T.U.A. and the Grass Roots, A Study in the Sociology of Formal Organisation*, University of California Press, Berkeley, 1953.

Theodore Sorensen, *Decision Making in the White House*, Columbia Paperbacks, New York, 1964.

James L. Sundquist, *The Dynamics of the Party System*, Brookings Institution, Washington, DC, 1974.

Ross B. Talbot and Don W. Hadringer, *The Policy Process in American Agriculture*, Chandler Publishing Co., San Francisco, 1968.

David B. Truman, *The Governmental Process*, Alfred Knopf, New York, 1951.

Harry S. Truman, *Years of Trial and Hope, 1946–53*, Hodder and Stoughton, London, 1956.

Luther B. Tweeten, *Foundations of Farm Policy*, University of Nebraska Press, Lincoln, 1970.

US Department of Agriculture, Economic Research Service, *Century of Service, the First 100 years of the United States Department of Agriculture*, USDA, 1963.

US Department of Agriculture, *Farm Commodity and Related Programs Agricultural Handbook*, No. 345, 1968.

US Congress, Eighty-fifth Congress, Second Session, Joint Economic Committee, Hearings on *Fiscal Policy Implications of the Current Economic Outlook*.

US Congress, Joint Economic Committee, Subcommittee on Agriculture Policy, Eighty-fifth Congress, 1958, papers submitted.

US Congress, House of Representatives, Eightieth Congress, First Session, 1949

198

Committee on Agriculture, *Long Range Agricultural Policy, A Study of Agricultural Adjustment Programs, 1933–41.*

US Congress, House of Representatives, Ninety-first Congress, Second Session 1970, Committee on Agriculture, *The United States Sugar Program.*

US Congress, House of Representatives, Ninety-second Congress, First Session 1970, Committee on Agriculture, *Food Costs, Farm Prices.*

US Congress, House of Representatives, Ninety-second Congress, Second Session 1972, Committee on Agriculture, *Government Subsidy Historical Review.*

US Congress, Senate, Eighty-fifth Congress, First Session 1957, Senate Committee on Agriculture and Forestry, *Possible Methods of Improving the Parity Formula.*

US Congress, Senate, Eighty-ninth Congress, First Session 1965, Senate Committee on Agriculture and Forestry, *Farm Programs and Dynamic Forces in Agriculture.*

US Congress, Senate, Ninetieth Congress, First Session 1967, Senate Committee on Agriculture and Forestry, *Parity Returns Position of Farmers.*

US Congress, Senate, Ninety-second Congress Second Session, Senate Committee on Agriculture and Forestry, *Farm Payment Limitations.*

Harman Ziegler, *Interest Groups in American Society*, Prentice Hall, New York, 1966.

Howard Zinn (Ed.), *New Deal Thought*, Bobbs Merrill, New York, 1968.

Articles, pamphlets, etc.

Anon., 'The political impasse in farm support legislation', *Yale Law Journal*, 1962.

Bela Ballassa, 'Tariff protection in industrial countries', *The Journal of Political Economy*, **73** (1965).

Prentice Bowsher, 'The Agriculture Department', *National Journal*, 3 January, 1970.

W. W. Cochrane, 'American farm policies in a tumultuous world', *American Journal of Agricultural Economics*, 1970.

Lewis Anthony Dexter, 'The Representative and his district', in R. Peabody and N. Polsby (Eds.), *New Perspectives on the House of Representatives*, Rand McNally, Chicago, 1963.

J. K. Galbraith, 'Economic preconceptions and the farm policy', *American Economic Review*, March, 1954.

Thomas Gilpatrick, 'Price support policies and the midwest farm vote', *Midwest Journal of Political Science*, November, 1959.

Don F. Hadwiger, 'The Freeman Administration and the poor', *Agricultural History*, **XLV**, No. 1.

C. O. Jones, 'The Agriculture Committee and the problem of representation', *APSR*, June, 1961.

C. O. Jones, 'The role of the congressional subcommittee', *Midwest Journal of Political Science*, 1962.

D. Gale Johnson, *Government and agricultural adjustment*, University of Chicago, Office of Agricultural Economics Research, Paper No. 73:16.

D. Gale Johnson, *Farm commodity programs, an opportunity for change*, American Enterprise Institute for Public Policy Research, Washington, D.C. 1973.

Roy Macridis, 'Interest groups in comparative analysis', *Journal of Politics*, **XXIII** no. 1 (1961).

Nicholas A. Masters, 'House committee assignments', *APSR*, 1961.

D. E. Morrison and W. Keith Warner, 'Correlates of farmers' attitudes towards public and private aspects of agricultural organisations', *Rural Sociology*, 1971.

J. Roland Pennock, 'Party and Constituency in Postwar Agricultural Price Support Legislation', *Journal of Politics*, 1956.

Wayne D. Rasmussen and Gladys L. Baker, 'A short history of price support and adjustment legislation and programs for agriculture, 1933–65', *Agricultural Economics Research*, **XVIII** (July, 1966).

Robert A. Rohwer, 'Organised farmers in Oklahoma', *Rural Sociology*, March, 1952.

E. L. and F. M. Schapschneier, 'Eisenhower and Ezra Taft Benson: farm policy in the 1950s', *Agricultural History*, **XLIV,** No. 4.

J. T. Schlebecker, 'The Great Holding Action: the N.F.O. in September, 1962', *Agricultural History*, **XXXIX,** No. 4.

Charles L. Schultze, *The Distribution of Farm Subsidies, Who Gets the Benefits*, The Brookings Institute, Washington, 1971.

Ross B. Talbot, 'The North Dakota Farmers' Union and North Dakota politics', *Western Political Quarterly*, **10** (1957).

Larry J. Wipf, 'Tariffs, non-tariff distortions and effective protection in U.S. Agriculture', *American Journal of Agricultural Economics*, 1971.

Interviews

As with the British section, interviews were invaluable. Those particularly helpful were:

Mr Wheldon Barton, Legislative Director, NFU Representative John Brademas

Charles Brannan, Former Secretary of Agriculture, now with the NFU

Mr Henry Cusso, Counsel, Senate Committee of Agriculture and Forestry Representative Paul Findley

Mr Roger Flemming, Secretary-Treasurer, AFBF

Representative Tom Foley

Mr Friedriche, Legislative Director, National Grange

Mr J. Hays, President, Alabama Farm Bureau Federation

Mr House, American National Cattlemen's Association

Mr Jenson, Colorado Farm Bureau Federation

Mr Clifford McIntire, Legislative Director, American Farm Bureau Federation

Mr MacMillan, American National Cattlemen's Association
Mr Kenneth Motz, Treasurer, National Farmers' Union
Mr Hugh Murray, Minority Counsel, House Committee on Agriculture
Mr E. Robinson, Natural Resources Division, Office of Management and the Budget
Mr John Schnittker, former Under-Secretary, US Department of Agriculture
Mr Leo Schaffer, Congressional Liaison Officer, US Department of Agriculture
Mr Charles Schultz, Former Director, Bureau of the Budget
Representative Jamie L. Whitten
Mr Volen Welch, Agricultural Stabilisation and Conservation Services

Index

Agriculture Act (UK),
  of 1947, 42–3
  of 1957, 14, 44
Agricultural Adjustment Acts (of United States),
  constitutionality, 58
  enacted, 57
  provisions of, 58
Agricultural Stabilisation and Conservation Service (of United States), 111–12
American Farm Bureau Federation, 165
  breadth of political activities, 167
  contemporary membership, 79
  divisions within, 83, 85, 87
  doubts about number of members who are farmers, 79, 80
  doubts about representativeness of leadership, 82 and *ff*
  early development, 76–7
  ideology of, 80 and *ff*
  ineffectiveness of, 87–8
  opposition to farm subsidy programmes, 82
  opposition to supply management, 67–8
  reasons for survival of leadership, 86–7
  role of New Deal, 78
  style of leadership, 85, 86
American Federation of Labor-Congress of Industrial Organisations, 69, 109
  alliance with National Farmers' Union (of the United States), 93–4

American Voter, The, 118
Amory, Rt. Hon. Heathcoat, 44
Anderson, Senator Clinton,
  as Secretary of Agriculture, 60
  as Senator, 156
Annual Review and Determination of Guarantees (UK),
  advantages of, 44, 170–71
  conduct of, 43 and *ff*
  criticisms of, 42
  legal framework of, 43, 44
Ashton, John, 47

Backbench Members of Parliament (UK),
  exert pressure for higher subsidies, 22, 26 and *ff*
  numbers with personal or constituency links to agriculture, 27
Barry, Brian, 7, 31, 32
Bauer, Poole and Dexter, 157
Beer, Samuel, 7, 32, 165
Benson, Ezra Taft, 172
  hostility to farm subsidy system, 62
  laissez-faire economic beliefs, 62
  limited success of, 62–3, 64
  loses support for Republicans, 119
  named Secretary of Agriculture, 62
  unpopularity of, 63
Beynon and Harrison, 20
Blythe, Robert, 25

Board (later Department) of Trade (UK),
as critic of higher farm subsidies, 47
role in Annual Review, 48
Brannan, Charles,
as Secretary of Agriculture, 61
failure of Brannan Plan, 61
Butler, Rt. Hon. R. A., on Conservative attitude to agriculture, 25
Butz, Earl, as Secretary of Agriculture, 114

Cabinet Ministers (UK),
reluctance to criticize each others' plans, 51
role as defender of special interests, 46
role as spokesmen for their Department's view and interest, 46
Central Policy Review Staff (UK), failure to challenge farm subsidies, 51
Conservative and Unionist Party, The (UK),
attitudes to agriculture, 25
fear of farm vote, 22 and *ff*
number and influence of backbenchers linked to agriculture, 27
Conte, Representative, work against farm subsidy system, 70–71
Cooley, Representative Harold,
as Chairman of House Agriculture Committee, 66, 68, 123, 133, 159
hostility to national leadership of the AFBF, 83
Council of Economic Advisers (United States),
as critic of farm subsidies, 109–10
limited power of, 109
Country Landowners' Association (UK), subservience to NFU on general questions of agricultural policy, 34
Crosland, Anthony, 46
Crossman, R. H. S.,
advocacy of farm subsidies to win rural constituencies and hence General Elections, 23
creation of Select Committee on Agiriculture, 27

Dahl, Robert, 6
Department of Agriculture (United States),
autonomy of certain agencies within, 11–12
clientele capture view rejected, 172–3
size of, 110–11
weakness of coordination with other Departments and agencies, 110

Eisenhower, President Dwight D.,
loss of popularity amongst farmers, 1952–56, 63
obfuscation on farm policy in 1952 election campaign, 61–2
orders Benson to reverse unpopular policy in 1956 election year, 121–2
Electoral Competition for farm vote in Britain, 171
by Conservative Party, 22–3
by Labour Party, 23–4
by Liberal Party, 24
Electoral Competition for farm vote in United States, 173
by Eisenhower, 62
by Johnson, 68
by Kennedy, 64
by Nixon, 71
causing Presidents to reverse policies, 117–18
volatility of farm vote in United States, 118, 119
Ellender, Senator, as Chairman Senate Agriculture and Forestry Committee, 141–2
Executive Branch and Agriculture (United States), 104 and *ff*
and alleged capture of the Department of Agriculture by its clientele, 105
Executive Branch and Congress, limited power over, 123

Farm Vote,
competition for in Britain, 20
importance of in Britain, 20–21
perceptions of its importance, 21
Farmers' Union of Wales, 32
and challenge to NFU, 34
Fenno, Richard, 136, 137, 140
Findley, Representative Paul, work against farm subsidies, 70–71
Foreign and Commonwealth Office (UK),
as critic of farm subsidies, 47
role in Annual Review, 48
Freeman, Orville, 172
failure to extract desired legislation from Congress, 66
loyalty to Presidential policy, 122
Selected as Secretary of Agriculture, 65
views on farm policy, 65

Galbraith, J. K., 116
Gilpatrick, Thomas, 121
Godber, Joseph, 180

Grange, The,
  as predominantly a social institution, 96–7
  legislative strategy of, 97–8
  reasons for apparent success, 97

Hardin, Clifford M.,
  named as Secretary of Agriculture, 171
  negotiates only postwar compromise Agriculture Act, 71
Home, Rt. Hon. Sir Alec Douglas (later Lord), insists on reaching agreement with NFU in 1964 Annual Revieew, 22
Howarth, Richard, 15, 16, 20
Hughes, Rt. Hon. Cledwyn, as Minister of Agriculture, Fisheries and Food, 170
Humphrey, Senator Hubert, 141

Interest Groups,
  defined, 5–6
  in Britain, 30 and *ff*
  in United States, 76 and *ff*
  lesser status in United States than UK, 168
  membership characteristics in United States, 76

Johnson, D. Gale, 4–5
Johnson, President Lyndon B.,
  change of policy to win farm votes in 1964 election, 68
  relations with Freeman as Secretary of Agriculture, 116, 122, 172
  works to secure passage of 1964 Wheat–Cotton Act, 69

Kennedy, President John F.,
  adopts 'supply management' policy, 64–5
  competes for farm vote in 1960, 64
  exerts formidable pressures to obtain 1962 Agriculture Act, 66–7
  initial refusal to continue subsidies without tight production controls, 67
Key, V. O., 6

Labour Party (of the UK),
  competes for farm vote, 23–4
  ideological predisposition to subsidy systems, 25–6
  organization of backbenchers' Food and Agriculture Committee, 26
  unsentimental attitude to countryside, 25

LaGuardia, Fiorello, and support for farm subsidies, 4, 59
Liberal Party (of the UK), and farm subsidies, 24
Lowi, Theodore, 111

MacMillan, Rt. Hon. Harold, views on backbenchers' committees, 26
Mayhew, David, 146
McGovern, Senator George,
  and role in passage of 1964 Wheat–Cotton Act, 68–69
  as favourite with NFU (of United States), 90, 91
Michels, Roberto, 36
Ministers of Agriculture, Fisheries and Food (UK), *see* Amory, Hughes, Peart, Prior, Soames, Williams
Ministries (UK), general tendency to represent established views and interests, 48
Ministry of Agriculture, Fisheries and Food (UK), (MAFF), 165
  representing farmers' interests in Annual Review, 170, 171, 45
Moore, Barrington Jr., 32

National Farmers' Organisation (of the United States),
  close relations with Democrats, 98
  compelled to enter political arena, 98
  formation as a marketing group, 98
National Farmers' Union (in United States), 165
  breadth of political involvement, 91
  distribution of membership, 89
  early history, 88–90
  embodiment of midwestern liberalism, 94–5
  farm policies of, 91–2
  ideology of, 90–91
  influence of, 96
  strucutre, 95–6
  style of leadership, 95–6
  ties to AFL–CIO, 93–4
  ties to Democratic Party, 92–3
National Farmers' Union of England and Wales,
  advantages to MAFF of its dominance, 32
  and Annual Review, 22
  and other British agricultural interest groups, 30

National Farmers' Union of England and Wales (*contd.*)
 and the Conservative Party, 38–9
 and the Labour Party, 38
 closeness of links to the MAFF, 35
 cohesion of, 165
 compared with agricultural interest groups in the United States, 165
 criticisms of leadership, 39–40
 effects on Union of close links with government, 37
 grass roots challenges to leaders, 34
 internal distribution of power, 36 and *ff*
 limitations imposed by close links with government, 49, 166–7
 relations with government as prototype for indicative planning, 26
 success in recruiting members, 31 and *ff*
National Farmers' Union of Scotland, 30
National Union of Agricultural and Allied Workers (NUAAW), 23, 25
 subservience to NFU on general agricultural policy, 34
Nettl, J., 32
New Deal, 4
 effects on agriculture, 59
Nixon, President Richard M.,
 claims to increase milk prices to win farm vote, 118
 conciliates farm voters, 71

Olson, Mancur, 31, 79–80

Parity,
 criticized, 58–9
 explained, 58
Peart, Rt. Hon. Fred, 49
Pennock, J. Roland, 7, 163, 165
Phillips, Morgan, hopes of Labour successes in rural constituencies, 23
Poage, Representative Bill, as member and Chairman of House Agriculture Committee, 71, 107, 133, 135
Price, H. Douglas, 157
Prior, Rt. Hon. James, 180
Public Expenditure Survey Committee, failure to affect Annual Review, 51

Quantities, standard, introduced in 1957 Agriculture Act (UK), 15

Roth, Andrew, 22

Schultze, Charles, 4, 72

Secretaries of Agriculture (United States), *see also* Benson, Butz, Freeman, Hardin
 firm views on farm policy, 114–16
 inapplicability of 'clientele' model, 115, 124
 minimal role of Senate in their appointment, 113
 need of heavy Presidential support in obtaining legislation, 116
 role as symbolic spokesmen for farmers, 113–14
Select Committee on Agriculture (UK), 27–8
Soames, Sir Christopher, as Minister of Agriculture, Fisheries and Food, 22
Special Interests, defined, 6
Status of farmers (in Britain), 24
Subsidies, agricultural, (United States)
 compared with size and distribution of British, 72–3, 164
 distribution, 72–3
 total value, 72
Subsidies, British system,
 before 1963, 13–14
 changes post 1963, 14, 15
 criticisms of, 17
 distribution of benefits, 17
 Exchequer cost, 14, 15
 political advantages of, 24
 general arguments in favour of subsidies, 2–4
 general criticism of agricultural subsidies, 2–4
 total value to farmers, 16

Textile Industry (of UK), compared to politics of agriculture, 175
Tocqueville, Alexis de, 6
Torrington, effect of by-election on belief in 'farm vote', 22
Treasury, The (UK)
 critic of increases in farm subsidies, 46 and *ff*
 reluctance to criticize established policies, 50
 role in Annual Review, 46, 47, 48
Treasury Payments (United States), political dangers of, 70
Truman, David, 6, 104
Truman, President Harry,
 support for farm subsidies, 60
 supposed importance of farm vote his 1948 election victory, 60

United States Congress,
  ideological divide on farm subsidies, 168–9
  impact of Committee system, 168
  inability to evolve coherent farm policy, 169
  partisan divisions in on farm subsidies, 168
United States Congress, House of Representatives,
  constituency interest and floor voting, 153–5
  ideological antipathy of Republicans to subsidies, 150–51
  ideological cohesion of Democrats on government intervention, 152
  importance of party, 147
  logrolling between urban and rural Democrats, 149–50
  Southern Democrats' approval of farm subsidies, 151
United States Congress, House of Representatives, Committee on Agriculture,
  determinants and characteristics of membership, 128–9
  importance of ideology as explanation of partisan divide, 133–4
  partisan divisions within, 130–33
  poor floor record, 135–6
United States Congress, House of Representatives, Committee on Appropriations, Sub-Committee on Agriculture,
  greater unity than legislative Committee, 137
  includes funds for non-agricultural pur-

poses to win floor votes, 138
  limited power of, 140
  reasons for higher prestige than legislative Committee, 137
  role in restoring cuts by OMB, 137
  willingness to accommodate wishes of the House, 137–8
United States Congress, Senate,
  floor votes compared to those in House, 156–8
  greater support for farm subsidies than in House, 155
  reduced partisan influence on floor voting, 155–6
United States Congress, Senate, Committee on Appropriations, Sub-Committee on Agriculture and Forestry, degree of unity, 144
United States Senate, Committee on Agriculture and Forestry,
  importance of logrolling, 141
  informal structure of, 141
  lack of partisanship, 142
  unity of Committee, 140
  weak floor record, 143

Whitten, Representative Jamie, as Chairman Agriculture Appropriations sub-committee, 136, 138, 139
Williams, Philip, 23, 24
Williams, Rt. Hon. Tom, 43
  and reasons for introducing farm subsidy system, 26
Wilson, Rt. Hon. Sir Harold, and Annual Review, 22
Williams, Sir Gwilym, 166, 35

DATE DUE

FEB 26 '82			
FEB 25 1982			
GAYLORD			PRINTED IN U.S.A.